SECRET
LIFE

BY THE SAME AUTHOR

The UFO Controversy in America

SECRET
LIFE

Firsthand Accounts
of UFO Abductions

David M. Jacobs

FOREWORD BY

JOHN E. MACK, M.D.

LONDON NEW YORK SYDNEY TORONTO

This edition published 1992
by BCA by arrangement with
Fourth Estate Limited

CN 3310

First published in the USA in 1992 by Simon & Schuster

Copyright © 1992 by David Michael Jacobs

The right of David M. Jacobs to be identified as the author
of this work has been asserted by him in accordance with the
Copyright, Designs and Patents Act 1988.

Printed in Great Britain by Hartnolls Ltd., Bodmin

TO IRENE

Contents

PART III. LIVING WITH THE SECRET

PART IV. THE SEARCH FOR MEANING

Foreword

The idea that men, women, and children can be taken against their wills from their homes, cars, and schoolyards by strange humanoid beings, lifted onto spacecraft, and subjected to intrusive and threatening procedures is so terrifying, and yet so shattering to our notions of what is possible in our universe, that the actuality of the phenomenon has been largely rejected out of hand or bizarrely distorted in most media accounts. This is altogether understandable, given the disturbing nature of UFO abductions and our prevailing notions of reality. The fact remains, however, that for thirty years, and possibly longer, thousands of individuals who appear to be sincere and of sound mind and who are seeking no personal benefit from their stories have been providing to those who will listen consistent reports of precisely such events. Population surveys suggest that hundreds of thousands and possibly more than a million persons in the United States alone may be abductees or "experiencers," as they are sometimes called. The abduction phenomenon is, therefore, of great clinical importance if for no other reason than the fact that abductees are often deeply traumatized by their experiences. At the same time the subject is of obvious scientific interest, however much it may challenge our notions of reality and truth.

The relevant professional communities in mental health, medicine, biology, physics, electronics, and other disciplines are understandably skeptical of a phenomenon as strange as UFO abduction, which defies our accepted notions of reality. The effort to enable these communities to take abduction reports seriously will be best served through scrupulously conducted research by investigators who bring a scholarly and dispassionate yet appropriately caring attitude to their work. In this way patterns and meanings may be discovered that can lead to fuller and deeper knowledge and, eventually, to the development of convincing theoretical understanding.

In this book Temple University historian David Jacobs has provided us with work of just this kind. In a field that lends itself to sensationalistic treatment, we have already come to expect of Jacobs a special standard of rigorous scholarship and careful observation. His 1975 book, *The UFO Controversy in America,* remains a classic history of the early years of UFO-related events. In the present work Dr. Jacobs presents his findings from the investigation of more than sixty abductees over a four-year period, using interviews and hypnosis to overcome their amnesia. His study uncovered more than 300 abduction experiences.

Dr. Jacobs's findings will, I believe, impress those who are open at least to the possibility that something important is happening in the lives of these individuals and countless others that cannot readily be explained by the theories and categories currently available to modern science. In Jacobs's cases, as in the work of other investigators, hypnosis has proven to be an essential tool in overcoming the amnesia of his subjects. Lest this lead skeptical readers to question the validity of Jacobs's findings, it must be pointed out that we have no evidence from this or any other study that under hypnosis abductees have invented or distorted significantly their memories of the abduction experience. On the contrary, memories brought forth in hypnotic regressions have been repeatedly shown to be consistent with what these and other abductees are able to recall consciously. Hypnosis appears to complete or add greatly to the process of remembering and has proved in this field to be a valuable therapeutic and investigative tool.

Dr. Jacobs's work covers a broad range of phenomena associated with UFO encounters. His focus, however, is upon the structure of the abduction experience itself. In case after case he demonstrates a pattern that is consistent—even in minute details and specific elements that are not available in the mass media—among individuals who have had no opportunity to communicate their experiences to one another. This pattern consists of what Jacobs calls "primary" experiences (physical examination, staring, and urological and gynecological procedures); "secondary" experiences (machine examination, visualization, and child presentation); and "ancillary" experiences consisting of various other physical phenomena, mental displays, and sexually related activities. At the heart of the abduction process there appears to be some sort of complex reproductive enterprise involving the conception, gestation, or incubation of human or alien-human hybrid babies. In Jacobs's words, "the focus of the abduction is the production of children."

Another investigator might place greater emphasis upon phenomena that Dr. Jacobs regards as less central, such as the visualizations of planetary destruction and their impact upon the consciousness of abductees. But whatever the emphasis or interpretation of these data, Jacobs's work has given us a solid foundation of carefully documented experience upon which investigators can now build as we add to our knowledge and explore further the meaning of this puzzling and disturbing matter.

Through his meticulous documentation of the structure and content of the UFO abduction phenomenon, Dr. Jacobs has deepened the mystery that lies before us while at the same time bringing us closer to some form of understanding. He has made clear that we are dealing with a phenomenon that has a hard edge, a huge, strange interspecies or interbeing breeding program that has invaded our physical reality and is affecting the lives of hundreds of thousands, if not millions, of people and perhaps in some way the consciousness of the entire planet. Jacobs has given us no explanation, but he has set forth explicitly the phenomena for which any theory must account.

Among ufologists and abduction researchers, explanations have generally fallen into psychosocial (or cultural) and extraterrestrial categories. Psychosocial hypotheses, at least in the Western materialist sense, are difficult to take seriously. For unless we are willing to extend our notions of the powers of the psyche to include the creation of cuts, scars, hemorrhages, and bruises, the simultaneous production of highly elaborate and traumatic experiences similar to one another in minute detail among individuals who have not communicated with one another, and all of the physical phenomena associated with the UFOs themselves, such explanations appear quite inadequate. At the same time a literalist extraterrestrial hypothesis must account for the relative paucity of solid physical information— the lack of photographs of the beings, for example—and the virtually insurmountable problems related to accounting for the location, origins, and lives of the aliens themselves within the framework of the physical laws of our space/time universe. This last frustration has led some ufologists to posit a "multiverse" and the intrusion into our familiar reality of other dimensions or forces outside of the known physical universe. Others have turned to alternative notions of the nature of the cosmos, more familiar to Eastern religions and philosophy, that depict the universe and all its realities as a vast play of consciousness with physical manifestations.

My own work with abductees has impressed me with the powerful dimension of personal growth that accompanies the traumatic experiences that David Jacobs so accurately describes, especially when these people receive appropriate help in exploring their abduction histories. An intense concern for the planet's survival and a powerful ecological consciousness seem to develop for many abductees. Whether this is a specific element, or even purpose, of the abduction enterprise or an inadvertent by-product of integrating a self-destroying traumatic narrative remains to be explored.

For me and other investigators, abduction research has had a shattering impact on our views of the nature of the cosmos. This has led me to offer at least a parable, if not a theory, to illuminate what is going on. Virtually all peoples throughout history, with the exception of the Western culture of the Newtonian/Cartesian era, have experienced the universe as possessing some sort of intelligence or consciousness in which human beings participate with other animate beings and inanimate things in an enterprise that has meaning, purpose, and direction, however unfathomable these may be. In the West, we seem, for reasons perhaps as mysterious as the abduction phenomenon itself, to have cut ourselves off almost totally from awareness of any form of higher intelligence. But let us suppose that such an intelligence did exist, and, what is more, that it was not indifferent to the fate of the Earth, regarding its life forms and transcendent beauty as one of its better or more advanced creations. And let us imagine that the imbalance created by the overgrowth of certain human faculties, a kind of technodestructive and fear-driven acquisitiveness, were "diagnosed" (perceived? fathomed? felt?—we really do not know how the divinity might experience itself and its creation) as the basic problem. What could be done as a corrective?

The two natural approaches of which we can conceive would be the genetic and the environmental. Is it possible that through a vast hybridization program affecting countless numbers of people, and a simultaneous invasion of our consciousness with transforming images of our self-destruction, an effort is being made to place the planet under a kind of receivership? This would not necessarily be for "our" good if this planet, on which humankind has broken the harmony of being, does not exist just for our pleasure, but in order to arrest the destruction of life and to make possible the further evolution of consciousness or whatever the anima mundi has in store. I do not say that this is true or offer it as a theory. I would merely suggest that if we could allow ourselves to reintroduce the possibility of a higher intelligence into the universe, and experience the numinous mystery of creation, this scenario is consistent with the facts of the abduction phenomenon.

David Jacobs has written in this book, "No significant body of thought has come about that presents strong evidence that anything else is happening other than what the abductees have stated." He has made his case well and has greatly enriched our knowledge of what the abductees have to tell of their experiences. We must now go on from here.

John E. Mack, M.D.
Professor of Psychiatry
Harvard Medical School

A Note to the Reader

This book is based on the testimony of some sixty individuals with whom I have explored more than 300 abduction experiences, and it includes transcripts or accounts of my interviews with more than twenty of them. A complete explanation of the techniques I used, including hypnotic regression, is included in Appendix A; Appendix B is a list of all abductees with whom I have investigated two or more abductions. In deference to the abductees' wishes, I have changed all their names, but I have included their active occupations and ages.

All the major accounts of abduction in the book share common characteristics and thus provide a confirmation of one another. I have not included one-of-a-kind accounts—no matter how dramatic —because no reliable inferences can be drawn from them without confirming testimony from other abductees.

Because the majority of abductees in this study are women, and because women seem to have a larger number of more complex experiences, I have adopted the stylistic device of using the pronoun "she" throughout the abduction event, except, of course, when discussing specific male experiences.

The transcripts have been edited for brevity and clarity, but the information and the meaning have not been altered. At the end of each transcript I have included the abductee's pseudonym, age at the time of the abduction, and year in which the abduction took place. Unless otherwise stated, I have personally investigated all of the abductions described in this book.

David M. Jacobs
Temple University

PART I
THE
BEGINNINGS

Chapter 1

A New Discipline

On an August day in 1986, I sat at my desk waiting for Melissa Bucknell to arrive at my house. Melissa was a twenty-six-year-old woman working in real estate management. She had experienced dreamlike recollections about strange little Beings examining her, and she suspected that she might have been involved in a UFO abduction. She was coming to me to learn if anything lurked behind these suspicions, and I was about to find out firsthand what such abductions were all about.

As I waited, I reflected on how I, a trained and seemingly rational historian specializing in twentieth-century America, had gotten involved in investigating anything as outrageous as UFOs and alien abductions. I am a tenured professor at an established university, where the majority of my teaching centers on political and cultural history. I have never seen a UFO.

Like many people, I didn't pay much attention to the subject of unidentified flying objects when I was growing up. Even though I was a child of the space age, Sputnik, and the program to put a man on the moon, I was never attracted to science fiction. But when I was an undergraduate university student, the UFO phenomenon captured my imagination. During my spare time I casually began reading articles about UFOs in newspapers and magazines. This seemed a harmless diversion, but it also had the tantalizing, although far-fetched, prospect of being the "real thing." Then in 1966, when I was a graduate student at the University of Wisconsin, the diversion became more serious for me. The April issue of *Life* magazine contained a large spread on an ongoing national wave of UFO sightings. I picked up a copy and stared at the published pictures amazed: something had been captured in the photographs. What were these objects?

Now I was more intrigued than ever. I read a few well-researched books in which credible witnesses consistently described apparently artificially constructed objects that seemed to be flying under intelligent control. I studied several debunking books as well, but it was obvious that these authors had their own particular axes to grind. In fact, except for perhaps a dozen or so books that presented solid, authenticated data based on responsible investigations, nearly all that had been written about UFOs, pro and con, was loosely researched and poorly documented; it was, quite simply, worthless. Still, enough was there for me to believe that UFOs were potentially an extremely important phenomenon that precious few people knew anything about.

In 1966 I read John Fuller's *Interrupted Journey,* the now-familiar story of Barney and Betty Hill, who claimed that aliens removed them from their automobile, gave them physical examinations (including a "pregnancy" test for Betty), and then released them. I thought this was a fascinating but highly improbable tale. The psychiatrist who had used hypnosis with the Hills to bring out the mainly forgotten story thought the case was an example of a shared dream, and I was inclined to agree, even though the aliens the Hills described looked very much like the UFO occupants that witnesses had claimed to have seen near landed UFOs.

In 1970 I joined several national UFO organizations and read their publications. I subscribed to the British journal *Flying Saucer Review,* which presented lively scientific debates and translations of the best articles from foreign periodicals. Even articles from skeptics, like Harvard astronomer Donald Menzel, appeared in its pages. The more I learned about the subject, the more adept I became at separating the wheat from the chaff. I began to understand the difference between good investigating and poor investigating, good research and poor research. I even began to do my own field investigations of UFO sighting reports.

Since my graduate training was in history, I began searching for historical patterns in the UFO phenomenon. I wanted to learn how society had "handled" UFOs since witnesses first reported them in the 1940s. I wanted to understand the role that the Air Force played in the UFO controversy. I wanted to look closely at the aura of ridicule that has surrounded the subject. I wanted to know why only a tiny percentage of the population had any solid information about UFOs despite the fact that sightings had been reported for so many years. I decided to write my doctoral dissertation on the history of the UFO controversy, even though only one dissertation had ever been written on a UFO-related subject, and that was in journalism. It certainly is not a common history subject. Professor Paul Conkin, who directed my studies and who was considered one of the most rigorous and systematic thinkers in the historical profession, was dubious when I first brought it up to him. He thought that UFOs were more related to social hysteria and fads than to anything else, but he allowed me to go ahead with the project. I finished my dissertation in 1973 and published a revised version of it in 1975.

After I received my Ph.D., I began teaching at the University of Nebraska and then in 1975 at Temple University in Philadelphia. At the same time I kept up my research on UFOs, published articles, and gave papers on the subject. As I continued to work in the area, I became aware of a major problem with the direction of that research. The study of UFO sightings was progressing well, but some of the most fundamental questions about the phenomenon were nowhere near being answered. Why, for instance, were these objects here? Why, if they were extraterrestrial, did they prefer to fly about and not make contact with humans? The answers to these and other questions could not be obtained from studying the outside shells of the objects. We needed to know more about what happened inside the UFOs.

The only UFO reports that described the interiors of the objects and what happened in them were the abduction cases. But the few cases investigators had collected in the 1970s were so different from one another that it was almost impossible to tell what, if anything, had actually happened. Two men said they were abducted by elephant-skinned creatures with long, sharp noses and claw hands. Another claimed to have been abducted for five days straight and to have seen not only small aliens but a "human" one as well. A woman said that little Beings came right through her wall and transported her to another planet. Some of the "abduction" stories involved benevolent Beings who had come to bring peace on earth and personal growth to the happy recipients of the contact. Still others told of prophecies of atomic destruction. Even though similarities existed between these cases—for example, all the abductees reported that they had been given physical examinations—it was easy to relegate this melange into the hoax and mind-game category.

Furthermore, there was the memory problem. Virtually all abductees suffered from a form of amnesia that prevented them from remembering exactly what had happened during the abduction. The preferred technique for retrieving these lost memories was hypnosis, but it was common knowledge that memories collected in this manner were not reliable. Indeed, some of the transcripts of the hypnotic testimony that I read revealed obviously leading questions and incompetent follow-up on answers. The lack of well-researched solid events did not inspire confidence.

In 1982 a friend introduced me to Budd Hopkins, an internationally celebrated artist who has been interested in the UFO mystery ever since his own sighting in 1964. Since the late 1970s Hopkins had specialized in examining abduction cases, and his first book, *Missing Time,* was published in 1981. In this pioneering work, he investigated a small group of people who he thought might have had abduction experiences. I was immediately impressed with his skillful research. Using a psychologist to administer hypnosis, Hopkins had collected data much more systematically than anyone had before. He meticulously uncovered important information about abductees having puzzling sustained lapses in time, mysterious scars, bizarre physical examinations, and screen memories (false memories masking what may have been abductions), and he even theorized a possible generational link between parents who were abductees and their children.

Hopkins's work was excellent, but I found that the overall situation was still confusing. After all, people have always claimed that many sorts of strange events have happened to them. They have lived past lives. They have been in communication with denizens of the spirit world and even Space Brothers. They have seen ghosts, danced with fairies, and had near-death experiences with religious implications. To my way of thinking, all of this might be a demonstration of the mind's mysterious workings. Perhaps these paranormal phenomena arose from the human tendency to create folklore. Or they might emanate from a collective unconscious. In any case, psychology rather than objective reality would explain these stories.

The same might be true of abductions. The problem was that when I read abduction accounts I could get no real sense of the progression of events during an abduction from beginning to end. Most of the reports consisted of snippets of stories, beginning in some logical order but then either ending abruptly or swerving off into wild, fantastic flights of fancy. As a historian, I required a chronological narrative. Before I could accept a psychological answer to all this, I needed a clear idea of exactly what the abduction accounts consisted of. I wanted to learn the details on a careful, rigorous, second-by-second basis, beginning with an abductee's first feeling that something extraordinary was happening to him and ending when the event was finally deemed to be over. I needed to be sure of my evidence.

I knew that if I were to make sense of what was happening, I would have to do abduction research myself. This meant that I would have to learn hypnosis. I had never hypnotized anybody, and it was a frightening prospect, but I was determined to learn. By 1985 Hopkins was doing his own hypnotic regressions, and he invited me to sit in on his sessions. I discussed hypnosis techniques with him and other researchers. I read books about hypnosis. I attended a hypnosis conference. I learned about the dangers and pitfalls of hypnosis.

Now Melissa Bucknell was on her way to my house, wondering if I could unravel whatever had been troubling her. She had written to Hopkins describing some of her unusual events and suspicions; because she lived in Philadelphia, he had referred her to me. I tried to exude confidence when she arrived, but underneath I was anxious. I had no idea what was going to happen, whether I could successfully hypnotize anyone or whether I could enable her to remember events in her past. Luckily, Melissa had been hypnotized before, so when I began the induction, she slipped quickly into a trance state. It was easy. The difficult part was asking the right questions, in the right manner.

In the first regression session, Melissa described being a six-year-old child playing in a field in back of her house with a friend. Before she knew it she was being transported into a UFO by aliens. Her clothes were removed and a physical examination was performed on her. Her genitals were probed with a needlelike instrument. She felt that some sort of implant was inserted near her left ovary.

I was amazed. On the first regression, Melissa had spontaneously "remembered" being taken on board a UFO, being given an examination, and having her genitals probed. What was I to make of this? I had no way of being sure of the truthfulness of what I had heard, although the material she recalled was very similar to what Hopkins had been finding. I did not know what to do with this testimony other than to just note it.

Melissa continued to come for sessions on a regular basis, and soon other people were coming as well: Ken Rogers, a professional bicyclist; Barbara Archer, a university student and reporter; George Kenniston, an attorney; Karen Morgan, a public relations specialist, to name a few. I decided that the best way to go about gathering systematic information was to conduct as many hypnosis sessions on as many "suggestive" events in an individual's past as was possible. Over the next five years I had more than 325 hypnosis sessions with more than sixty abductees. The abductees were, by and large, average citizens who did not desire publicity, who were not trying to commit a hoax, and who, with one exception, were not mentally disturbed. They were Protestant, Catholic, Jewish, white, black, male, female, younger, older, professional, nonprofessional, married, single, divorced, employed, unemployed, articulate, and inarticulate. The people who came to me fit the random quality among abductees that Hopkins had also found.

I discovered that, in general, it made little difference where the abductions occurred. The people I interviewed described being abducted from every region of the country (and around the world as well), from cities and rural areas, highways and isolated roads, single homes and apartment complexes. Although in the main they did not know each other, they all told the same stories: They were abducted by strange-looking Beings, subjected to a variety of physical and mental "procedures," and then put back where they had been taken. They were powerless to control the event, and, when it was over, they promptly forgot nearly all of it. Most were left with the feeling that something had happened to them, but they were not sure exactly what it was. I also found that some of the abductees remembered events without the aid of hypnosis; their stories were the same as those whose memories were recovered with hypnosis.

The events that the abductees related were completely implausible. Time and again they would describe physically impossible situations, such as floating through a closed window or communicating telepathically, that made no scientific sense whatsoever. But the abductees were not asking me to believe them. For the most part they were just as puzzled as I was about the meaning of what had happened to them. Often they would describe abduction events that I had heard perhaps a hundred times and then look and me and ask, "Has anybody ever said anything like that to you before?" Most of them were grateful for having the opportunity to recall what had been locked up inside them, sometimes for many years, and for having somebody who would listen to them without ridicule.

Whether or not their experiences were real, they were all people who had experienced great pain. They seemed to be suffering from a form of trauma related to a combination of Post-Traumatic Stress Disorder and the terror that comes from being raped. Nearly all of them felt as if they had been victimized.

As I listened to them, I found myself sharing in their emotionally wrenching experiences. I heard people sob with fear and anguish, and seethe with hatred of their tormentors. They had endured enormous psychological (and sometimes physical) pain and suffering. I was profoundly touched by the depth of emotion that they showed during the regressions. I did my best to reassure and to help them, but I felt almost as powerless as they did.

Dealing with my own emotions was also a difficult task. During the first year of my research into abductee narratives, my impulse was to deny everything I heard. I reasoned that I had probably been glimpsing an unknown form of psychological fantasy that was causing the abductee tremendous fear and pain. Anything seemed better than the possibility that what people were describing had actually happened to them. Yet I could not ignore the convergence of minute detail, the lack of personal content, the physical evidence of unusual scars and other marks on their bodies immediately following an abduction, the missing time lapses during the supposed abduction, the multiple abductions, and other witnesses. There must be explanations, but no one seemed to be coming forward with a psychological theory that fit the evidence.

As I continued the hypnotic regressions, it became apparent that, as incredible as it seemed, it was possible that these accounts might be true. The stories I was told seemed to take on an air of greater reality as I became more competent in my hypnosis techniques. My questioning became so close and so careful that I began to uncover information no one else had ever heard. For example, Lynn Miller came to me because of missing time episodes that she had experienced over the past few years. I took a history of her background, and, among other events, she remembered that when she was twelve years old she had "flown with the angels." When we conducted a session about this event, it turned out to be another abduction episode.

She said that during the experience one of the procedures performed on her had involved a tall Being giving her a piece of "paper" with "boys' names" on it. She was told that she had to remember the names, and that the Being would come back to her later and retrieve the names. She stood there looking at the paper. "What could this be?" I thought to myself. Why would they want the names? Why did she have to remember them? Why couldn't they remember the names themselves? I had absolutely no idea what was happening in this account. As I tried different lines of inquiry, I at last hit upon the right question. The answer opened up a world of completely unknown testimony about supposed procedures. *Question:* "What is he doing while you are doing this?" *Answer:* "He seems to be staring at me."

I was surprised by this answer. When I asked the question I had thought that perhaps the Being was doing something in the room while leaving Lynn to her task. But as soon as she said that he was staring at her, I began to be suspicious. Perhaps the point of this event had very little to do with memorization. I asked other abductees what the Beings were doing when they said that they were required to observe or concentrate on something. In virtually every case the answer was that the Being was staring at them, very closely, and usually at their eyes. I began to realize that this event might be part of a complex series of mental procedures that were administered to abductees.

No one had ever heard these procedural accounts before. It seemed unlikely that so many people would independently come up with the idea that they were being stared at closely. What kind of a psychological mechanism was this? It became evident to me that this and many other details that were described to me would be extremely difficult, if not impossible, to attribute to internally generated psychological fantasies.

I wanted to discuss the research I was doing with my fellow UFO researchers. Although sympathetic to my work, most of them were still involved with investigating the sightings of UFOs and knew very little about abductions. They also felt, as I once had, that abductions were probably psychologically induced. When I broached the subject with my colleagues at the university, I was met, with few exceptions, with instant ridicule. Jokes about my sanity followed as they tried to humor me. And who could blame them? The material seemed so outrageous and ridiculous that expressing interest in it was obviously a waste of time. Some criticized me for veering from my normal history research. A few pointed out that my academic career could be effectively halted by this research.

I knew I was on shaky ground in terms of both my own analysis and science. I was using primarily anecdotal evidence as the basis of my research. Stories that people tell are a weak form of evidence for most scientists. Stories of space aliens abducting people and performing strange biological procedures on them were not going be considered evidence for anything other than mental aberration. In the discipline of history, one spends years learning how to analyze documents and other forms of evidence, put them together into a coherent, logical whole, write serious historical works, and make knowledgeable contributions to the field. In order to do this the historian has agreed-upon events to guide him and a chronology to structure the evidence. Discovering previously unknown historical facts adds dimension and insight into a larger body of known material.

This was not the case in abduction research. I had no ground rules or signposts except Hopkins's work to help me make sense of these abductions. In the beginning of my investigations, I floundered with my data. When I started doing regressions it was immediately apparent that significant parts of the stories were impossible to understand, and some of these were pretty "wild." The more I learned, the more I understood that some of what was being told to me was the product of confabulation (the unconscious invention and filling in of memories), false memories, and dream material. I had to learn to distinguish the unreliable material from what appeared to be legitimate memories. After much trial and error, I finally became confident in my ability to perceive what was happening in various abduction accounts and to make connections. I now was ready to put the material into some sort of theoretical framework.

I noticed that the abduction accounts were forming themselves into distinct patterns of activity. Practically all the abductees said that they were experiencing similar physical, mental, and reproductive procedures. Each abductee contributed a piece of the puzzle, but no single abductee related the entire structure of the abduction. The more data I gathered, the more I began to realize just how structured this phenomenon was. Certain physical procedures were almost always followed by other procedures. Certain reproductive procedures led to other reproductive procedures. The same was true of the mental procedures. I devised a matrix consisting of three tiers:

Primary experiences, which involve procedures that the aliens perform the greatest number of times on the greatest number of people and that set the structure for all other procedures to come.

Secondary experiences, which occur less frequently. All abductees have some secondary experiences, but not during every episode, and some procedures might never be performed on individual abductees.

Ancillary experiences, which involve specialized sexual and other irregular procedures. These happen infrequently to the abductee population as a whole, but may recur many times to an individual abductee.

I arranged these experiences into the physical, reproductive, and mental categories that abductees described. I worked on this matrix for two and a half years—revising, adding, subtracting, and rearranging the data and the categories as I gained more information and as my understanding of events became more sophisticated. The structure of the abduction was bizarre, fantastic, and alien. Yet it had fit neatly into a pattern. All the procedures appeared to be linked in some way. Even the smallest details of the events were confirmed many times over. There was a chronology, structure, logic—the events made sense. Like any scientific or historical inquiry, my investigations had lent themselves to systematic study, and they displayed an extraordinary internal integrity. I found areas that were difficult to understand because the abductees described apparently superior technology and biotechnology, not because the events were nonsensical.

The more I learned about these abduction stories, the more I felt that I was peeking into a hidden world. If these stories had any semblance of reality to them, many people had been leading secret lives, unbeknownst even to them. They were being abducted and subjected to strange procedures. As a result, humans were being employed to produce another form of life—a secret life. And all this was being carried out by an alien form of life that existed secretly in our environment.

In writing of these abduction experiences, I am not out to convince the reader they are really happening. The material is inherently unbelievable, and I assume that many readers will be skeptical of it. It is entirely possible that a psychological explanation for the abduction accounts will be devised that fully explains the origin of these accounts. Rather than build a case for their reality, what I have done is to put the accounts that I have collected into a coherent whole, so that we can see what they add up to. It is up to the reader to make up his or her mind about the reality of the accounts.

If, however, the abductions are occurring as the abductees describe, then this book can serve not only as a guide for future abduction research but also as a warning to everyone about something incredible and ominous that is, in fact, happening—something that can have a profound effect on us all.

I now invite the reader to take an extraordinary trip with me, a trip to what might be the farthest reaches of believability. First, we must understand the history of the UFO phenomenon in order to place the abductions in a historical context. Then we proceed on a step-by-step journey through common, or typical, abduction experiences from the first few seconds of an abduction to the last few. Next, I draw a composite picture of the appearance and behavior of the aliens. I then discuss some of the serious consequences that abductions have had on victims' lives and examine methods of resistance and intervention to the abductions. I also examine alternative explanations for what abductees are describing and, finally, explain some of the implications and meanings of the abduction experience.

This trip may be shocking to some, especially the descriptions of sexual procedures, but it is a journey that has to be made. If not, we may be playing ostrich in relation to an event of such fundamental importance that our failure to recognize it will be the subject of amazement for future generations.

Chapter 2

Sightings and Abductions

The modern UFO phenomenon emerged full-blown in the summer of 1947 when witnesses described a wide variety of geometrically shaped objects in the sky. These objects were not the earthly rocketships or space travel contraptions commonly found in science fiction literature. Nor were they technological variations of the new jet planes that had captured the public's imagination in the mid-1940s. They were something completely new and were unrelated to popular culture in general. The UFOs seemed to come out of nowhere.

Although a puzzling "mystery airship" wave had taken place in 1896 and 1897, it had long since been forgotten. Strange aerial objects known as "foo-fighters" and "ghost rockets" had been in the news occasionally from 1944 to 1946, but the public had taken little notice of them. In fact, there hadn't been any science fiction radio programs with extraterrestrial invasion themes (with the exception of the 1938 *War of the Worlds* broadcast, which did not include UFOs). The first Hollywood motion pictures with plots of alien visitation were not produced until 1949. Many films had been made about earthlings traveling to other planets (Buck Rogers and Flash Gordon, for example), but no major films had aliens from outer space invading earth. UFO sightings did not spring from one of the important shapers of popular attitudes—mass media science fiction.[1]

At the time, not enough information was available to establish just what people were seeing, but the prevailing assumption was that the objects were real and could probably be explained as secret weapons or other "conventional" phenomena. Nonetheless their mysterious nature was enough to rattle the nerves of the United States government. In 1948 the government assigned the Air Force the task of investigating the UFO reports to determine whether or not these objects posed a threat to the national security. Government interest in UFOs also spilled over into the Army, Navy, and CIA, which mounted small-scale investigations of sightings. Even J. Edgar Hoover, sensing Communist hanky-panky, had the FBI investigate UFO witnesses for their possible "subversive" capabilities.[2]

In these early days of UFOs, the Air Force and the public fell prey to several outlandish hoaxes and rumors. A citizen in Maryland reported that a flying saucer had crashed in his backyard and that he had recovered it. The Air Force sent men to investigate; the three-foot-wide toy of aluminum foil made headlines across the country before the Air Force decided that it had been victimized. Other hoaxes proved all too easy to perpetrate before investigators were able to distinguish them from legitimate UFO reports, and rumors of crashed flying saucers abounded almost from the beginning.

From 1948 to 1953, the Air Force and its scientific consultant for UFOs, astronomer J. Allen Hynek, actively investigated the UFO phenomenon. After the Air Force satisfied itself that the objects were not secret weapons from this or any other country, and having found no "hard" evidence for the existence of UFOs, it reasoned that the witnesses were simply mistaken, no matter how detailed the report or how credible the observer. Project Grudge, the Air Force's official UFO investigation unit, came to the convenient conclusion that any UFO that defied conventional explanation could be accounted for in psychological terms—specifically, that they were attributable to misperception of conventional phenomena, abnormal psychological or physiological states, "societal stress," and hoaxes. Whatever reports remained were categorized as "unknown." In the end the "unknown" category became the solution to the mystery—the objects were unknown, case closed. Project Grudge made no attempt to analyze the character of the unknowns, to look for the common properties in the narratives, or to compare the witnesses' backgrounds.

Project Grudge quite easily assigned psychological answers to this physical puzzle. Although there was no evidence that UFO witnesses

had serious psychological problems, it seemed "right" to suggest that
this might be the case. Therefore this scientific judgment, based on
no evidence whatsoever, was issued to the public as fact. The scientific community, assuming a perceptual and psychological answer,
did not question this evaluation. Scientists preferred to accept this
explanation because it conveniently seemed to solve the mystery.
The same was true of the "societal stress" argument. No scientist
ever attempted to verify the theory that stressful events in the society cause people to look into the sky, see strange objects, and then
report these observations as a way of alleviating their personal stress.

From the very beginning, the scientific community, instead of testing the assumptions about conventional explanations of UFOs, gave
the military a free hand in UFO analysis and never seriously attempted to confirm its results or investigate the UFO phenomenon
independently. A pattern was set: the scientific community assumed
that the phenomenon was "illegitimate" and allowed the Air Force
to investigate it without questioning either the Air Force's assumptions and methodology or its own assumptions.

Once the Air Force "explained" UFOs and found no threat to the
national security, it attempted to distance itself from the subject, first
by proclaiming that UFOs were misidentifications of conventional
phenomena, and then in 1950 by dissolving Project Grudge in the
hope that the entire fad, now free from government validation,
would soon disappear. But by 1951 it was obvious that the Air Force
had not solved the UFO problem. UFOs were still being sighted, and
even high-ranking Air Force officers were seeing them. The Air Force
decided to reopen Project Grudge. Unknowingly, the Air Force's
actions validated one of the critical findings of UFO research: The
UFO phenomenon has no relation to societal events. No matter how
the Air Force tried to manipulate public opinion or to suggest that
UFOs had no objective reality, sightings continued, unaffected by
these activities and pronouncements. Even a 1952 Air Force study
of publicity surrounding UFOs and its effect on the number of sightings reported failed to show any cause and effect relation between
publicity and UFO sightings.

Eager to put the issue to rest, the Air Force appointed Capt. Edward Ruppelt as the head of Project Grudge, later renamed Project
Blue Book. Ruppelt made an enthusiastic attempt to study UFOs in
the spring and summer of 1952. His efforts would constitute the

high point of Air Force involvement in UFO analysis. He developed plans to equip a special diffraction lens on a camera to analyze the spectrum of the light emitted by a UFO; he was going to photograph radar screens and measure radiation from UFO fly-overs; and he enlisted electronics and weather experts to help him.

But in 1952 the Air Force and Ruppelt were caught off guard. The Air Force found itself swamped with reports. During one month, more reports came in than the total for the previous five years. A series of spectacular sightings over the White House and Capitol Building created sensational publicity and convinced the Air Force that too many people were reporting what it still believed to be bogus sightings, in spite of Ruppelt's ongoing investigation. The UFO problem was getting out of hand, and something had to be done before it presented itself as a threat to the national security.

The Central Intelligence Agency then entered into the picture. It put together a panel of scientists to study the situation. The CIA convened the Robertson Panel in January 1953 and changed the course of government involvement in UFOs for the next sixteen years. (Ruppelt and others were invited to give a briefing before the panel, but Project Blue Book did not formally participate.) After only twelve hours of briefings and study, the panel concluded that UFOs were not a threat to the national security. It did find, however, that the UFO *reports* were a threat because the Soviet Union could use "UFO hysteria" and public criticisms of the Air Force's UFO investigations as a psychological warfare weapon against the United States. The Robertson Panel endowed the Air Force with a new mission: to mount a public relations effort to convince people that all UFO phenomena were explainable. Once educated to the great variety of things seen in the sky, the people would forget about UFOs, and the entire ridiculous affair would soon disappear. Solving the UFO mystery was no longer the objective. Public relations became the focus.

With this, the Air Force's (and the government's) efforts to study the phenomenon ended. All of Ruppelt's plans to study UFOs systematically were scrapped. Never again would the government scientifically investigate the UFO mystery. Never again would it consider the UFO problem as anything more than a public relations headache. After 1953 it acted as a "soothing agent," trying to calm fears and persuade the public that it had everything under control, hoping that eventually the fad would end and the reports would cease. No one within the scientific community critically examined the government's actions.

The Air Force was unwittingly aided in its attempt to prove that UFOs were nonsense by the "contactees." These colorful individuals began telling their stories in the early 1950s and fundamentally altered people's perceptions of the UFO phenomenon. Led by "Professor" George Adamski, "Doctor" Daniel Fry, Truman Bethurum, Orfeo Angelucci, and Howard Menger, the contactees claimed in ever-escalating sensational accounts that they had not only seen flying saucers but that they had met the occupants of them, engaged in long conversations with them about the differences in their respective planets, and took trips in flying saucers to visit distant worlds. They claimed that the benevolent beings they called Space Brothers had given them a mission to perform on earth, which usually involved giving a message to mankind to stop atomic wars, stop atomic testing, live together in peace, and so forth.

The contactees gained adherents and in the process attracted widespread press attention with their spectacular (and often demonstrably untrue) claims. Many unsuspecting people interested in UFOs were drawn into the web of charlatanism. To complicate matters, a small but growing number of reputable witnesses were reporting small Beings seen in or near UFOs. These reports were all but disregarded in the confusion as the contactees' media splash resulted in increased public ridicule for all UFO witnesses. The new UFO organizations were horrified at the contactees and spent large amounts of time and energy trying to dissociate themselves from them.

UFOs continued to be an "illegitimate" area of study for scientists, both because of the Air Force's debunking policies and the ridicule that stemmed from the lack of tangible evidence of their existence and the negative publicity the contactees generated. In 1952 the Air Force's UFO consultant, J. Allen Hynek, conducted a survey of forty-five astronomers and found them very frightened of ridicule and afraid of jeopardizing their careers if they showed any interest in UFOs.

Since the scientific community and the Air Force had dismissed the validity of the sightings out of hand, it was left to "lay" people to investigate the persistent UFO mystery and to deal with the contactees. In their efforts to distance themselves from the contactees, most researchers reacted negatively to all UFO "occupant" sightings, and a wave of conservatism swept the UFO research community. A split developed. Some organizations accepted the occupant reports, while others rejected them summarily, fearing that they smacked of "contacteeism."

The quality of investigating, analyzing, and reporting was wildly inconsistent. Some of the work was excellent, but much of it was worthless. Debunkers exploited the weaknesses of these amateur investigators and suggested that the phenomenon itself was illegitimate because most of the people who studied it were not scientifically trained. This reinforced the notion within the scientific community that UFOs were truly an illegitimate field of study. It was a self-fulfilling prophecy. The longer the scientific community rejected the subject, the more amateurs filled the void. The amateurish quality of the work, along with the contactees' gibberish, indicated to scientists that the entire affair was a "silly season" fad unworthy of scientific analysis.

But some UFO organizations in the mid-1950s tried to impress upon the public that the UFO phenomenon was legitimate and that the Air Force investigation was inadequate. Organizations such as Jim and Coral Lorenzen's Aerial Phenomena Research Organization (APRO), the New York–based Civilian Saucer Intelligence, and the National Investigations Committee on Aerial Phenomena (NICAP), under the leadership of retired Marine Corps Major Donald Keyhoe, became more convinced than ever that UFOs were most likely extraterrestrial and that the government was covering up this fact. They mounted intense efforts to make the Air Force reveal its findings and investigate UFOs openly and fairly.

By 1958 it was clear that the Air Force's continued attempts to eradicate reports were failing. UFO sightings appeared to be unaffected by Air Force policy, contactee yarns, scientific attitudes, and public ridicule. They had continued at a steady pace from 1952 until 1957, when there was another enormous wave of sightings.

The 1957 wave prompted much public criticism of the Air Force's handling of the problem. When the 1957 wave hit, much of the press began to realize that Air Force statements about UFOs—that they did not represent a threat to the national security and did not display technology in advance of our own—seemed disingenuous. The press put increased pressure on the Air Force to "come clean" and tell what it knew about the UFO mystery. By 1958 the Air Force, frustrated with trying to eliminate reports, and tired of increasing public hostility, was also trying to rid itself of the UFO program entirely.

The Air Force's policy of secrecy, however, and its attempts to identify the UFOs at all costs (to implement the recommendations of the Robertson Panel) were firmly entrenched. Only J. Allen Hynek had civilian access to the Air Force data, and he still believed that the UFO phenomenon was the product of conventional sources, although he was beginning to have his doubts.

The Air Force felt that it was under siege. Its efforts to relieve itself of the burden of UFOs intensified. But no matter where it tried to have the UFO project transferred—to NASA, the Brookings Institution, or a scientific area within the armed services—the Air Force could not get rid of it. No one else would assume the public relations headache that went with it.

By 1966, the Air Force was ready to try anything to rid itself of Project Blue Book. The opportunity presented itself in March, when a few sightings in Michigan seized the public's attention. Eighty-six college students at Hillsdale College had seen a football-shaped object hovering over a field. The object ducked behind some trees when automobiles approached and then hovered again when the cars left. In Dexter, Michigan, a farmer and his son, along with many other witnesses, saw a large red object come flying out of a wooded and marshy area.

The Air Force dispatched J. Allen Hynek to investigate the reports. Hynek had been the Air Force consultant on UFOs on and off for eighteen years. He had begun as a debunker and had been severely castigated by UFO buffs as an Air Force stooge. But over the years, and especially in the early 1960s, Hynek had agonizingly rethought his opinions and had come to the conclusion that UFOs were probably extraterrestrial. In his role as Air Force UFO specialist, however, his job was to go to Michigan and explain the sightings. After a perfunctory look into the cases, he issued a press statement saying that the sightings might be caused by a spontaneously igniting release of methane gas caused by rotting vegetation, sometimes known as swamp gas.

A howl of ridicule went up in the press. Hynek's investigation had produced exactly the opposite effect the Air Force had intended. Instead of quieting the public's interest in UFOs, the swamp gas explanation seemed to give credence to the people who were charging that the Air Force was engaged in a cover-up. *Life* magazine published a feature article on the sightings with dramatic UFO photographs from around the world.

Pressure on the Air Force mounted as Congressmen Gerald Ford and Weston Vivian, sensing Air Force ineptitude, called for hearings on the Air Force's handling of the UFO problem. The first of those investigations was held in April 1966. A House committee strongly urged that the Air Force allow universities to look into the UFO matter. As a result, the Air Force contracted with the University of Colorado to conduct a study of the UFO phenomenon and issue findings on whether the objects represented a threat to national security. If UFOs were not a threat, then the Air Force could gracefully retreat from the UFO battleground and close Project Blue Book. Noted physicist Edward U. Condon led a committee of about a dozen scholars that was to take a fresh look at the UFO evidence and recommend whether further study was warranted.

But Condon's flip attitude toward the subject, his controversial managerial style, and internal disagreements over procedures and evidence severely hampered the committee's investigation. In spite of the committee's serious split, Condon recommended in the 1968 final report that the Air Force give up UFO investigations because "further extensive study of UFOs probably cannot be justified in the expectation that science will be advanced," and UFOs do not "pose a defense problem."[3] For Condon, the entire UFO affair was an enormous waste of time filled with hoaxes, bogus contactees, and weak-thinking UFO enthusiasts awash in the "will to believe."

Based on these recommendations, the Air Force closed Project Blue Book in December 1969, and its public investigation of UFO reports came to an end. It had never mounted a serious full-scale investigation of the phenomenon. It had never systematically analyzed reports. After 1952, the main thrust of the Air Force's UFO policy was to treat it as a public fad.

In fact, the Condon Report left an unsolved mystery. Even though it had come to strongly negative conclusions, the report still presented a strong case for UFOs as anomalies. The committee could not identify more than 30 percent of the cases it had investigated. Many of the reports were simply labeled as unidentified. In one case a UFO was called an "extraordinary flying object, silvery, metallic, disk-shaped, tens of meters in diameter, and evidently artificial."[4]

Buried within the report was a solid body of evidence that this was a phenomenon requiring at the very least more study and attention.

The Condon Report, however, did its damage. Scientists who had not bothered to read the entire report concluded that Condon's recommendations were the final word on the subject and that the UFO mystery had been laid to rest once and for all. UFO "buffs" dropped their membership in UFO organizations, assuming that there was no further reason to support research into the subject. The media played up the "case closed" angle. Although the Condon Report hurt UFO research, it had absolutely no influence on the UFO phenomenon itself, which continued to be reported, unaffected by societal events.

In 1973 another massive wave of sightings took place, but for the first time since 1947 the Air Force stayed out of it. The wave occurred in exactly the same way the other waves had—without reference to societal events and displaying the full range of UFO activity: high-level sightings, low-level sightings, "trace cases" where the object left evidence of its existence in the form of an affected environment, reports in which witnesses claimed to see UFO occupants, and even a few oddly puzzling abduction cases.

But in the absence of government interpretations of these objects in the sky, the American people could at last indulge in unrestrained interest in the phenomenon. Hynek, now fully committed to the extraterrestrial origin of UFO sightings, took the opportunity during the 1973 wave to announce the opening of the Center for UFO Studies, which was to be the first scientific organization devoted to studying the mystery. In addition, the new Midwest (later Mutual) UFO Network came to the fore as a leading UFO investigative organization, and the two groups worked together to collect and analyze reports.

By the end of the 1970s, the study of UFOs had become much more sophisticated than ever, and a great amount of knowledge had been acquired about UFO patterns, effects, appearances, and residues. But UFO researchers felt frustrated by the seeming decline in public interest, and they had great difficulty in piercing the armor of mystery around UFO behavior. And even though Hynek and others strenuously tried to convince the scientific community of the importance of the subject, ridicule still remained a critical negative factor for its study. The scientific standing of UFOs was still very much where it had been from the beginning: intriguing but "illegitimate." Yet even though the Air Force was ostensibly out of the UFO business, documents released in the mid-1970s showed that it was still doing investigations of UFO reports made by military personnel or on military installations. Some documents spurred concerned UFO researchers to continue searching for evidence of even more extensive clandestine government activities.

Underneath the surface of these public events were some remarkable cases strongly suggesting that the UFOs were involved in the abduction of humans. January 1965 brought the first publication of an abduction case. The event had occurred in 1957 in Brazil. Antonio Villas-Boas was the son of a rancher. He was working on his father's farm at night when he saw a UFO land near him. Four large-headed, small Beings quickly came out of the object and forced Villas-Boas inside. They took off his clothes and spread a clear, odorless liquid over his body. They then cut his chin and collected some blood into a cup. Villas-Boas claimed that a small, naked female Being then entered the room. She had thin blond hair, large slanted eyes, high cheekbones, an ordinary nose, a small, thin-lipped mouth, and a sharply pointed chin. Her body looked human, her feet were small, and her hands were long and pointed. She was about four and a half feet tall. She began to hug and caress him. He became uncontrollably sexually excited. They had intercourse twice. Then the female Being abruptly broke off their intimacy and left Villas-Boas with the feeling that he was being treated like "a good stallion to improve their . . . stock." He was then let off the object.[5]

To UFO researchers at the time, this report seemed ridiculous and lurid; it reeked of pulp science fiction. Having spent the better part of the 1950s battling the contactees, they did not need another outlandish case to complicate their job of winning scientific legitimacy for the phenomenon. But Villas-Boas's story and actions did not match those of the contactees. He received no messages to relay to mankind. He had no mission given to him. He made no money from the story. He simply told his story and then retreated to the normal activities of his daily life. (He eventually went to law school and became a respected attorney. He maintained the truthfulness of his account until he died.)

While this case stood out for the next few years as an embarrassing anomaly, another case came along that was more difficult to dismiss: The Barney and Betty Hill case not only became a source of great debate, but it also ranks as perhaps the most important and well-known case in the history of the UFO phenomenon. It was the subject of a two-part story in *Look* magazine in 1966, a popular book in the same year, and a 1975 NBC television movie.[6]

The Hills said that while driving from Montreal to Portsmouth, New Hampshire, small Beings with large heads and eyes abducted them from their car into a landed UFO. The Beings separated them into different rooms and subjected them to physical examinations. They inserted a needle into Betty's abdomen and told her that they were giving her a "pregnancy" test. They obtained scrapings of the Hills' skin and performed other physiological tests. A larger Being, whom Betty thought was the "leader," communicated with her telepathically. After the "medical" procedures were completed, and after some other events happened, the Hills were allowed to exit from the object and watch its departure. They immediately forgot what had happened to them, resumed their trip, and arrived home about two hours later than they should have. All they remembered was that they had observed a UFO close up. They recalled nothing of the abduction. Over the next few months they were bothered by strange dreams of being on board an alien craft; when they suffered continual anxiety related to their UFO sighting, they sought help through psychological counseling. They were referred to Benjamin Simon, a well-known psychiatrist proficient in hypnosis. Through the use of hypnotic regressions, they recovered the memories of what had transpired that evening.

Although John Fuller's 1966 book about the episode, *Interrupted Journey,* described the "pregnancy test" performed on Betty, he decided not to include the fact that the Beings had extracted a sperm sample from Barney. This was too embarrassing for the Hills and for Fuller in the mid-1960s, and he did not mention it lest it detract from the veracity of the account.

The Hills' story broke like a thunderbolt in the UFO research community. They were an interracial couple whose credibility was above reproach. Barney Hill was a member of the NAACP and the New Hampshire Civil Rights Commission, and Betty Hill was a social worker. They were respected, churchgoing members of their community. This was not the type of couple who liked to attract "lunatic fringe" attention to themselves. But did the events as the Hills described them actually happen? Researchers had no way of knowing.

The Hill case split the UFO research community. Many UFO researchers agreed with University of Arizona atmospheric physicist James E. McDonald when he complained that because of the relationship to the contactee stories, the Hill case put UFO research back twenty years. But, like the Villas-Boas case, the Hills' account seemed to be unrelated to the 1950s-style contactee claims. The Hills were not concerned with making money from the tale (although they received money from the publication of the book), nor did they embellish and change the story as time went on. They did not receive a "mission" from the Space Brothers. They did not say that they were chosen for any particular reason. They were not members of a flying saucer cult. In fact, until his initial sighting Barney had been hostile to the idea that UFOs existed.

A crucial aspect of the Hill case was that their information was retrieved through the use of hypnosis. Benjamin Simon, the psychiatrist who administered the hypnosis, was never convinced that an abduction had actually occurred. He preferred to think that the two had experienced a "shared fantasy" or a condition known as *folie à deux*, even though the details of their "fantasies" were quite different because they had been put in separate rooms and had different experiences. The transcripts of the hypnosis showed that Simon spent a considerable amount of time unsuccessfully trying to get the Hills to admit that the events had never really happened, or to catch them in contradictions.

After the Hill case, other reports of abductions slowly began to surface, but the number was still so small that they caused very little comment among UFO researchers. They represented an anomaly outside the more conventional sighting reports that dominated the field. Yet the abduction claims persisted. In October 1973, two residents of Pascagoula, Mississippi, said that strange-looking aliens floated them into a UFO and physically examined them. In 1975 forest worker Travis Walton claimed that he was taken aboard a UFO and, while he thought he was gone for a few hours, he appeared to be missing for five days. Inside the object he remembered lying on a table and seeing small Beings with large heads and eyes. That same year an Army sergeant saw a UFO headed for him while he sat on the hood of his car. A numbness spread over his body before the object left. He noticed that he was inexplicably missing about one and one half hours of time. The next few days brought a sore and inflamed back and a rash from his chest to his knees. He later remembered small Beings with large heads and eyes performing a medical examination on him while he lay on a table.[7]

In January 1976 three women in Kentucky observed a bright-red object hovering some distance from their car. The next thing they knew, they were eight miles down the road and it was an hour and a half later. They continued home and experienced burning sensations on their faces when water touched them. They then noticed that they had similar red marks on the backs of their necks. Hypnosis was administered by Leo Sprinkle, a professor of counseling psychology at the University of Wyoming and an early investigator of abductions. The three women remembered being physically examined by small, gray, humanoid figures while they lay on tables. One woman felt that they were conducting an experiment on her to learn about her emotional and intellectual processes. Another woman could see a human she didn't know lying on a table next to hers.[8]

In 1977 a ten-year-old report came to light in Massachusetts. Betty Andreasson claimed that she and her family were put in a state of "suspended animation" when five small Beings entered their home by walking through a wall. She was taken to a bizarre location where, among other things, she was examined, saw strange animals on another planet, and saw a giant phoenixlike bird rising from ashes. She also reported various events that she interpreted as profoundly religious. UFO investigator Ray Fowler wrote three books on her experiences, but the events were so bizarre that UFO researchers were at a loss to separate reality from fantasy.[9]

By the late 1970s and early 1980s, abduction accounts began to be reported in ever-increasing numbers. Some researchers were beginning to theorize about an apparent reproductive link that recurred in these accounts. As early as 1972 researcher Marjorie Fish hypothesized that a needle inserted in Betty Hill's navel might have been for experimentation with human eggs, and in 1977 psychiatrist Berthold E. Schwarz discussed the idea of a laparoscopy (a method of examining internal organs by using a viewing scope) being performed on Betty. Based on cases that she investigated, in 1980 researcher Ann Druffel suggested that aliens might be interested in human sexual life-styles.[10]

Most UFO researchers, however, still considered abduction reports to be exotic and bewildering anomalies—perhaps true and perhaps not. Although patterns were slowly emerging from the abduction stories and the people involved seemed to be credible, the specter of the contactees still intimidated most UFO researchers. In fact, some 1950s-style contactees were still around, claiming trips to the planets and gab sessions with friendly aliens. To complicate matters, some abductees who seemed to be sincere individuals and who did not fit the contactee model were reporting contactee-like abduction experiences. They claimed that they were given prophecies of death and destruction for our society, or that they had experienced Christian religious experiences. Others were enamored with kindly, handsome, space people who were here on a benevolent mission of some sort. How these reports could fit into the scheme of "legitimate" abductions was impossible to comprehend.

To make matters worse, there was the increasing popularity of "channeling," a process in which, by placing oneself in the proper mental state, a person could contact benevolent aliens at will. Prior to the 1950s, channelers, whose activities are related to automatic writing, speaking in tongues, and a number of other "psychic" phenomena, had mainly communicated with spirits. Now aliens, a phenomenon that had been known in UFO cult groups for more than thirty-five years, became the contacts of choice. In channeled messages, the Space Brothers, frequently said to be from the Pleiades or Zeta Reticuli star systems, freely discussed their reasons for visiting Earth, the propulsion systems of their vehicles, and life on the idyllic planets where they resided, and their philosophy of life. They took Earth people to task for befouling the environment, causing wars, and so forth. They expressed love for Earth and Earthlings, and gave advice on how we should be more loving to each other. Much of the channeled information was taken up with trivial matters along the lines of "pop" psychology and self-help advice—urging vegetarianism and other health measures, providing metaphysical and spiritual messages, and discussing the place of Earth and its people in the universe. Ultimately they wished to lead us through a spiritual passage into a New Age. For some UFO researchers, channeling confused the issue and made the abduction phenomenon seem all the more improbable.

In 1981 UFO research was fundamentally altered by the publication of Budd Hopkins's *Missing Time.* Unlike most UFO researchers, who treated abduction cases as simply another "sighting" category, Hopkins investigated seven abduction cases for patterns, similarities, and convergences.[11] He found that the question of inexplicable one-to two-hour gaps of time was more pervasive than had been realized in the past. Among other things, he discovered the significance of an unaccountable bodily scar that often accompanied abduction reports. He demonstrated that a person could be an abductee without having a UFO sighting and that abduction accounts could be hidden beneath the surface of strange "screen memories." Hopkins's research confirmed the prevalence of the examination that seemed to take place with nearly every abductee. He showed how the people who had experienced these events were normal people who had not manifested serious mental disorders. He also demonstrated that many of the abductees had family members who were also abductees and that the phenomenon might be intergenerational.

In *Missing Time* Hopkins invited readers who felt that they might have been abducted to write to him. He received hundreds of letters as a result of the book and more after his subsequent radio and television appearances. UFO researchers began to realize that the scope of the phenomenon was far larger than anyone had imagined.

Yet the question remained: why were there so many abduction accounts now and not after the Hill case? The answer may be that when John Fuller published *Interrupted Journey* in 1966, he did not embark on a television and radio tour for the book and make the idea of abduction accessible via the media to millions of people. Nor did Fuller include a note in his book asking people who might have had these experiences to write to him. Therefore, abductees did not have an easily reached outlet for their stories. Furthermore, as researchers looked back at older cases, it became evident that some abductees did try to report their experiences as they remembered them, often with fragments and screen memories, but UFO researchers could not understand the import of what they were hearing. For instance, people would report that they had had a close view of the underside of a UFO; or that they had the strange feeling that they had floated out the window upon seeing a UFO; or that they had seen a UFO from their car, had the urge to stop the car, and become confused over what happened next; or that, although they had seen a UFO hovering 100 feet from them, they had the idea that they could tell what was inside. The UFO investigators would record the details of the case, but there would be no back-up or in-depth investigation other than of the sighting itself.

If the UFO investigators had suspected that there was more to the case than a simple sighting, they had no idea how to investigate it. Since most investigators lacked expertise in hypnosis, the majority of cases went uninvestigated. Even when competent hypnotists were called in on cases, they were not well versed enough in abduction research to ask the proper questions. They could not tell if the subject was "filling in" with false information, if the witness had slipped into channeling, or if they were hearing dream material or "screen" memories. And because the investigators did not know exactly what happened during an abduction, they could not identify false memories purposely placed in victims' minds.

Furthermore, most abductees did not report their experiences because they simply did not remember them. If they did remember something, they often linked the event to a psychic or religious experience and thus had no reason to call a UFO organization.

Even with the investigating problems, by the mid-1980s there were so many of these reports that researchers could not keep up with them. The amount of data from each abduction experience was so extensive and rich in detail that even the most cursory look indicated that something extraordinary was occurring. In 1987 Dr. Thomas E. Bullard published a massive study of 270 published abduction cases. Although most of the cases were not investigated as carefully as they should have been, and many contained untrustworthy material, Bullard's careful analysis was still able to show numerous structural similarities.[12]

Most researchers still did not understand the implications of the new data. They had been schooled in the older sighting-analysis techniques and were ill-equipped to study abduction cases with new "internal" methodology. Most of the analytic procedures that had been developed for deciphering what a person observed no longer applied as UFO research moved into the delicate area of recovering memories locked away in the mind. But once a few researchers, like Budd Hopkins and Dr. Richard Haines (who developed a more planned method of questioning abductees) slowly began to develop proper techniques of investigating abductions and to unravel the tangled web of data that the abductees related, the victims' stories began to take on a coherence and a structure, with extraordinary detail that had never before been revealed.

In 1987 Hopkins published *Intruders: The Incredible Visitations at Copley Woods,* which for the first time revealed the extent of the UFO phenomenon's intrusion into peoples' personal lives. Hopkins found that, in addition to examinations, victims described aliens performing genetic experiments on them that included the taking of ova and sperm. He uncovered the idea that aliens were having abductees physically interact with odd-looking babies presumably grown at least in part from the abductees' eggs and sperm. He also began to realize the extent of victimization that had occurred among abductees as a result of their experiences. The people he investigated were traumatized individuals whose lives had been profoundly affected by their abductions.[13]

By the late 1980s the phenomenon had begun to yield some of its secrets. The abductions, once considered the fringy "stepchild" of the UFO phenomenon, were irrevocably changing UFO studies. Researchers had begun to realize that the abduction phenomenon yielded far more information about UFOs than sightings had revealed. At last we had literally and figuratively entered inside the UFOs.

PART II
THE ABDUCTION EXPERIENCE

Chapter 3

Getting There

"THIS IS NOT A DREAM."

Going from a normal environment into a UFO can be a shattering experience. People are engaged in normal activities when suddenly they are removed from their surroundings against their will and taken into the fringes of reality. The abductors seem to make a conscious effort to take people when they will not be missed or when their lives will not be overly disrupted. That still allows a wide range of opportunities for an abduction.

TRANSPORT

An unsuspecting woman is in her room preparing to go to bed. She gets into bed, reads a while, turns off the light, and drifts off into a peaceful night's sleep. In the middle of the night she turns over and lies on her back. She is awakened by a light that seems to be glowing in her room. The light moves toward her bed and takes the shape of a small "man" with a bald head and huge black eyes. She is terrified. She wants to run but she cannot move. She wants to scream but she cannot speak. The "man" moves toward her and looks deeply into her eyes. Suddenly she is calmer, and she "knows" that the "man" is not going to hurt her.

This is a typical beginning of an abduction. Virtually all abductees have experienced this. From the first few seconds of an abduction, nothing is within the realm of normal human experience. It is an instant descent into the fantastic and bizarre. Technology and bio-technology that seem like magic are immediately apparent. Once the event begins, humans are powerless to stop it. When it is over, most victims cannot remember it.

Often the abductee forms "screen" memories that mask the begin-ning of an abduction event. For example, one abductee said she saw a wolf in her bedroom one night. The wolf was standing squarely on her bed looking her in the eyes. She clearly remembered its fur, fangs, and eyes. Other abductees have claimed to have seen mon-keys, owls, deer, and other animals. Some say that they have seen an "angel" or a "devil." Through the use of hypnosis to recover the details of these events, each of these cases turned out to be the beginning of an abduction sequence. It is common for abductees to refer to out-of-body experiences that they had or, more commonly, that they succeeded in "preventing" at what was the beginning of an abduction. They sometimes remember that they felt themselves floating out of bed but then "fought it" and were able to lower themselves back onto the bed and abort the experience. When these memories have been examined, they have turned out to be a com-bination of the first few seconds and the last few seconds of an abduction.

Secrecy appears to be critically important to the aliens in deter-mining the opportunities for abductions. They commonly take place when the abductee is in an automobile, alone in the daytime, or with a small group of people. Victims have reported aliens doing proce-dures on them in their homes without being abducted. The majority of abductions, however, begin at night when the victim is alone, either awake or asleep. No abductions have surfaced that took place in the middle of a very large group of people, in full view at a public event.

The greater the victim's seclusion and the less others will miss her, the longer the experience tends to last. If a person is alone and is not likely to be missed for hours, she will experience more events during the abduction. Similarly, an abduction of a person walking alone in a secluded place will last longer than an abduction originat-ing in a small group of people. Most abductions last from one to three hours.

Nighttime and Sleep

Nighttime presents an ideal time for an abduction. During the night, the abductee's disappearance has a greater chance of going unnoticed and the aliens can maintain maximum "cover." Also, if the abductee is asleep, the event can become concealed as part of a dream. Although the "dream" may be much more vivid and have a different quality than usual, it is still within the acceptable cognitive realm.

At the beginning of the nighttime abduction, the Beings enter into the room through a light source coming from the window. How the use of light can transform and transport matter is unknown. The frightened victim is calmed when the Beings come close to her and stare into her eyes. A Small Being then touches her shoulder or arm. She finds herself floating up and out of bed. She is drawn to the light and enveloped in it. She floats toward the light. Small Beings are with her. Then, without hesitation, she and her escorts go directly through the closed window to the outside. She has no particular physical sensation when passing through the window.

Although abductees frequently report going directly through walls and ceilings, the Beings appear to seek out a window. Sometimes the aliens will take abductees out of their bedrooms and into another room and then out through a window there. Windows that are blocked, for example with boxes after a move, are avoided in favor of unblocked windows. One woman was visiting friends with her son. They slept in two different rooms in the basement. An abduction sequence began, and the aliens took her out of her bed and walked her into her son's room. Then they took her son and walked both of them into the bathroom. She wondered why they were crowding into the bathroom and then she realized that the bathroom was the only room in the basement with a window. Soon a bright light entered and they flew out the window.

In spite of hundreds of accounts of people flying through closed windows, it is exceedingly rare to find an outside witness who has observed it. Therefore, although it sounds impossible, the physical mechanism that allows people to pass through solid objects probably renders them invisible, at least for this part of the abduction experience.

Floating can be extremely unpleasant. Many abductees experience nausea and dizziness, compounded by their fear and confusion. As the abductee travels up, rooftops and treetops recede, and then stars come into view. During the transition upward she is only vaguely aware of her body; she may not even be able to see it. As she continues her journey, she approaches the source of the light and is floated into a UFO.

When I met Barbara Archer in 1987, she was a petite, twenty-one-year-old university student who was studying to be a journalist. She was overwhelmed with fear and anxiety when she remembered snippets of bizarre events that had dominated her life. During the course of her six hypnosis sessions with me she was able to recall vividly her extraordinary experiences. One night when she was sixteen years old, she was getting ready to go to bed when she noticed a light coming in through the window. When she closed the shade, the light continued to illuminate the entire room. She looked outside but could not see the source of the light. During a hypnosis session, she remembered what had happened in the beginning of the event. I asked her how she felt when she saw the light.

Well, I think when I first realized that the light was in my room it made me feel scared, but like I couldn't figure it out.

So you're puzzled?

Yeah. I should look out the other window, because I could see more of the sky. But I just didn't.... There's all this light still. I start to feel like, I sit there for a while and I look out the window, and then I turn around because I think that there might be somebody there. I first thought that it might be the dog. After a while I just stop looking out the window because there's nothing there to see.

Do you sort of look back in, though, can you get the sense that ...?

Well, the light seems to be going away. It's not filling the whole room as much anymore. When I turn around there's somebody standing over by the closet.

Is this a big person, or a medium person, little person?

He's smaller than me. I'm not all that shocked to see him standing there.... I think he came toward me when I was standing
there by the window.... I think he touches my arm. He sort of
touches me around my wrist area, between my elbow and my
wrist sort of. It feels better then, I mean, I'm not scared or
anything now.

When he touches your wrist, what happens next?

Well, I turn around toward the window again, the side window
that I had been looking out of. I just sort of go up.

Okay. Is this through the shade?

Yes. I think I left the shade down. I don't remember putting it
up, anyway. And we just go out. Oh, I feel so dizzy.... It feels
terrible.

Do you get a sense that you're going horizontally?

No, up.

Is it straight up like an elevator, or ...?

Yes. It's up straight.

Can you get a sense of movement, or do you just feel that you're
going up?

I feel sort of like I'm on an elevator except there's no walls or
anything around it, it's just up, fast....

Can you see anything outside?

When we went out the window we went straight in between
the two row houses, my house and my next-door neighbor's.
The houses go back a little bit and there's like a room in there

between my bedroom and the bedroom across from me, it sort of goes back, like a little cove sort of thing. And I go straight up from in between there. So I can see everything. I can see all the row houses on my street, in the driveway. I feel really nauseous. . . . I hope I don't get sick.

[I assured Barbara that the feeling would subside and she would not be sick.] Can you get a sense of if you're headed toward a specific point?

We're going straight up. I looked down and I saw the trees and everything on my street, and it makes me feel kind of scared because I don't really like heights. Not scared, but it just makes this nauseous feeling a little bit worse, I think. But then after that we're just going straight up. I know that we're going to some place.

Do you get a sense of weather? Can you feel breezes? Is it cold? Do you get a sense of being outside?

It doesn't feel cold or anything. Just kind of feels like body temperature.

Do you get a sense that you might be enclosed in something? Is something protecting you from the weather?

Not that I can tell. I can't feel anything, or touch anything.

So you still continue to go up.

Yes.

Can you see yourself approaching something?

Yes. When I look up I can see the bottom of, kind of a big, I think it's roundish, but longer, though. It's like an oval maybe. I can see the bottom, sort of gray, dark gray.

Is it big, or small, or are you a little too far away to get that sense?

Well, it's big, but it's not huge. I can remember from before, and it's not that big.

Do you sort of get closer to it then?

Mm-hmm. It feels like there's sort of light around me, that we're following up. And we're getting closer to the point of where that's coming from, inside that big thing.

Are you heading toward the center of it, or off to the side?

Yes, the center, underneath. We just go right in through the bottom.

Is this other person still with you?

Yes. I think he's still there. When we get there, there's somebody else waiting for us at the inside.

(Barbara Archer, 16, 1982)

Other abductees report floating horizontally across buildings and fields, and then coming down in a field or secluded area. The UFO is in a clearing and the abductee and aliens walk to it, sometimes a considerable distance. Why this happens is not known.

When the abductee is near other people, they are usually rendered unconscious or immobile while the abduction is going on. Typically they sleep through the abduction; if they are awakened at the beginning of it they are made to go back to sleep immediately. This "switching off" procedure presumably allows for secrecy to be kept and for minimal disruption in the life of the nonabductee. When the abduction is over, the nonabductee will be switched on once again and resume normal activities.

In spite of the aliens' ability to control human behavior, from time to time an abductee will see another person being abducted. "Tom," for example, told me an intriguing story. He was making love to his wife "Nancy" (the couple asked that their names be changed) when she complained that she felt an "electric jolt" go through her hips. He said that he did not feel anything. He looked at the clock and was surprised to find that he had been engaged in lovemaking for about forty-five minutes. This seemed odd because he felt that he had not been doing it for more than a few minutes and there were no "gaps" that he was aware of. When I questioned him during hypnosis, Tom remembered seeing two Small Beings come into the room. He was switched off and the Beings moved him off his wife.

> She turns her head for a moment, and it's like she drew a quick breath. . . . But it's like, there's something pulling us apart, but it's like we look like a couple of rag dolls, it's like we're completely poleaxed, whatever you call it, shot with a tranquilizer dart, like a couple of grizzlies or something. It's like we're just completely limp, but I'm just facedown on the bed. I don't know where she is.

> Do you sort of feel yourself going limp just before you realize you are like a couple of rag dolls?

> Yeah, I just felt clammy, like I was losing energy. It was like I felt like I had been at it for a couple of hours or so, which isn't usual. . . .

> Now, you say that you sort of go limp like rag dolls, so that means that you must be lying on her.

> Yes, I'm lying on her. They pull me off, and I'm on my side, but my eyes aren't moving. I can only see what's in the field of vision, and I'm on my side. I can see, it's like everything's sideways because I can't turn my head up, and they're there, and they've got her, and there's a flash, it's dark.

> Is she standing?

> No, she's gone!

Oh, you say they've got her. Do they stand her up? Do they get her out of bed that way? Does she walk?

It was like they rolled her off. As they were rolling her off the edge of the bed, she just faded out with them, just like a flash. And yet I'm thinking she'll be back.... It's like I'm shutting down. I'm just there, that's all. It's like my eyes, I'm trying, I can't move my eyes.

Are you still on your side?

No. Well, my head's turned to the left enough so my left eye still has slight field of vision to the edge of the bed, but there's nothing there to see, and the other eye is just staring into the blanket. I can't move my eye. I can't move from left to right.

But your eyes are open?

Yeah, they're open, but it's like nothing's happening.

While you're lying there, and she's gone, do you get a sense that anybody touches you?

I don't think so. I'm just lying there, I might as well be asleep, except I don't know why I'm not. I'd like to move, but I can't move, so I just don't.... I've got a headache, I know that, and my left arm's cramping.

Can you move your left arm?

No, I can't move it, but it's cramping. And the right, my right leg, the tendons from the knee down to the ankle, they're trying to cramp up, but I can't do anything about it.

You can't flex your foot or anything?

No, all I can feel is a tingle, like the muscles are trying to pull but they won't pull. I can't do anything about it, but I have a hell of a headache.

Now, you're looking over somewhere?

Yeah.

When you look there before, Nancy was in your field of vision as they rolled her off the bed.

Yeah.

Can you see her coming back now, or at least coming into view?

It's like, I can't see them, but I can see her. It's like she's—it's eerie—it's like she was down on the side of the bed the whole time, and it's like if you could imagine the bed like a conveyor belt, if I'm not moving, and it is, it's almost as if she was down on the side of the bed and she just nonchalantly rolled back up onto the bed, not under her power, but just under a conveyance. She was suddenly there, but I didn't see anyone around her. . . . She comes into view.

From your . . . ?

From below my field of vision, below the bed, up onto the bed. Then I can sense myself, I'm getting poked and pushed around, I'm being pulled back and we're being moved, manipulated around. And yet I can move again, and it's just like we never missed a beat. . . .

So suddenly your wife is back in bed.

Yes.

Is she alert, or is she out of it?

No, she's awake.

This is before you get back on top.

No, oh, before that, she's limp, completely, totally limp.

Are her eyes open or closed?

Closed.

Do you see yourself getting back into the position that you were in before?

I'm being *put* into position. That's odd, that's real odd.

I'm going to ask you another horribly embarrassing question.

That's all right.

How did you get an erection? Is it just there?

I still had one.

You mean the whole time that you were . . .

Yeah, that I know.

So that . . .

It's got to be a record.

So the blood never essentially drained . . .

No, everything is as it was . . .

So then you finish?

Yeah. She says, "Ouch!" She said she felt an electric shock. I said, "Where?" She said, "Right there," and pointed to her hip. And I remember looking at the clock and I'm thinking it's around, I know it's midnight, I'm thinking 12:05.

("Tom," 1988)

I asked Tom not to discuss the incident with his wife, who had been thinking of coming to see me to investigate some unusual events that had happened to her. When she came I asked if we could hypnotically investigate the incident of her feeling an electric shock going through her hips. She was surprised when I mentioned it because she had not thought about it since it happened, and it did not seem to be related to abductions. After the hypnosis session began, she started to describe the lovemaking episode and then she saw a blue light in her room pointed at her.

It's aiming right at me.

From in front of you, or on top of you, or . . . ?

I think it's behind me.

What is behind your bed, there?

At the time, a window and the heater.

There was a window there, you say?

Yeah.

So the blue light is sort of aiming at you from behind.

Uh-huh.

As you notice this blue light, what is Tom doing?

Nothing.

Has he stopped?

No, it's like he's not there. It's like he's in a trance, he's just lying there.

He's lying there on your side?

He's sort of next to me. He's not moving.

But he was on top of you just before?

Yes, he was.

Now, as you see Tom lying there, there's this blue light, do you get the sense that you and Tom are alone in the room?

Not anymore.

What's going on in there? What do you see?

When I saw the light it's like the window disappeared. It's like something came through it.

You mean, sort of from over your head?

Yeah, because I was lying down [their heads were at the foot of the bed].

When you say something came through, what kind of a sense do you get of that? What do you think it might have been?

... I kept telling them to leave me alone, to stop using me because I told Tom I want another baby and I can't get pregnant if they keep bugging me, if they're messing my cycle up.

Are you saying this in your bedroom right then and there?

I feel like I'm still in the bedroom. I don't feel like I've left.

When you say "them," are you talking about more than ...

I think there were two of them there.

Are they big, medium, small?

They were shorter than I am.

Where are they in relation to you?

They're standing up against the bed.

Do they come up to you? Of course, if they're next to the bed they're fairly close, I would assume.

Mm-hmm. . . .

Well, let's sort this out then. You're lying in bed, you see a blue light, you see these little guys in the room. Tom is off to the side now.

Uh-huh.

He's sort of in a trance. Are his eyes open, or are they closed?

I can't see, he's not facing me. They've got him moved from the way he was.

And these guys sort of come up to the side of the bed?

Right, they were standing up next to me.

Do you sit up, for instance?

I try, but they kept telling me it was all right, just to lie down. And I couldn't move, I felt like I was just frozen in that position. . . .

Nancy went on to describe an abduction event filled with physical and mental procedures that happened while her husband "waited" for her. The Beings then returned her to her original position in the bed.

What happens next? Do you just continue to lie there, or . . .

I don't think they were there that long, I don't remember how long it was, but they left and, I think, the next thing I remember is, Tom was on top of me again, and that's when I felt the shock.

("Nancy," 1988)

Automobile

An abduction from a car usually begins with a UFO sighting. The abductee may be driving alone when suddenly she sees a strange object flying through the air or even hovering off the side of the road. The victim pulls over and gets out, ostensibly to take a better look at it. Then for no apparent reason she walks toward the object now on the ground. As she gets closer she notices that the Small Beings are apparently waiting for her near it. She is not necessarily frightened, but she is uneasy, yet she cannot stop walking toward them. She comes up to them and they escort her into the object.

If she is driving and spots an object that appears to land out of view, she might stop the car and walk to an area off the road, with trees or heavy foliage, where she thinks the object has landed. She comes to a clearing where a Small Being joins her; they walk for a short distance toward a UFO resting on the ground and enter it.

If the person is in the car with other people, the aliens switch off the nontargeted individuals. For example: Several people are riding at night and the abductee is one of the passengers. Suddenly they spot a strange light in the sky that gives off an eerie glow and begins to move closer to them. Inexplicably, the driver pulls the car over to the side of the road and stops. The UFO shines a light directly on them. The abductee is excited and frightened; she yells at the driver to keep going, but it is too late. The driver and the other two people have "vacant" looks on their faces, and their heads are leaning against the window or the seat. The victim realizes in horror that her friends are "unconscious." Their perceptions and information processing have been disrupted, and they no longer are in control of their senses, memories, or wills.

Then the light beam that was shining on the car takes on a different character. It has a physically compelling or pulling effect on the abductee. Her consciousness is altered, and it is difficult for her to understand what is happening. Before she realizes it, she floats up off her seat and heads directly through the windshield and up. She ascends as if she were on an invisible elevator until she reaches the UFO.

Will Parker, a computer programmer, was driving with his first wife, Ginny, through Virginia late one night in 1974. He inexplicably pulled into a closed gas station in a small town, turned off the motor and the lights, and waited in the darkness. A hypnosis session with

me fourteen years later revealed why he had performed this seemingly inexplicable act.

So we're sitting there. I keep thinking. I don't know why we
keep waiting. Nothing's come by. There's nothing out there.

Are you talking with each other while you're waiting?

Yes, we're just talking. We're both kind of jumpy. . . .

You sit there talking.

Yes. She's telling me to be quiet, she thought she heard something.

Okay.

I don't see anything, I'm looking around. I don't know. I didn't
hear anything, but she said she did.

Does she hear a noise that's coming from the front, the back,
the side?

She didn't say, she just said she thought she heard something.
She didn't say what kind of noise, she said she was sure she saw
a light.

While you're sitting there, or before?

Before. She said that there's someone out there. Oh, shit.

What is it?

Yeah, I see them. Ginny, she's shocked. She's praying.

What do you see?

Little guy, he's outside the car, and he's not human. He's, he
ought to be cold because he hasn't got a coat on. I've seen this

before, but I didn't remember it until now. Now Ginny is quiet. I'm turning to her, but she's just, she's asleep is what she is.

Are her eyes closed?

No, they're not, but she looks like she's drifting off. They got me out of the car.

Do you open the car door, or do they . . . ?

I don't remember, I don't think I opened it. I'm out of the car now, and she's sitting in the car. I keep thinking I want to lock it up, but I can't get to the car. I don't want anyone to get in to her, because she's by herself.

Does she get out of the car also?

No, she's asleep.

They don't take her out of the car?

No. I keep thinking I don't want them to take me away from the car, but I'm afraid she's going to be scared when she wakes up and I'm not there for her. We're going around the building. It's dark. There are a bunch of them.

How many do you think there are?

Four, maybe five. It's weird. I'm saying, "Where are the rest?" But they don't say anything to me.

When you talk to them, are you verbalizing?

I'm not sure. I think so, but it's like they're not talking back to me, but . . . they told me that they'll bring me back. They're not going to hurt me. I'm not scared. I'm surprised, but I'm not scared. I'm scared for Ginny because I don't know how she's going to, she's not going to remember . . . They told me she's not going to remember.

The Beings took Will around to the back of the service station where they all stood around in a tight group.

We're just in the back of the building. It's dark.

You're behind the building?

We're behind the building. We're just standing there, like in a group. . . .

Do they say what they're waiting for, or what's happening?

I know what they're waiting for, they're waiting to be picked up, but they . . . it's here. It's not very big. It's bigger than the building, but it's not huge. We're going underneath it. We're just, it's like it's opening up, but I don't see any door. It's just like it's open. We're going up inside.

How do you go up inside?

I'm not sure. It's like we're on an elevator, but it's open. I'm not sure. We were on the ground a moment ago, now we're inside. It's like we were lifted up, but nothing grabbed hold of me. I can still see the ground and earth underneath, but it's closing off. I can't see it that well. It's not all that bright inside either, it's kind of dark.

(Will Parker, 19, 1974)

Sometimes the abductee will inexplicably get into her car and drive to a specific location where the abduction will take place. The abductee does not think about why she is doing this, or she invents a reason so that her behavior conforms to logic and reality. For example, the abductee tells herself that she "wanted to take a ride" or that she was "going to visit friends." When asked where she went, she is at a loss to remember or makes up another excuse that she later realizes is not true.

The critical point is that the abductee's activity can be altered somewhat to conform to the dictates of the intelligence that is directing the behavior. Barney and Betty Hill raced down the highway trying to get away from a UFO when suddenly and for no particular reason Barney made a left turn onto a little-used dirt road leading nowhere. He made it with such confidence that Betty thought he knew exactly what he was doing and did not question it.

Patti Layne, a high school teacher with an ivory complexion and dark hair, indicated to me that she had a few memories that had upset her, but she did not know what had prompted them. Subsequent hypnotic regressions with me uncovered a series of abductions throughout her lifetime. In one that took place on her twentieth birthday, Patti decided to get into the car and go for a drive in the mountains. At the time she was attending college in a small town in Pennsylvania.

> I was living in the apartment complex on campus, right in front of the health center, and I had my own car, and I just wanted to get out. I had to get out.

> Why?

> I don't know, I wanted to get out, and I knew I had to go by myself.

> Do you think it's because you were excited about your birthday, or . . . ?

> No, depressed, but nothing I couldn't handle. I just had to . . . find this place in the mountains and I would feel better. I wouldn't feel depressed.

> So you got into the car and drove off toward the mountains?

> Mm-hmm.

> I want you to sort of see yourself driving there. Do you kind of know where you're going?

> Kind of. I went out the campus, to the left, down English Street, make a left on Queen Road, go out to Mountain Street. . . . I

stayed on Queen Road until I got to Pine Road, and went right, and I just stayed on that for a long time. I made a right on Bluff Road . . . I got up to the mountains, to the foot of the mountains, and there were some dirt roads, and I don't know where those dirt roads were. I don't know what direction off of Bluff Road they were.

Did you turn off Bluff Road onto one of the dirt roads, though?

Hmm, I think I made a left on Aviation Road after Bluff Road, and I think I went out that, and there were some dirt roads up near there off of Aviation Road, and I could see the roads better. I didn't know where, I forgot where Bluff Road went until just now, and it goes to Aviation, and I made a left on Aviation and then I kind of draw my blank, but I know there were dirt roads, and I followed one up to the mountains. There are some real ramshackle houses.

What are you thinking while you're doing this?

Why am I doing this? I have a night class tonight, I should be studying for it. Why am I out here by myself?

You drive out past these ramshackle houses. Do you remember stopping the car, or the car stopping?

The car stopped. It just stopped on this road, and there weren't any houses nearby. And I started to try to start it up, and I wanted it in reverse to get out of there, and I rode backward. I think it started again, I went backward.

Now before it started again, when the car stopped, did the car just die?

Maybe I stopped it. I think I put it in park and sat there and waited for something.

And as you're sitting there for a while, can you tell me what's happening as you're sitting there waiting?

I wanted to get out of there. I put the car in reverse, and I turned around, and I found another dirt road and it went to a dead end.

(Patti Layne, 20, 1982)

This time Patti waited for a while and then the car door opened. She was taken out and the abduction began.

In spite of the aliens' ability to make nontargeted people unconscious during an abduction, entire cars—abductees and other passengers as well—have been lifted up off the road and taken on board a UFO. In 1979, Tracy Knapp was driving from Los Angeles to Las Vegas with two girlfriends when they spotted a strange light swooping down toward them.

So you see it approaching the car a little bit closer, then?

Mm-hmm, but fast, not slow. . . . It seemed like it dropped down by the window too, like whizzed by.

So it whizzes by, what happens next, then? [Tracy suddenly became upset.] Are you okay? How are you doing, Tracy? What are you thinking?

That the car's spinning around.

Do you get a sense of movement?

Like I'm in a teacup, like I'm spinning, like the car's turning, and I'm grabbing onto the seat and we're screaming.

The three of you?

Mm-hmm.

[Tracy was crying now and I calmed and reassured her. After a short time she was able to continue.] So you get the feeling that you're spinning around; therefore I would assume that you're not on the ground, or you are on the ground.

That we're not on the ground.

Do you get the sense of motion up, or sideways, or diagonal, or can you tell that?

Like we're being spun up, like we're moving forward and getting spun, and I'm holding on to the car.

How do you feel physically? Do you feel dizzy, or anything like that?

A force, a pressure. Heavy. Like I'm weak, weighted.

Do you say anything to your friends, or is everybody too alarmed, or . . . ?

I can't talk. Nothing's being said at that point.

What are your friends doing in the front seat? Are they looking at each other? Are they animated or not, or can you tell?

They were not. They're going limp.

Are you going limp also, or just sort of observing them going limp?

I'm not going limp. I don't feel like I'm going limp. I see or feel myself have one hand on the door and one hand on the car seat, and I'm looking out the window watching this whole thing and wondering what's going on. . . .

What happens next, then? [Again Tracy became too upset to continue and I calmed her.]

They just leave them alone. It's me, and they're just taking me out of the car. . . . It seems like the window's open, and they put their hand through the window and they touched me, and then at that point I'm back now.

You're back against the seat?

Yeah. I'm laid back now. And I'm getting limp then. And then I see a hand coming through the window, and they were touching me and I'm feeling limp now, and they open the door and I feel like I'm being picked up out of there.

(Tracy Knapp, 21, 1978)

The Beings took Tracy out of the car; she lost sight of her girlfriends until the three of them were back on the ground in the car.

Small Groups

Sometimes the abduction will begin in the midst of a group of people who are engaged in some outdoor activity. Generally they are in small groups of not more than ten. The abductors control the environment by switching off the nontargeted people or causing them to develop an all-encompassing fascination with some object on the ground or in front of them. The object may be a worm, a leaf, something imaginary, etc. They are compelled to look at it and not at what is happening around them. The abductee is, in effect, separated from the herd.

The abductee may then feel an urge to walk toward a secluded area, which may be on the other side of a hill or a stand of trees. The walk may be a long one, going over one hill after another through underbrush, between trees, and so forth until she approaches a clearing where a UFO has landed. On these journeys, either an alien appears near the small group of people and accompanies the abductee all the way to the UFO or an alien waits for the abductee about halfway to the UFO and goes with her from there. When the abductee returns, her friends have been switched on again, but they do not notice that she was missing. Sometimes one youngster in a group of children feels compelled to wander away; the other children are not switched off and continue their play as before without noticing that the abductee is gone.

Janet Demerest is an attractive woman with strawberry blond hair. She and her sister Karen were subjected to a prolonged series of abduction experiences. When Janet was nine years old she was playing with some of her friends a short distance from her house. (She thinks her friends were part of her Brownie troop.) Suddenly they all gathered around something on the ground and stared at it.

I just want you to remember the one part about the little girls playing there. Can you tell me how they're playing, and what they're doing?

They're kneeling and sitting on the ground.

Is this a wooded area, or in a playground, or is this somebody's backyard, or can you tell at all?

I can't tell. I can see the grass, it's green.

What kind of game are they playing, or are they playing a game?

I think they're looking at something. . . .

And where are you observing this from: Are you standing up there, or sitting down also, or a member of this group?

I was sitting down and I got up. . . .

Now you sort of get up and what do you do now?

I'm watching them.

You're standing now?

Mm-hmm.

And do they just continue to do whatever they're doing there?

Yeah, they're all looking at something. I think it's a bug or something.

Now when you stand up are you still in that little group of kids, or do you stand away from them a little?

I'm a little bit away, a couple of steps.

Now can you tell me what happens next?

There's a man there.

Is this a man you recognize?

No, I ... he doesn't look like a person.

Is he tall, or is he medium, or is he short? In other words when
you look at him, do you look straight at him, or do you look up
at him, or do you look down at him?

Just about straight at him.

How did you first notice him?

He was standing outside the circle.

Does anyone else notice him?

No, they're all looking in the circle.

But you notice that he's there?

Yes, and I got up and went over to where he was.

And why do you do that?

Because I was supposed to.

Okay, and what happens next?

We walk away.

Now when you walk away is he sort of next to you, or is he in
front of you, or behind you, or is he leading you, or are you
leading him, or does that apply?

He knows where we're going but I think we're walking next to each other.

Is he the only one there, or is there someone else also?

He's the only one.

Can you sort of see where you're walking?

Into the trees, into the woods.

And what happens next then?

I don't know. It doesn't make any sense, why would I just go?

Well, that's okay, just sort of go with the flow. You're walking along, and he's on the side of you. You walk into the woods, you keep walking, I assume.

I think he's holding my hand.

When he holds your hand, how does that make you feel? Do you have feelings about that, when he touches you?

I'm happy to be going with him. I want to. . . .

What do his hands feel like?

It's not bigger than mine. I feel safe.

Does he communicate with you?

No. I don't think so.

Now you continue to walk, do you walk a long distance or not?

Not very far. We walk down a path, to a place where there aren't any trees, to a clearing. And I see something, but I don't have any idea of what it is. . . .

(Janet Demerest, 9, 1964)

Janet could see a landed UFO in the clearing. The Small Being who was with her led her up a ramp and into it.

When Patti Layne was in college she and some of her friends went to a secluded mountainside picnic area to drink some wine and to have fun. She had to relieve herself; so she walked into the woods and the abduction event began.

So, do you set the blankets out?

Mm-hmm, right at the car. And we pass around a bottle of wine, and we tell stories, silly stories. Talking about how we teased Margie earlier this year at lunch. We told stories about her, and we finished about half of the bottle of wine, just passed it around. I had to go to the bathroom, so I took a little walk down. It wasn't really a trail, I just kind of blazed my own back into the woods. I walked down to the left; actually, we were to the left of the car, I was wrong. I walked kind of left into the woods, further away from the road, but also up to the left. And I'm kneeling down, and a light shines on me.

Where is the light coming from? Can you get a sense of that?

It's kind of coming from the right, deeper in the woods, from the right. And I thought that darned Freddy is bugging me again. If he's not kicking the bathroom doors in at the apartments, he has to shine a light. I think he's obsessed with this, disturbed. I get kind of mad and I laugh, and I yell "Cut it out," but I don't hear anything.

You don't hear yourself yelling?

No, I don't hear them talking. They were laughing a while ago. so I got scared, and I started to walk back. There was a whole lot of them [aliens] standing there with my friends.

How do you mean?

There's just about six of them standing there with them. They got James by the arm, and he's standing there, leaned over.

He's standing, leaning over?

Like he's going to throw up. The rest of them are sitting there, real still, but they got James.

What are the Beings doing with the other ones?

Looking at them, touching them with something, real fast.

You mean, with an instrument of some sort?

Yeah, with a stick. And they're all quiet.

What are you doing? Are you continuing to walk toward them?

I'm frozen in my path.

About how far away are you from them?

About five feet now.

Oh, so you walked all the way back, essentially?

Mm-hmm.

You're five feet back, away from James and June?

James is closest to the road, and they've got him by the arms. And he looks sick, he looks really sick.

Does he see you?

No, he doesn't know what's going on.

Are they walking with him, or . . . ?

. . . it's not moving, I don't know what they're doing, it's just everything's standing still, including me. And he just looks like he's going to vomit. . . .

Is he sort of doubled over?

Mm-hmm, he's doubled over, and one of them comes over to me and takes me very gently by the arm, the one I've seen before. I think he has a scarf on.

A scarf?

Yes, like a winter scarf. The dumbest-looking thing.

Around his neck?

Mm-hmm. But I don't know if he's got much of a neck anyway, but he's got a scarf around his head.

Does it have a color to it?

It's red, a red scarf. But he doesn't have anything else on.

Does he look the same as the other ones?

Mm-hmm, but they don't have a scarf on. They look more military. They have an insignia.

An insignia?

Mm-hmm.

Can you sort of see what this insignia looks like?

Birdlike. But he doesn't have anything on. He doesn't have any genitals either. Just kind of like a Barbie Doll.

Just kind of smooth, there's no bulge or anything?

No. It's like nothing. But anyway, he looks friendly, and he comes over very warmly, and he like grabs my arm like an escort would, and he walks me toward where they have James, and one got on one side of James and the other got on the other side of him, and they both kind of linked arms with him, kind of marshaled him along.

Does James stand up at this time, or is he still doubled over?

He's kind of being dragged.

I see.

They must be strong because, well, James is not real big, but he's bigger than they are. There are six of them. One has me, two have James, and I don't know what happened to the other three. I think there were six of them. Maybe they were staying with my friends.

What are your friends doing at this time?

They're frozen. Freddy has the bottle in his hand, kind of resting in the gravel. Freddy has his mouth open. Kathy is looking down at the ground. June is looking at her car. Where's Barry? I don't know where Barry is.

You don't see Barry sitting there?

No. I don't know what happened to him. I don't see him at all. But, anyway, we walk down the road. James was in front with the other two, and I was in back, walking along. We walk kind of down the road a little bit, and off into the woods again, to the left. We kind of walk deep back into the woods.

And they're still sort of carrying James?

They're just dragging him along. He just really looks bad, and I'm really worried about him.

They're dragging him . . . ?

He'll get a foot down, and then his knee will sag, and then he'll put another foot down, and his knee sags again. It sounds like he's making retching noises.

I see. So they're not dragging him and his heels are scraping along, it's more the tops of his shoes, or something?

Mm-hmm. He's kind of moaning. . . .

Do they seem to have much trouble with James? I mean, is it easy for them to . . . ?

No, it looks like it's a pain for them. I don't know why they don't float us, but they're not. They took us deep back into those woods; it's pretty creepy back there. And there was a craft, it's kind of like a bubble with a hatch, and it's really not terribly big. It's not a saucer anyway, it's a bubble. It's kind of black.

Is there any light emanating from it? In other words, I guess what I'm asking is how you can see it if you're outside and it's black.

There's some light inside. There's like windows, a whole little row of windows around the top, and we walked in the little . . . It wasn't much of a ramp, just like a little walkway inside it.

Is James still there?

They got him in first. They took me into the first room on the right, and he went along down further. It's like next door in another room.

(Patti Layne, 21, 1984)

Although it is uncommon, individuals who happen to be near an abductee will also be taken in an "opportunistic abduction." When Patti was fifteen years old, she and about eight other students were on an overnight camping trip as part of a high school club. At night they decided to go "skinny dipping" in a nearby reservoir. As they approached the reservoir, they saw a strange light in the sky. Suddenly the light was shining on them and all of the students were lifted off the ground and taken on board a UFO.

Alone in the Daytime

Abductions can occur when a person is alone in the middle of the day. For instance, nine-year-old Jill Pinzarro was returning home after checking out several books from the library. They were in the basket of her bicycle and she was reading one of them on the handlebars as she walked alongside her bike. She cut through a park to go to her house about a mile away.

Do you decide to go through the park that day?

Yeah, I always go through the park. I don't know another way to go. It's overcast. It's about, it must be about four o'clock because I think I have to be home about five o'clock for dinner.

And you go into the park, and you start walking, and what happens then?

It's troublesome to walk and read, and push the bike. So I stop at a bench near the statues. . . . I put the books on the bench because the bike won't stand up with the books in the basket. I guess I don't want to go home because then I'd have to stop reading to do stuff, get ready for dinner, I don't know. I don't really know why, maybe I just want to read the book. It might be a Lucky Star book.

Are you still on the bench?

Yes.

Do you continue to read then?

Yes.

What happens next?

I go to the trees. I don't know why. But it's, I'm just there at the trees. I don't know where the books or the bike is.

Is the stand of trees dense, or is it just a few trees?

It's a lot of trees, not a forest. But I'm at the edge of the trees. Something is, there's something there in the trees. I'm being brought to the trees.

You're being led to the trees, or carried to the trees, or walked to the trees?

I feel as if I'm walking, but I feel as if I'm standing there and looking and there's someone at my elbow. And I don't want to —it's not that I'm apprehensive. I don't feel as if I can resist . . . I think that there's something that's making me come, not that anybody is there. It feels like there's somebody right behind me, or beside me, but I don't think there is. It's just as if I were being brought there.

[Then Jill remembered what was there.]

There's something that's lit up, or glowing. And that's what I don't like about it. There shouldn't be . . .

Is this the outside of something, or the inside of something, or . . . ?

It's the outside. It's not a bright light, it's glowing. But there shouldn't be a glow in there. There's something over, I've walked up to something. I'm under something. All right, I climb up something metal, ladder-type thing. . . . Now it's dark, when I come close to it, it got dark.

(Jill Pinzarro, 9, 1958)

Jill climbed up the ladder and entered into the object.

ENTRANCE

The actual entrance into the craft may be difficult to remember. The abductee may be extremely frightened; often she is confused, dazed, and nauseated, and her vision is impaired. It is difficult for her to orient herself. Furthermore, her entrance procedures may vary according to the size of the craft that she is brought into. Abductees describe UFOs that range in size from thirty-five to hundreds of feet in diameter. In smaller and medium-sized craft the abductee usually enters directly into an examining room, but, for reasons that are unclear, in larger craft she is almost always brought into an entrance room. There she either lies on a table or stands up. In neither case is she able to move, but she reports feeling "tingly" and that something "physical" is happening to her. Sometimes there are machines around the wall, and she might find herself surrounded by a gray "mist" or "fog." The Beings who have accompanied her during transport stand around and watch her. After a short while, a Being comes over to her. He helps her take off her clothes and leaves them there. He puts his hand on her elbow or her wrist and guides her down a hall toward the examination room.

On rare occasions, the abductee might also have to stay in a waiting room until a table in the main examining room becomes free for her to lie on. In these cases, she is brought from the entrance room into a narrow, curved waiting area with benches in arched indentations in the wall. This happened to Karen Morgan in 1981. Karen is the sister of Janet Demerest and a businesswoman who owns her own public relations firm. When she was thirty-eight years old, she wrote to me saying that she "had an experience" that might be related to my research. I interviewed her and eventually we had more than twenty hypnosis sessions together. The strength of Karen's personality allowed her to resist whatever happened to her during her abductions, and she was extraordinarily articulate in describing her experiences. In one abduction episode, she was strapped into a bench in a curved area while she waited. She saw other people sitting in alcoves near her, including a red-haired woman.

Are these alcoves sort of real close together, or are they spread apart?

Well, they're apart. What I see is here's me, and here's someone else, and here's someone else, and here's someone else. [Gestures with her hand.]

So they're across from you?

Uh-huh, but I can't see them. I can just see their bodies. I can't see their faces.

Are these men or women?

There's a man across from me. I don't know about the other two. He's wearing heavy work jeans and boots, and I think a flannel checkered shirt. It's not flannel, it's a cotton checkered shirt. It looks like what you think flannel shirts look like. He's "out of it," I think. . . .

I see.

I'm just sitting there, thinking, trying to get my thoughts, trying to get ahold of my thoughts.

You can sit, though, as opposed to falling forward?

I think they strap you in. I don't know why I think that, but I do. They do, I'm pretty sure they do.

So is your back up against something, or . . . ?

A smooth surface.

Are you sitting on wood, or metal, or plastic?

The closest it is, is plastic. It's some synthetic, I think. It's not wood. It's very smooth. I'm not very conscious of everything, though, because there's no . . . but it looks smooth. I'm trying so hard to get ahold of my thoughts. I'm telling myself not to panic. I'm thinking, "Don't panic. Don't panic because you've been through this before. This isn't a dream, this is really happening. Look around, look around. Figure out what's going on." So I do.

Are you able to look around now?

I'm trying to stay calm. . . . And then I see he has very thick, brown wavy hair. He's young, in his twenties. He's slumped, like that.

Are his eyes closed?

No, it's horrifying. They're wide open.

Is he looking around, or . . . ?

He's staring, he's gone. Okay, then next to him, it's hard to see. Somebody with short hair, I think it's a woman. Short red hair, much redder than mine. A very petite woman wearing pajamas.

Is she young, or . . . ?

Early thirties. I can't see to the immediate right of me because of the way the alcove is. I can only see the legs of the person. I'm trying to think, I'm confused now. I think this person is wearing sandals and has nothing on, a woman, her legs. So there's three women [including me], and one man. . . .

Do you make eye contact with [one of the women]?

Yes, I do. Oh, she's so frightened. Her eyes are just pleading. She's scared. . . . She's terrified, she's just terrified. Oh, that's so sad. It's awful to see someone that scared. . . . Maybe I look that scared too, though. . . . But I'm not as scared as she is.

While she sat waiting to be taken into the examination room, two aliens came and took off her clothes. Now it was time to go into the main room.

You know what, they don't come for us one by one this time. They take us all together. It's just like Auschwitz, just like Auschwitz.

How many Beings come in?

I can't believe this. There's eight, two for each person. I can't believe this. I'm so mad. I'm so mad. It is just like being in a concentration camp. They come in and they just take you.

Do they unstrap you?

Yes. There are straps here, and here. They might even have them on your legs. I think they do.

Is that to sort of prevent you from falling over?

From getting up and running away, and smacking them, and fighting with them . . .

Now, does everybody sort of stand up when they [take off the straps]?

Well, the guy's "gone." He's just sort of falling over.

Do they support him?

He's big, and I don't think that they can move him very well. He's big. They use something to poke you with. Maybe it's their arms, but maybe it's not. I can't see him now because they've got him around the corner. I don't think they had an easy time with him. And then one puts his hand on my elbow, and I pull it and it feels like I want to pull it so hard, but it just comes out like I'm under water or something. . . .

Do they sort of get you all real close together, or are you separated from each person?

This part is so hard to see. There's like a measured distance. Six feet, eight feet.

Can you see the red-haired woman?

She's going around that way. She's very petite. I feel very sorry for her. . . .

Are you first in line, or second, or third?

Last.

So even when you're at the end you could be the first, closest to the big room. They turn you the other way so you wind up being last? I'm assuming that the redheaded woman was first?

Second, the man was first. . . . And they push me along. And I just tense my arms hard, to push them, to try to resist them. It just makes them go faster, they push more. I'm not going to look like all those people just going in order like that, though. I want to shake their arms off me, their hands off me.

(Karen Morgan, 32, 1981)

If the abductee has waited in an entrance room, it is now time to take her into the main examining room. The transport and entrance phases of the abduction experience are over.

These stories are characteristic of all the other aspects of abduction accounts, which are remarkably detailed and remarkably similar. The accounts display a predictable routine common to most abductions. The Beings have an agenda to carry out and, once the event begins, nothing can stop it.

Chapter 4

Physical Probing, Alien Bonding, and the Breeding Program

Once the abductee has been transported to and entered the alien craft, the primary experiences begin. These involve those procedures that the aliens perform the greatest number of times on the greatest number of people, including physical and mental examinations, and reproductive procedures that are ultimately directed to the production of offspring. The primary experiences usually occur close to the beginning of the abduction episode, and the dazed abductee has little time to accustom herself to the event, even if she has had a number of previous abductions. Although the primary experiences that I describe are typical, one must bear in mind that they are a composite of many. All the procedures may not happen during one abduction, but all do happen during the primary phase.

During the entire abduction experience, communication between aliens and abductees is telepathic. The abductee either "hears" the communication or receives an impression in her mind. She knows she is being addressed and what the Beings want from her. The alien's communication to her is almost always reassuring. For instance, she may ask, "Why are you doing this?" and the answer might be, "We are not going to hurt you" or "You will be all right." The Beings deflect the subject's questions with palliatives and do not give substantive answers. Usually the abductee receives only an "impression" of what the Beings are communicating and has difficulty repeating specific words and sentences, although some people "hear" sentences in their minds and can recall not only the sense of the communication but the words as well. So far no cases have emerged whereby Beings and abductees communicate mainly through sound waves.

The aliens bring the abductee into the main examining room. Although disoriented, she can still observe what is happening to her. She sees frightening-looking Beings who are busily going about their tasks, seemingly paying no attention to her. But other aliens are waiting for her. They are small—about three and one-half to four feet tall. These Small Beings are usually gray, tan, pale white (not Caucasian), or "colorless." They have bald, bulbous craniums. Their immense eyes are dark, with no pupils or corneas. They either have no nose or it is so slight that it is unnoticeable, and their small, slit-like mouth does not move. They have no ears. Their bodies are very thin. They either wear nothing or what appears to be form-fitting clothing.

The examining room is small and circular. It might contain a ledge or "walkway" around the perimeter that appears to be part of the wall itself. Sometimes apparatuses or machines are in the room, often attached to the walls and ceiling. The room lighting is diffuse. It can range from bright to dim, but the origin of the lighting cannot be seen. The entire room closely resembles a hospital operating room. It is serviceable and functional; it is neat and clean. The dominant colors of the "metallic" walls and floor are white and gray.

The central feature of the room is the table. It is made of a "metallic" or plasticlike material supported by a pedestal. Stationed around the table are carts that contain instruments and other machinelike devices. There might be from one to four tables in a small room and up to two hundred in a large room.

When the aliens escort the abductee into a very large room, she silently passes other tables containing naked humans lying in rows in various stages of examination. It is eerily quiet. She hears only the clanging of instruments, the shuffling of feet, and an occasional moan from the victims.

The Small Beings lead the abductee to the table and, if she still has her clothes on, assist her in removing them. They allow the clothes to fall to the floor and remain there for the duration of the experience. She then gets up on the table and lies down. Karen Morgan was escorted to a table in a typical way in 1981.

They take me around the corner. I hate this room. There's tables. I only see four tables, but I think that there's more. . . . This room seems more like an operating room than any of the others.

How so?

Mainly because I'm trying so hard to pay attention. I'm able to see more shelves, the shelf that runs around the room, and instruments and stuff. This room is much more in focus. I think they're going to do that physical examination again. Oh, they take off my clothes. They're all moving in unison.

You mean everybody's having their clothes taken off at the same time, or . . . ?

I mean exactly at the same time. Allowing for the fact that some people have more buttons, or whatever, than others. . . . I am wearing a red shirt. I really did like the shirt. And they take it off. I won't put my arms over my head.

How did they get it off?

They pull my arms up. I always have the impression they're saying, "Come on, come on, come on," like that. I remember they unfasten my blouse. I remember everything.

Do they untie your shoes?

They pulled them off my feet. I don't think they untied them.

Are you standing, or are you sitting?

Sitting on the table.

How do they get your jeans off?

They turn me around, and lay me down. They pull off my jeans, my underpants. They strap me onto the table.

(Karen Morgan, 32, 1981)

Lynn Miller was told to get her clothes off herself.

Does anybody say anything to you?

I'm told to undress. I don't want to.

Do they help you get undressed then?

They're sort of pulling my clothes.

What are you wearing?

A nightgown.

And what happens next?

They force me to take my clothes off, and they make me get on the table.

(Lynn Miller, 31, 1986)

Sometimes the Beings place Velcro-like (and often metallic) restraints around the abductee's upper arms and her legs. From the position on her back she gets a good look at the ceiling, which might be smoothly domed or have "ribs" or "latticework" on it. In the center is a circular area that is "buttonlike" or shiny. Sometimes she can see windows around the dome of the ceiling.

Her mental state is altered. She has no concern for what she was doing before the abduction. If she is abducted with her son or daughter and they are no longer in sight, she may quickly forget about their plight. Brothers and sisters may forget about each other. Although the victim may have had many abductions before, she has only a limited sense of familiarity with the situation she finds herself in. Almost everything that is happening to her during the abduction is forgotten as her attention is continually fixed on the present. Some abductees have more of a continuity of memory, but it is severely restricted at best. Janet Demerest explained it: "When I'm there it's like one thing happens, then the next thing happens. I completely forget about the first thing that happens. I have no sense of who I am." While she is in this state and trying to get her bearings, the Small Beings begin the physical examination.

THE PHYSICAL EXAMINATION

Between two and four Small Beings surround the abductee while she is on the table. She is powerless to move or to speak. But, although she may be confused and terrified, she still has her wits about her. Her eyes are open, and she is able to observe and record what is happening.

The entire examination may not last much longer than ten to twenty minutes. The Small Beings work fast. They are dedicated to performing their tasks. They are quick, efficient, and focused. They target specific anatomical sites for a poking, feeling, "touch procedure" type of palpation. Their fingers move rapidly. One abductee said it was like they were operating a typewriter on his body.

The standard pattern is to begin at the feet. The aliens carefully observe and touch the soles of the abductee's feet. Sometimes they take a sharp instrument and scrape it down her soles, causing her feet to curl in an apparent reflex test. They quickly touch her ankles and twist her foot from side to side. They push and press against her calf muscles. Sometimes they squeeze hard and painfully between the bone and calf muscle. They look closely at her knee and bend her leg a few times as if they are observing the action of the joints.

During the examination of the legs and knees, the Small Beings might make a painless incision in the calf, thigh, back of the knee, or arm. The incision may be in the form of a scoop, or a long, thin cut, or a wide, messy cut. The abductee usually reports no blood and no prolonged healing process. A scar forms almost instantly. The subject may be vaguely aware of what the aliens are doing at the time, but after the abduction she does not remember how she got the mysterious scar.

The Small Beings palpate the abductee's thighs and separate women's legs. They conduct a quick gynecological examination of women. A Small Being might "scrape" the vaginal or uterine wall and extract the material with an instrument in a manner similar to a Pap test procedure. He uses instruments that sometimes resemble butter knives. Sometimes he only palpates and observes. Men's and boys' genitals are palpated, lifted, and carefully observed.

After the genital exam, the Small Beings closely look at the subject's ribs and rib cage. Sometimes the aliens make a small incision
on the abductee's left side. They then raise the subject's arms over
her head while they examine and palpate her underarms and possibly her lymph nodes. When they are finished they return her arms
to her side.

For women a breast examination is next. Sometimes the abductee
feels a powerful and painful squeezing around the nipple as if the
Beings were trying to express fluid. If the woman is not pregnant and
some fluid is expressed, the aliens collect the fluid onto an instrument and either put it into a container on the table or take it out of
the room. Sometimes women feel "heat," "heaviness," or swelling in
their breasts during and immediately after the palpation. The Small
Beings also express milk from pregnant women; even women who
are not pregnant have reported that they inexplicably begin to lac-
tate.

The Small Beings now concentrate on the subject's head. One of
them places his hands on either side of the abductee's temples and
carefully rolls her head from side to side. Next they examine the ears
with an instrument similar to an otoscope, and look into each eye,
usually with a light-emitting device like a physician's ophthalmo-
scope. The Small Beings then open the abductee's mouth and look
in. Frequently they insert something into her mouth and scrape the
back of her throat. They may jam a large wad of material into the
subject's throat and then withdraw it, causing her to gag and cough.
They then examine the abductee's teeth and gums. They feel inside
with their fingers. They might excise a piece of gum for examination.

The Small Beings next palpate the neck and carefully feel around
it, giving the thyroid glands special attention. The abductee might
gag a little when this happens. Sometimes it is unnerving because
the victim thinks she is being choked. Usually the Beings do it gently,
causing little discomfort.

After the abductee's head examination is completed, the Small
Beings lift her up, as several abductees have stated, "like a rag doll,"
to a sitting position. Her muscle tone is still almost nonexistent. Her
legs are out in front of her, and the Beings balance her so that she
does not fall to one side. Once she is in this position, the Beings
carefully examine her back and vertebrae. They might take a tissue
sample from her back, but more often they continue the palpation

that is a constant feature of the entire physical examination. They methodically touch and press each individual vertebrae from the neck to the coccyx; they may repeat this process several times. The Small Beings pay very careful attention to the coccyx, and several of them may palpate it in turn. They take a long time with the vertebrae as their fingers manipulate each bone structure.

After they have examined the vertebrae and back, the aliens roll the abductee onto her left side. From this position the Small Beings may once again examine and feel the vertebrae. After this, they conduct a rectal examination. They use a variety of instruments, one of which resembles a small wire whisk. They insert the instrument and withdraw it. When the rectal exam is over, the Beings roll the woman completely on her stomach. They once again examine the back of her legs. They may take tissue samples, especially in the area behind the knee. Frequently the abductee reports that she thinks the Beings are "measuring" her from her hip to her heel or up her side. Finally the Beings turn the abductee on her back again.

Essentially this ends the examination. But many variations exist. The Beings may start at the head and work down and then back up again. They may begin with the gynecological aspect of the exam. They may begin with the examination of the vertebrae. Wherever they begin, they work systematically around the body until the exam is completed.

If the subject has been abducted before, any significant change in her physical status since the last examination immediately draws attention. For instance, Melissa Bucknell had part of her black hair dyed blond, and this instantly aroused the Beings' concern; after much feeling and examining, they decided that she had been ill and needed treatment. In her late thirties, Karen Morgan was fitted for braces on her teeth; during a subsequent abduction experience, the Beings immediately focused their attention on her braces and asked her what they were for. When she refused to tell them, they cut out a small triangular-shaped wedge of tissue from her gum for analysis.

I see them with the instrument. Cutting it out . . . It doesn't hurt. I can't believe this. This is absolutely unbelievable. There is actually a discussion going on about my braces. . . .

What are they saying?

Honest to God, I thought . . . I can't believe this! They're saying, "What are these?" They're looking at them. And I think, "You jerks, I'm not going to tell you what they are. You figure it out!"

How do they respond to that?

They don't pay attention to me. They say . . . it's almost like somebody's saying, "You shouldn't be afraid by now!" or, "You shouldn't be afraid." Of course, they always tell me that. And I say, "I know you guys do this to me all the time, but if I don't remember it I won't care." Because I haven't remembered it ever, really.

Are you standing up?

Oh no, I'm lying down. . . . They're cutting out a piece of my gum. I'm terrified, just terrified. I'm absolutely terrified. And yet I know . . . I can't describe all the emotions I'm feeling by now. I feel absolutely terrified. I feel like this is psychological torture, but I'm not afraid for my life. And I'm furious. There are no words to describe how mad I am because I feel like they're just torturing me. And I'm saying, "This has got to stop." . . .

Did they tell you why they were taking this sample of your gum?

I say, "Don't you guys have enough of me by now? What do you want?" I said, "How long does it take you to study somebody?"

And what do they say?

They say it can go on for years.

(Karen Morgan, 38, 1987)

Scabs, infections, or other body marks and changes attract their curiosity. For instance, a woman who had given birth by cesarean section had new scars that drew the attention of the alien who told her this was not the way *they* did it. In another instance, Jill Pinzarro had fallen off her bike when she was eleven years old and was later abducted:

> They're looking at my knee, and the reason is, I think is, I fell off my bike, and there's a bad scab there. They seem to know about it because it's the first thing looked at, they're just looking at it.

> Is this your right knee or your left knee?

> Left. Got all sorts of dirt and gravel in it. They're just looking at it, look at it, touch the edges of the scar where it's a little infected probably. It's kind of pus-y, it's a bad scrape. But they cover it up [with a "sheet"].

(Jill Pinzarro, 11, 1960)

Such changes often elicit discussion among the Small Beings as they try to discover the origin of the change on the abductee's body.

Implants

Toward the end of the examination, the aliens either implant a small, round, seemingly metallic object in the abductee's ear, nose, or sinus cavity, or remove such an object. The object is as small as or smaller than a BB, and it usually is smooth, or has small spikes sticking out of it, or has holes in it. The function of this device is unknown: It might be a locator so that the targeted individual can be found and abducted; it might serve as a monitor of hormonal changes; it might facilitate the molecular changes needed for transport and entrance; it might facilitate communication.

The ear is a commonly described place for the implant. The abductees report that Small Beings will insert the object with a long, thin instrument far into the ear canal, sometimes rupturing the ear drum, and leave it very near the brain. When asked during hypnosis what the aliens are doing, abductees frequently reply that they "know" the aliens are placing an implant there. How they know this is not apparent, but sometimes an abductee describes a small object shaped like a ball bearing on the end of the instrument that is inserted; when the instrument is withdrawn, the ball is gone.

The nose is another place for tiny implants to be left. Abductees say that the aliens insert an instrument way up in their nasal passages between their eyes. Sometimes nosebleeds occur after this procedure. Both child and adult abductees have seen physicians for nosebleed problems, and have discovered odd holes inside their noses. Several abductees have reported that a ball-shaped object either dropped out of their nose or was expelled when they blew their nose. All of these expulsions happened before they knew they had been abducted; in each case they thought that they had inexplicably inhaled something and discarded the object or lost it.

The third most common place for an implant is in the sinus cavity underneath the eye. The Small Beings sometimes insert a sharp, thin needle downward into the tear duct and then into the sinus cavity below the eye and above the cheek. Like the other procedures, it is not painful, although it can cause swelling and sometimes black-and-blue marks. Once again people report that they "know" the aliens left an implant behind.

Abductees tell of other areas of implant placement, such as near the ovaries and in the lower abdomen in women, and even in the penile shaft in men, but the preferred places appear to be in the head.

STARING PROCEDURES

Throughout the abduction, both as a way of communicating with the abductee and, presumably, of examining and altering her mental and emotional state, the Beings stare deeply into the abductee's eyes. For instance, during the first moments of an abduction, often before the abductee has been transported to the UFO, an alien inexplicably stares deeply into an abductee's eyes. When the abductee is very excited or frightened during the abduction, an alien stares into her eyes, calming her. Staring can also alleviate an abductee's pain. However, the most profoundly affecting of the staring procedures is Mindscan.

Mindscan

After the Small Beings complete the physical examination and implant the device, they stand back from the abductee. Then a Taller Being walks into the room. The Taller Being closely resembles the Small Being except that he is slightly taller, he might have subtly different facial features, he sometimes wears noticeable clothes, and he has an air of authority about him. He gives orders and the Small Beings obey. People often have strong and divided feelings about the Taller Being. Some hate him because he is clinical and brusque, and because he does "bad" things to them. Others feel he has more of a range of emotion and they can relate to him better than they can to the Small Beings. Abductees sometimes call him the doctor because of his demeanor and his task. He is usually very businesslike, with a detached, matter-of-fact attitude.

When the abductee attempts to communicate with the Taller Being, he usually responds with reassuring phrases, much as the Small Being does. But when "pushed" he will not respond directly to the questions asked. When an abductee asks, "What are you doing?" he may answer with a cryptic, "You know what we are doing." When an abductee asks if they will ever stop doing this to her, the Taller Being might respond with, "You are very special to us" or, "This is very important and you are helping us."

At times the Taller Being will perform the physical exam himself, but Mindscan is the focus of his attention. Mindscan entails deep, penetrating staring into the abductee's eyes. Abductees commonly feel that data of some sort is being extracted from their minds. We do not know what the information is, how it is extracted, or what the Beings do with it. One abductee thinks that they transfer it to other Beings' minds.

During Mindscan, the abductee lies on the table and the Taller Being stands next to her. He bends over and comes very close to the abductee, who may feel extremely frightened and threatened. He may even be close enough to touch foreheads with her. When asked how close the Taller Being is to them during Mindscan, Will Parker, Patti Layne, James Austino, and Lydia Goldman gave typical answers:

He's right up in my face. Not quite touching my nose with his face, but he is almost that close.

(Will Parker, 33, 1988)

If he had a nose, it doesn't seem that he does, not much of one anyway, it's just pressed down as close to my nose as he can get without specifically touching.

(Patti Layne, 23, 1985)

How close is his forehead to you?

He is touching it. He is leaning right over and touching it. . . . My nose touches his face.

(James Austino, 21, 1987)

I just see what I am looking at and I see this thing moving and it looks like a monkey.

How close is this face to you?

I would say inches. . . .

(Lydia Goldman, 4, 1936)

The Taller Being then gazes deeply into the abductee's eyes. His black eyes, which lack pupils, occupy a huge amount of space on his face. They are spellbinding, riveting. He locks eyes with the abductee. Even though she tries, she cannot close her eyes or take her eyes off his. Most abductees feel overwhelmed by the procedure. They feel as if they are "falling into them [the eyes]" and achieving some sort of connection with the Taller Being. He may order her to "look at me!" to ensure proper contact.

I'm looking into those eyes. I can't believe that I'm looking into eyes that big. . . . Once you look into those eyes, you're gone. You're just gone.

How do you mean that?

I can't think of anything but those eyes. It's like the eyes overwhelm me. How do they do that? It goes inside you, their eyes go inside you. You just are held. You can't stop looking. If you wanted to, you couldn't look away. You are drawn into them, and they sort of come into you. . . .

Are your eyes open or closed?

My eyes are open, but my mind is sort of gone. I have no will. I have no will. I am absorbed and I'm not fighting it.

(Karen Morgan, 9, 1958)

Some people say that they feel that the Taller Being is "stealing their memories." Others say that the effect is calming and soothing, and they are not as frightened as they were before. Both men and women report feeling vulnerable and violated. They are powerless to prevent this procedure from happening. If the abductee tries to close her eyes, the Taller Being tells her she must open them, and she does. Often the Taller Being's hand is on the abductee's head or shoulder while he completes his procedure.

Bonding

During Mindscan, the Taller Being can elicit specific emotions in the abductee, such as fear and terror. Often he will create an instant rush of pleasurable emotions in the abductee that "bonds" her to him. As he stares deeply into her eyes, she may feel that the Taller Being is really a "good" individual. She wants to help him. She wants to be with him. She wants to give herself to the Beings' "program," to help in any way she can. She does not want to leave. Sometimes there is a romantic and even sexual quality to these thoughts. Some women say that they "love" the Taller Being. They want to give themselves to him fully and completely. Men have similar feelings, especially if they perceive the alien to be "female." Bonding can be a totally overwhelming experience.

Very young children undergo the same experience. But instead of strong romantic or sexual feelings, they usually consider the Taller Being to be "nice" and a "friend." During abductions they are comforted that their "friend" is present to protect them. With children over age ten, however, the Taller Being might induce mature bonding feelings.

Lynn Miller was a Mennonite woman who had experienced a series of inexplicable events in her life. In one hypnotic regression, she remembered being abducted from her car near Tuckahoe, New Jersey. During the event, the Taller Being stared into her eyes intently and began the bonding procedure.

Can you tell if the person that's looking in your eyes is the same one that was in the room when you first came in, or is he different?

Different.

How is he different?

Bigger.

So when he looks in your eyes, does he just do sort of a cursory examination, or does he go from one eye to the other eye, or is he just kind of staring into your eyes?

He's staring into my eyes. . . .

Is he touching you?

Yes.

Where is he touching you?

My head.

Now, as you look at him, what kind of feelings go through your mind?

Love.

By love, do you mean directed toward him, or just sort of amorphous?

It's for everything.

Are you looking into his eyes also?

He makes me.

So he looks into your eyes and you get this sort of rush of pleasurable feelings again?

Yes.

When you have this rush of pleasurable feelings, is there sort of a sexual component to this as well?

Yes.

Is it because of the situation of the vulnerability of it all, or . . . ?

I think from what he's projecting. . . .

So he looks into your eyes for a while, and then what does he do?

Then he goes down and does a gynecological exam. . . .

(Lynn Miller, 31, 1987)

When Barbara Archer was twelve years old, she found herself in a room with forty or fifty tables. After her examination the Taller Being came over and performed Mindscan on her. I asked her if he was looking at her.

Yes.

Was he just kind of looking at random, or . . . ?

He looked into my eyes, and I really like him.

You looked in his eyes too?

Mm-hmm, but I just felt happy and I just lay down.

Did he kind of look in your eyes for just a short instant, or for a little bit longer?

No, for a little while. But I don't feel sick anymore, I just feel a little chilly.

Now when you look into his eyes, what kind of feelings do you have?

He makes me feel happy. I think that he likes me.

Do you feel positive toward him?

Mm-hmm, he doesn't scare me when I see him. The smaller guy scares me, but he's okay because I feel like I know him, but not like this. . . .

[The Taller Being then left Barbara for a short time and when he came back to her he resumed his bonding procedure.]

Then the tall guys comes back, and he asks me how am I doing, and I say I'm fine. And he looks at me again, looks at me for longer.

What kind of a feeling do you get when he looks at you?

I feel wonderful. I think that he's wonderful.

Now when you're looking at him, does this sort of have an almost romantic type of feeling to it?

A little bit, yes. He just makes me feel okay, makes me feel good.

[I asked her delicately if there was a sexual component attached to these feelings.]

Yes, I think that there is.

. . . you look at him and he looks at you, and you get this rush of positive feelings. Is that the way to describe it best?

Yes, I just feel like I fall into it.

Does he say anything, communicate anything while this is going on?

No, just a general happy feeling.

What do you think he's doing?

I don't know, I think he...I don't know. I think he can read what's in my mind, he knows what's in my mind....He makes me feel grown-up, sort of. When he says things to me he talks to me like I'm really young, but I feel womanly or something, I guess because I think that he thinks I'm attractive or something.

(Barbara Archer, 12, 1979)

Twenty-three-year-old Patti underwent a bonding procedure that attracted her to the Being. She struggled to explain what it was like.

So now he comes over and he sort of stares into your eyes. Do you have those same feelings of liking him?

Yeah, kind of liking him. Not being really threatened by him. Kind of sympathizing with his purposes, whatever they would be.

Patti, do any of these emotions seem sort of bordering on romantic feelings or anything approaching that?

Well, I don't think he means it to be that way, but I may interpret it to be that way. Like he's just so curious, and he's looking at me with such questioning eyes, and maybe I interpret it that way. But he gives me a feeling, just kind of a head rush. A real head rush, just all different emotions. He's trying to tap into me, maybe he's just evoking things from me, it's because he's curious as to what they are....A real powerful feeling, but it's really, you can't really describe it adequately. Romantic is just too shallow....I think you become one with this thing. You're happy. It's just like a symbiotic relationship. It's like you exist together with him, there, while your eyes are locked and you just kind of feed on each other, charge each other. It's really a very hard thing to describe.

Do you have a feeling you have a certain vulnerability in this?

Yeah, I really do. Because he's definitely the dominating one.

Do you feel that you've sort of given yourself over to him?

Um-hmm. Like possession in a way.

Does this have a sort of sexual component to it?

Yeah. In a way. It's not unpleasant, though. It's like you are meant to do this.

(Patti Layne, 23, 1985)

At times a female Being will perform Mindscan and bonding, especially with abductees who are children. (Somehow the abductees know that the alien is a female even though they see no anatomical differences.) The female Being is kind and sympathetic. She explains that they are not going to hurt the abductee. She considers the abductee to be a "very special" person who is helping them. She is grateful for this help. The alien might state that the abductee may even be "one of us." She is very gentle and empathetic. The abductee cannot help but be fond of, or even love, this female Being.

When Jill Pinzarro was ten years old in 1959, she received a strong "friendship" impulse during the bonding procedure. A Taller Being stared at her, and she began to feel positive emotions.

It's quite reassuring for some reason. I don't know why it's reassuring. It's not love or care or anything like that, but there is a sense of connection to this Being, and it's not false. . . . I guess there's a sense of not even guardianship, but of being personally important in some way to this Being. . . . And the sense of protection too. I know I won't come to harm, I know the Being cares about me to the extent that it cares, and that . . . it's not cold, it's limited but it's not cold. In fact, in some ways it's more than human beings give because even though it's not as intense, it's unconditional.

While he's looking down at you and you're getting this sort of feeling, does he touch your forehead or anything?

I can't think of this as a he.

Do you think it's female, or does that apply?

It's more like a she than a he, more like a nonsex than either.

But sort of leaning toward the she?

Yeah, just because of the nonmasculine quality of its personality. Maybe it's the unconditional warmth or something. I don't know. I don't think men are so unconditional, maybe that's why I'm picking this up.

Does this Being put his or her hand on your forehead while you're thinking about all this?

As a matter of fact, yeah. I almost think that it wants me to look into its eyes, then it links up with me in that caring way, and then it touches my forehead and I feel quite calm and at peace. I think this one is a little different from the others in some way. I don't mean physically. . . . I do feel such a strong emotional . . . emotional isn't really the right word, but bond. I trust. I, to a degree, love, I think, because I so much need what is being given.

Does this feeling, as you're lying there, have a slight sexual component to it as well, not necessarily directed toward them, but more amorphous?

Wait a minute, let me get ahold of this. There is, yeah, if you want to say that willing surrender is sexual, it's there.

Is this a little bit confusing to a ten-year-old girl?

It's not a child's emotion. But who analyzes like that? It's just something new.

Is it embarrassing?

It doesn't have . . . no. I don't think it's embarrassing. I don't have words. It's desirable, good, beautiful, and shocking and traumatic, without having as much intensity as those words imply because I can't analyze it, it's just there.

Now this feeling that's being created in you, does this feeling last very long? Do you feel it sort of ebbing away as you're lying there, or does this maintain a high level of intensity for a long period?

It ebbs away slowly. It does have a slightly sexual component which I don't recognize at the time. But in another way it can never leave. It's there, as a perfect experience, and you always try to recapture those, don't you? . . . I don't think I'd want to give it up.

(Jill Pinzarro, 10, 1959)

From time to time the aliens will induce rapid, intense, sexual arousal and even orgasm in a woman as part of their Mindscan procedures. A few abductees report that arousal occurs through manual genital manipulation during Mindscan. Others think that it is a combination of physical and Mindscan procedures that quite suddenly creates sexual feelings. Most women, however, know that the feelings are being elicited from them almost as if the aliens were pushing a mental button. In spite of their attempts to fight it, sexual arousal builds to a peak in a few minutes and then subsides. As often as not, orgasm will take place. The orgasm is not a pleasurable event—it is usually something to be endured until it is over. Some women, knowing what is happening, become very angry and humiliated when this procedure begins, but control is not theirs.

When Mindscan is completed, or when the sexual arousal procedures are at their peak, the Taller Being immediately begins a set of gynecological and urological procedures.

REPRODUCTIVE PROCEDURES

Reproductive procedures are a constant feature of the abduction experience and are ultimately directed to the production of off-spring. Women endure a complex series of gynecological procedures designed to collect and implant eggs and to extract fetuses. For men, the urological procedures are focused on taking sperm.

Egg Harvesting

The Taller Being breaks off from performing Mindscan and begins what is reported to be ova harvesting. With one hand he presses on the woman's abdomen in the region above the ovaries, and with the other he inserts a variety of instruments into her vagina. The first is a speculumlike instrument that creates an opening large enough to work with. Then he inserts a long, thin, flexible tube that women report goes in very far. One woman described it as being as thin as a "daffodil stem." The women then realize that the tube is going to an ovary. Most women in some way know that he is taking an egg. As this procedure goes on, the women may feel ill, they may feel a "twinge" of pain, cramping (a little like menstrual cramps), or pressure. Some women perspire, feel dizzy, nauseated, and weak.

In another common procedure, also presumably for egg harvesting, the aliens insert into the woman's navel a thin needle attached to a "syringe" apparatus. When they did this to Betty Hill, the Beings evasively told her that they were performing a "pregnancy test." Other women have reported that the Beings told them they were taking eggs. Still other abductees have felt that the procedure was related to both but not specifically to either. One woman stated that the needle in the navel was used to take an egg from the ovary when she was menstruating. On some occasions a slightly larger tube is placed in the navel and a liquid is injected. Abductees feel cramping when this procedure is performed. Sometimes the insertion of the needle is painful, but most of the time the aliens succeed in blocking any discomfort.

Now they come up and they're poking at my bellybutton. . . .

When they poke at your bellybutton, do they use their hands or do they use an instrument?

An instrument.

Can you describe what this one is like?

It's long and pointy. It's like a needle. . . . It pinches.

Do they insert it into your bellybutton?

Yeah.

Does it hurt?

Yeah.

Do they stop the pain, or . . . ?

They put their hand on my head.

Does that stop it?

It seems to take it away.

(Lynn Miller, 30, 1985)

After the egg has been harvested, the Taller Being puts it into a container and places it on a cart or gives the egg container to a Small Being who quickly takes it out of the room. After he is finished with the egg-harvesting procedure, the Taller Being goes over to the woman's head and stares into her eyes again. Some women "black out" or go to sleep when he does this as a wave of irresistible calmness overtakes them. Then the Taller Being turns around and walks out of the room.

Embryo Implantation

Implanting a fertilized egg into the abductee is another critical procedure of the primary experiences. Usually the woman knows that something is being inserted into her and left there. She receives the impression that she is now pregnant. She does not want to be pregnant, and she certainly does not want to be pregnant under those circumstances. The Beings ignore her objections. Karen, for one, was furious at the gynecological procedures performed on her during an incident.

And now...I'm wondering what he's doing, and I say in my mind, "You son of a bitch, I'd better be all right," and he says, he's down at the other end of the table, he says, "But you are all right," or that he's just making sure. And then he comes back up....I think he takes an instrument, and I think he's taking... it always reminds me of a Pap smear, but I think that's what he does next....I remember it feels like a long, rounded instrument.

Thin, or...?

Thin. I can feel it. A long...I don't know what he's doing. This part is mystifying to me. I can't see and I don't know. It's a long, rounded instrument.

You mean, sort of tubelike, or...?

That's what it feels like. I must have seen it at some time, too, because I have a better image...

Is it something that would just sort of take a smear, or is it something that has an apparatus on the end of it?

It definitely has an apparatus on the end of it, and it definitely has a hole somewhere on it, or an impression. I can see it. It's sort of like a bullet. It's something, it's got a bullet in it. I don't know how I know this. I don't think this is for removing an egg, I think this is for inserting one.

For inserting an egg?

Okay. That's why he gave me that exam. That's why they were worried. He's implanting an embryo in me, I'm positive of it. There's absolutely no doubt in my mind.

How do you know?

I have no idea, I just know it. I have the impression of something being shot into me, or put into me, but I can see this instrument and I don't know why. Stapled into me is a better way. I don't know how I know this. But I know it, even while it's going on. He must have told me, or I could see it in his mind. Because I'm saying, "This is repulsive! You're not going to get away with this. I will not let you do this!" And he said, "Yes, you will let us do it. It's very important." They never say, "There's not a damned thing you can do about it," they always give you some reason. And I say, "I'll remember this and I'll have an abortion." And he said, "You won't remember this." That's a suggestion he's giving me. He's saying, "You will not remember it." It's hypnotic. And I'm saying, "I will, I will." But then I'm thinking really fast in my mind, I can never get an abortion. How can I go into someone and say, 'I'm one day pregnant'? And then I think, there's got to be a way to get it out, because I know when they put it in they've got to take it out, and that means I've got to go back. And then he says, "You know there's nothing to worry about. We've done this before." And I think I know they've done it before, and it always makes me feel sick. I can't believe it, they really are doing this. They really are doing this. And there's nothing I can do.

Does this take a while, or is this a very short procedure?

Not as short as some of the others. But it's not long and drawn out. They're very careful. The other times they rush around, they give you a real fast exam. They usually focus on one part more than another, depending on what interests them. This time they're focusing on this and they're really careful, not because of you but because of the disgusting old hybrid embryos that they're sticking into you. I feel like a cow. I'm so mad, but I'm also so exhausted. And I now there really isn't anything I can do.

What does he do when he finishes with this?

The instrument stays in a while, and then he pulls it out. I have the impression there's a lot of goo involved, but I never remember feeling it. . . . And he pulls this thing out and he . . . I don't know if he hands it to someone or puts it down. He might hand it to someone. And then he pats my stomach or touches my stomach and says, "There we go." I say, "You're disgusting, get your hand off me! Take your hand off me! Take your hand off me!" And he does.

Where was his hand, on your stomach still?

He took his hand off my stomach, and he sort of shakes his head as if he's puzzled. Shaking is too violent a term, he moves his head as if he's puzzled, as if to say, "I don't know what's the matter with this one."

(Karen Morgan, 28, 1977)

Karen woke up in the morning with a sticky, gelatinous substance between her legs. She was puzzled about how she got it and washed it off in her morning shower.

Lynn Miller was with her son when they were driving to Cape May, New Jersey. They saw a huge object hovering by the side of the road, and Lynn felt compelled to pull the car over and stop. In the ensuing abduction, the aliens separated Lynn from her son, inserted a needle into her bellybutton, and then implanted something in her.

He puts something inside.

Do you feel whether this is going in just a little way, or a long way, or . . . ?

It's all the way in.

Left side or right side?

I don't know. I can't tell.

Can you describe what this feels like? Does this give you any pain, or pressure, or cramping?

It hurts.

Now, is this after they do the bellybutton procedure, or before?

After.

And what happens next?

It feels like there's something still in there, but they're done.

Do you think that they put something in, or they took something out?

It feels like they put something in.

Okay. And what happens then?

Then they make me get off the table.

Just before that, now, this taller one, does he come over to you, say something to you?

They tell me they're implanting me.

Does he say with what?

No. He said I was implanted.

Do they mean internally?

I don't know.

What do you say when they say that?

I don't remember saying anything.

(Lynn Miller, 30, 1985)

Janet Demerest has also had events in which she felt that something had been left inside her. As it was for Lynn, it was difficult for her to tell what was happening during one of them.

At some point the guy is there with this long metal thing, like a needle. But I don't know what context [it is in]. . . . I think he stuck that thing inside me, and I thought it was going to hurt.

Now when you say stuck inside of you, do you mean through your stomach or . . . ?

Vaginally.

What do you think he's doing there? What is your impression?

My impression is that he is putting something inside of me. . . .

Do you feel any pain?

No, but I'm scared.

Do you say anything to him?

No, I'm afraid to move. . . .

I asked Janet what the thing looked like that had been left in her. She said that it was "a little round thing." When the procedure was completed, a female Being helped her off the table.

Somebody helps me sit up, pushing me from the back. I think it's a woman, I don't know.

Okay. You sit up on the table?

And all I can think is that I want to have a baby.

And what happens next?

Well, I think I kind of tell that to the woman, that I want to have a baby.

Does she respond?

No. She has no expression on her face at all.... I feel like I'm
going to have a baby, and that I want to have a baby.

Do you think that might be related to seeing that thing put
inside you?

I don't know. I don't know why all of a sudden I would want to
have a baby.

(Janet Demerest, 33, 1987)

The procedures for implanting an embryo seem similar to harvesting an egg, and often the abductee cannot tell the difference. Similarly, it is often difficult to tell when the aliens extract an embryo or
fetus from the abductee.

Embryo and Fetal Extraction

The extraction of the implanted embryo is the third critical gynecological procedure in the primary experiences. The abductee with
the implanted fertilized egg may not realize that she is pregnant even
though she stops menstruating. The abductee may have been extremely careful in her use of birth control, or she may not have had
sexual relations of any sort for many months, and therefore there
would be little or no reason to believe that she was pregnant. Nevertheless, her breasts swell and retain water, she may have morning
sickness, and she may have a "pregnant feeling." She may take a home
pregnancy test that shows positive, and then she may go to a physician for a blood test that confirms her suspicions—she is pregnant.

But about six to twelve weeks later her period begins again. She is
inexplicably not pregnant. She has no miscarriage, no expulsion of
fetal material, no indication that something was "wrong." She goes
to her physician, who confirms that the fetus has suddenly disappeared.

Sometimes the pregnant woman decides to have an abortion.
When the abortion takes place the physician is puzzled and mystified:
There is no fetus. It has mysteriously disappeared.

We cannot be sure of the exact number of times a woman has
undergone the implantation and extraction procedures unless we
know the number of pregnancies that are terminated in the first

trimester. Even then, the pregnancy may be terminated after a very short time, and the subject may assume that she simply missed a period or two and never know she was pregnant. We also have indications that some extractions are completed just before the first menstrual period is missed so that the woman has virtually no overt signs of pregnancy.

Lynn Miller described being painfully poked in the side by the Taller Being and told, "It's time to take it." The Taller Being began by using a speculum-type instrument followed by a long, black instrument with a "cup" on the end of it.

Can you tell me what this looks like?

It's long and it's black. It's got sort of a cup on the end or something.

Okay, you can go on.

With a suction or something.

Is this instrument attached to anything, or . . . ?

To a machine.

Is the machine on?

There's buttons lit up.

Do you hear any noise from it?

No, it's silent.

So he inserts this suction-cup device, and what happens next?

It feels like he's tearing something inside at first. . . . They're not too gentle. I keep on telling them it hurts.

Do they respond to that?

No.

Does he try to make it stop hurting?

No.

Does he say anything to you while this is going on?

No.

Okay, you can go on.

He seems to pull something out, and he puts it right in something else.

What does he put it in?

Sort of a container with water or something in it.

Is this container near the table, or does somebody give it to him?

He gives it to him.

I mean, when he first got it does somebody bring it to him to put whatever . . . ?

Yeah, one of the little guys. He wants me to see it. I don't want to see it.

Does he show it to you anyway?

Yes.

What are you looking at, then?

I'm looking at a fetus.

Is this a live little fetus?

Yes, it's in the bag.

Why does he want you to see this?

He says, "This is your child and we're going to raise it."

Does this look like a normal fetus?

Yes. I told him it was part of me and they didn't have any right.
He says, "It's our right."

That's all he says, "It's our right"?

Yeah.

Now, what does he do with this container?

He puts it in the machine.

Is there a door or a drawer for it, or an opening?

There's an opening on the top; he lifts it up and puts it in.

Does it disappear into the machine, then?

I can still see it. It must be glass.

Do you ask him why he's doing this?

No. I just tell him it's mine.

Does he volunteer any information as to why he's doing this?

No, he just said it's all right.

What happens next?

He told me I'm done, get dressed.

(Lynn Miller, 31, 1986)

Although the majority of fetal extraction procedures are per-formed when the abductee lies on a table, Anita Davis had a fetal extraction while sitting in a special chair.

It's almost like a birthing chair, it's at an incline this way, and he's adjusting straps, or stirrups, or something. I don't get the feeling it's to tie me down or anything. I know that I'm going to somehow sit on this thing.

... So this looks more like a chairlike device.

Like a chair that you'd squat in, like something that if you were to give birth in, it would be a good thing. It would go along with the force of gravity, and it would have you in the squatting position with one foot on each thing. I want to go back to the table. I don't like this.

But you don't actually see a table in the room?

No, I don't think so. I tried to.

Okay.

It's very obvious that what they put in now has to come out. It's almost time to give birth to it, but yet, they're not doing one of those birth numbers, but yet ... It has, it's time to take it out so they can have it. There's a sense of relief with that.

Is it more than one of them who are adjusting this?

He's adjusting this. He's doing it all. The little guys are just standing there, almost hands behind their backs, at ease.

So what are you doing?

We're talking back and forth.

I see.

It's almost like the obstetrician. I don't have any sense of dread or anything; it's like "Yeah, this is part of the procedure." He gets it ready, I get into it, sort of, there's no pain or anything. . . . He straps my feet in. It feels just like going to the obstetrician, though. There's no sense of "Oh, what are you doing to me?" I know what's happening. . . .

So you get into this contraption. And they kind of . . .

Strap my feet in.

Where are your arms?

There's like handles on the sides. . . .

So now you're . . . sitting upright?

Mm-hmm.

Your legs are . . .

Kind of bent, like a frog.

What are your feet on?

On little foot platform things, kind of. . . .

What are the little ones doing?

Just standing there.

And the taller one?

He positions himself underneath . . . with maybe something made of glass . . . something to catch it in. And he has me bear down once. There's no pain, it's not like I'm simulating birth or anything. And for some reason it just comes right out. There's a sense of relief. He gives almost a little Pyrex thing to one of the little guys, and he takes it out.

Can you see that little Pyrex thing?

Yeah, if you want to know what it looks like, it looks like what you'd expect a very early miscarriage to look like.

(Anita Davis, 33, 1991)

Twenty-year-old Tracy Knapp found herself the subject of a fetal extraction procedure that provoked intense feelings of sadness and depression in her.

There's one man here and one man on this side, and there's one man here and they're pressing. My legs are up, and I'm getting snipped, but internally. Something's snipping. . . . Something burned, burned. A fluid burns me, burns. There's a fluid put on me and it burns me. It's put inside of me. It burns me. [She cries.]

Does anybody say anything to you at this time?

No. [She cries.]

[I comfort her.]

They're pressing and there's snipping.

They're using instruments for this, I guess, then?

Very tiny, tiny, long, very long, little, bitty scissors things but very, very tiny.

What do you think they're snipping at? Can you get a physiological sense of that?

Yeah, it feels like . . . snipping on both sides. Somehow they like, I just feel like an uneasiness. I don't know where they're coming into . . . I don't like it. I don't like it. They're not taking eggs out of me. They're just snipping, it's like they're snipping. They're releasing, they're snipping. It's like they're cutting threads or something. They're cutting something, I don't know, I don't know.

Do you get the sense that they're . . . ?

Removing something.

Is this a long procedure or a short procedure, or . . . ?

Pretty long. . . . I can't fucking believe this!

Do you kind of see them finishing up?

Yeah.

Do they remove their instruments?

Yeah, they removed something out of me. They removed like a, like a little baby or something. And they removed the sac or something. They removed the . . . but it's tiny, it's real tiny. It's not a baby.

An embryo you mean?

Yeah, it's like . . .

What do they do with it when they remove it?

There's a cylinder or something. It seems like it's being placed .n this cylinder, like a silver cylinder, I don't know, tube—silver, probably three inches wide by [gestures with her hand].

Is the cylinder portable? In other words, are they holding it, or . . . ?

They're holding it.

What do they do with the cylinder then?

Well, you know how, they got other . . . God! It's like they've got other babies there. They're in like drawers in the walls; it's like little drawers that pull out, and there's babies, like little, little somethings in these drawers that pull out like in a lab or something.

(Tracy Knapp, 20, 1977)

Tracy described drawers on the wall containing many fetuses. This is where they put the fetus they took from her. She thought that the drawers were acting as incubators for the fetuses.

Sperm Collection

For men, the expression of sperm is a central aspect of the abduction experience. All males after puberty experience the sperm-collection process. The aliens initiate sperm-sampling procedures either directly after or during Mindscan. They place a tubelike apparatus or a funnel with a tube attached on the end of the penis, and they attach the other end to a machine. They then somehow extract the sperm. Sometimes they place a metallic, cuplike machine over the penis to extract the sperm (this is what happened to Barney Hill, among others). The apparatus acts as a pumping machine. An erection sometimes takes place but is not needed. There is ejaculation but not necessarily orgasm.

Often the subject is so distracted with an ongoing Mindscan that he is only vaguely aware of the sperm-collection procedure. At other times it can be quite painful, and it can be extremely embarrassing, particularly for adolescents. Very often a "female" alien will perform a bonding procedure during the extraction of sperm or immediately before it. With a combination of bonding and envisioning (see next chapter), the alien will make the abductee think that he is engaging in sexual relations with a human woman. This facilitates the sperm-collection procedures. At other times a male Taller Being will perform the sperm extraction.

Some men have said that while the sperm is being extracted, the aliens press or "knead" the right side of their lower abdomen. Ken

Rogers had his side massaged during a sperm extraction procedure and was at a loss to understand why.

Does he communicate anything to you while this is going on?

Not that I recall. I don't know what he says at all. I don't think he says anything. I just feel kind of like a baby, a little. Very safe, calm. I get the feeling these guys are guys who were busy doing something down there.

What do you mean?

I think they're hooking up a machine. They hook up a machine on a tube, with a suction cup end. So now they put it on my penis. I don't remember this or feel it, but I can see it happening now. That's where sexual feeling comes.

This is happening while he's staring at you?

Yeah, then he'll break away, and I think he touches me somehow. That's when I ejaculate. At least that's the way I see it. And I think while one little guy hooks up the machine the other one pumps my stomach for some reason. That seems to be the procedure. When he looks into my eyes, I get this bonding feeling. When the machine's all hooked up and ready, he strokes me or something. It feels pleasurable. And I ejaculate into the machine. That's the way I see it all the time.

So you think this is the same as before, then?

Yeah, it seems to be the same thing. Then they take it away. They wheel this thing away. And then he either bends down, or waits a little, and looks back into my eyes. I think he looks back into my eyes for a short time. Then I get this feeling of "Till we meet again" or something. A real close, ongoing relationship that will continue. Then he gets up and leaves, and I lie there for a while.

(Ken Rogers, 28, 1988)

Will Parker experienced the same method of sperm extraction, but his was even more mechanical than Ken's. One time he felt that there was a "self-contained" unit attached to his penis; at other times he described a hoselike appendage attached to his penis and then to a machine.

Are there just these two who are doing this?

There are others. They've got this comb-shaped gimmick over my crotch, and it's a buzzing, vibration type of sensation. It's a very functional kind of thing.

What do you think is happening?

Well, they're taking a sperm sample, obviously, because it's not piss they're pulling out of there.

Do you feel something flowing out?

Definitely; there's an erection and there's no sense of release or anything orgasmic; it's just like a literal drawing out.

. . . Can you get a sense of what it [the apparatus] looks like?

The only glimpse I could get of it, and I remember seeing some-thing like it before, a long time before, but it's like a, it looks like polished stainless steel, aluminum, chromium I guess you'd call it. It fits over the penis and it's got a rounded lower section that fits up over the testicles. And it's like you're enclosed in this thing. It looks like a piece of machinery that no good mistress of domination would be without, something rather kinky, in a different environment of course. But it looks, it's completely metallic.

Some people report that there's like a tubelike thing that goes to a machine on the side of them.

I don't see any tube or anything. This looks like it's self-con-tained.

I see.

Of course, I can't see if there's anything coming out of the lower section of it, or maybe where I can't see, but from where I can see it doesn't look like there's anything attached to it, it's attached to me and that's it.

(Will Parker, 33, 1988)

James Austino was a student at Temple University when he realized that certain puzzling and frightening events in his life might be due to the abduction phenomenon. We had several sessions together; in the course of one, he recalled having sperm extracted by a device similar to Will Parker's. The Beings began the procedure by pulling an apparatus that resembled a "dentist's light" close to him from its attachment underneath the table.

Oh, this is the "dentist's light"?

Yeah, he grabs it and moves it down toward my waist.

How does he get ... if it's down that low ... ?

He can just reach up and touch it and move it. He pulls it down pretty close to my waist, like maybe two feet above my waist. This part gets embarrassing.

Is this the genital business?

Yeah. The tall guy fumbles around down there, and I'm looking up, and I keep getting the feeling "It's okay."

So they're reassuring you?

Yeah. Don't worry about it, it's not going to hurt. I still get the feeling that he's instructing, like the other guy ... he's kind of showing him, because he presses right here [above pubic hair line] ... and he's still looking at the other guy, and he looks down and moves it around a little bit. He goes underneath and lifts it up a little bit and starts touching down there and stuff like that. I'm a little uncomfortable.

Absolutely.... So, he's sort of showing this other guy your genitals, and sort of manipulating the whole thing?

Yes. I feel like a lab animal, just sort of lying there and taking it, like a cat at the vet.... One of the arms has tubes running from it, and they're bringing it down to my genital area. I say out loud, "What's that for?"

You mean, through your mouth?

Yeah, and the big guy quickly glances over at me, and he moves toward my face. He puts his left hand on my forehead, and he comes down pretty close to my face.

How close is he?

About two inches away from my face right now. It's almost like I'm locked with him.

While you're locked with him, what's going through your mind? Is he generating any feelings?

No, but he's giving me a picture of Monique [his friend who was switched off during the abduction] with no clothes on. That's just the image I get.

So suddenly you get this image of Monique?

Yeah.

When you get this image, what setting is she in, or is it just disembodied?

It's just disembodied...

In other words, you don't get an image of Monique, let's just say, in another room next door?

No, it's just an image, like a flash in my mind.

Right.

Then he pulls away, and they're moving the arm away.

What was going on down there while he was staring into your eyes?

I felt like they were attaching it.

Mm-hmm.

But I didn't feel anything.

Do you get the sense that you have an erection, or not?

Yeah, one's going away now. As soon as they pull the machine off, and he moves away.

Okay. Some guys say yes and some guys say no, it doesn't seem to matter much, for their purposes anyway.

I'm like, "What happened?"

The part that attaches over your genital area, can you get a sense of what that looks like?

Yeah, I can. It's like a little ball with the end cut out of it, and it goes over the tip. It doesn't go all the way down. . . . This table is pretty useful, multipurpose. It's like everything's kind of attached to it on the sides.

So they move this thing away, then?

And I lift my head up a little bit and look down. I'm a little bit embarrassed.

(James Austino, 14, 1980)

From time to time a woman will be abducted with a male companion. When that happens, she can sometimes describe the procedures being done to her friend. Their descriptions may vary on the details of what the extraction devices look like, but they are all describing the same event. One woman was abducted with a boyfriend when she was seventeen years old. During the event she noticed that the aliens were attaching something shaped like a "distributor cap" over his penis. Similarly, Melissa Bucknell also had an abduction with a boyfriend during their lovemaking. She was placed on a table next to him, and she watched the aliens attach a hoselike apparatus with a cap on the end to his penis. The hose went to a machine on the ceiling.

Another woman watched in horror as her teenaged son was placed on a table near her. She could see a female Being perform Mindscan, sperm sampling, and presumably bonding on him. This was obviously an emotionally wrenching scene for her.

Do they start on Richard now?

I can't even watch it . . .

Is Richard still asleep while this is going on?

Yes, he's asleep. But I can't watch it. I know that he puts his hand on Richard's head.

The tall one, you mean?

They're really not very big, but they seem big compared to the other ones.

Is he looking at Richard when he does that?

It gets Richard to open his eyes. I can't really get into the telepathic conversation they're having, but I know what they're saying to him because of what they say to me. And I'm frantic, I'm just frantic. I can't even watch it. And they're giving me this exam, and they're hitting my back, and they're doing this stupid stuff to me, and I'm trying to get rid of them. I'm saying, "Get

THE ABDUCTION EXPERIENCE 129

out of here! Leave me alone!" And I'm thinking, "Don't do that to him." And I'm thinking, "I wonder if I can get my mind into what he's saying. If I could just concentrate, if they'd leave me alone." They're just all over me and I can't even think.... I'm so mad, and I'm so helpless. And it looks at me. It must hear me.

The one who's next to Richard?

Yeah, the creature looks over at me—it must hear me. That's good though. That's good because that distracts him. And I think, "Keep your hands off him! Get away from him!" I know that they're taking a sperm sample from Richard. I don't know how I know it, but I know. I must have seen it. I think it . . . of course it would hear me. It knows that I'm saying something. . . . It either leaves Richard or it comes over to me next.

The same one, you think?

I have the impression it's the same one. The same . . . either it says it from over there or coming over to me. It says, "Why do you interfere? Why do you want to interfere?" And I say, "You have got to be kidding! You filthy, disgusting creature. You can't possibly be asking me that question." It doesn't understand all that; it just says, "Why do you interfere?" I say, "Leave him alone! Leave his mind alone!" And then it says that he belongs to them. And I say, "No he doesn't! He belongs to me." And then all it does is look at me. And it's saying that I belong to it too. And I say, "No, that's bullshit! I don't buy that. I don't care what you had to do with him when he was conceived. I don't care what you've done to him, he's not yours and I'm not yours. I'll never be yours." . . . I want it to leave Richard alone. It tells me that they've only begun with him. Why should I worry? No harm will come to him. I've got to get Richard out of this. Every time I have one of the encounters with one of those creatures, it just depresses the hell out of me.

Does he still stand there with you?

I don't think, no. He does for a while but then he leaves. I don't think they're capable of altering what they're going to do, so I'm sure he didn't interrupt himself with Richard. On the other hand, I think he did know that I was trying to interfere. I don't have the impression that they took eggs or anything this time, but I wasn't paying any attention to that at all. It's so hard to focus on anything to begin with, and when I saw that thing put its hand on Richard's forehead, you know, I'm sure it was the same one who came over to me. But there may have been... there's more than one running around. It seems there's another one over with Richard now, sort of a smaller version of the bigger one.

Is it bigger than the little guys?

Yeah.... It's something to do with sperm samples.... It seems like this one has to do with one of the female creatures.

What do you mean?

I have the impression that there's a female creature that's involved. And God knows what she's doing to him, or telling him.

Is she standing next to him?

Yes. And even though she's repulsive and horrible, there's something seductive about the whole thing. I have the impression that she's opening his eyes.

And is he still lying there?

And she's opening his eyes. They're too big. They're too big. He's frightened. I just want to scream at the top of my lungs and get her away from him. I'm moving my head from side to side because I'm so upset. I have to make a commotion. I have to make trouble. I have to do something. I'm screaming in my mind. I have the feeling... that she's doing something to his mind. Like they do with mine. There's something about it, like the other one was doing with him, but this is more intense or something. How does anyone survive this? They're putting something in his nose. I know this happened before me. I saw this. They put something in his nose.

They inserted something?

Or they took something out. And I think, "I always knew there was something there, he used to get nosebleeds." I think that. I'm so furious at this whole thing.

(Name omitted by request)

The taking of sperm or the ending of the gynecological procedures usually signals the conclusion of the primary experiences. The Taller Being has left the room and only one or two of the Small Beings remain. The abductee continues to lie on the table for a few minutes. Then the Small Beings get her up, help her to her feet, and guide her out of the room. But the ordeal is not over.

Chapter 5

Machine Examinations, Mental Testing, and Hybrid Children

"ISN'T THIS A BEAUTIFUL BABY?"

By the time the abductee has finished the primary experiences, most of her dizziness, nausea, and confusion has passed, although her consciousness and visual perception are still altered. Her emotions are a mixture of fear, anger, and calmness. The intense alien bonding feelings have ebbed, but she may still feel emotionally attached to the Taller Being. She is now ready for the secondary experiences.

Like primary experiences, the secondary experiences involve physical, mental, and reproductive procedures. The sequence of secondary events is variable, and as always there are significant variations in each procedure.

MACHINE EXAMINATIONS

Either the abductee remains on the same table or the aliens lead her into a different room and help her up onto another table. This table is similar to the one that she has just left, except that it may have mechanical contraptions around or on it. She lies down, and the aliens quickly bring one of the machines over to her. They may pull it down from the wall or the ceiling, or "wheel" it over from a side area. It may be attached to the table, or the table may be rolled to it. They turn the machine on, and the abductee can hear a whirring or humming sound. She sees lights on the machine. It may remind her of a "dentist's light." The machine is trained on her. The lights are intense. They may be blue or white or yellow.

Sometimes the machine comes down from the ceiling and gets closer and closer to the abductee. It is aimed at her head, her chest, or, more commonly for women, her lower abdomen. The lights become more intense as the device gets closer. If she feels any sensation at all, it might be a "tingling" where the machine is aimed. If the machine is pointed at the abductee's head, she might see vivid colors. She is unable to move. The machine may be stationary, or it might slowly circle her body from top to bottom and back again. It is not uncommon for the light to focus on her lower abdomen and genitals. The entire table may revolve with the axis at the feet while her body moves from one apparatus to another.

The variety of machine examinations is great, although the exact purpose of the machines is unknown. Most abductees think they are recording devices, much like X-ray equipment. Somehow people know that the machines are scanning them, "taking pictures," or making neurological measurements. When Marva Roberts was eight years old, the aliens used a machine on her that was beyond her ability to understand. During most of the hypnosis session she talked from an eight-year-old's point of view.

Yeah, I know that they're not going to hurt me. . . . But it's okay. It's okay. They're not going to hurt me. But they just . . . What are you going to do, guys?

What are they doing now?

They're just staring and that little noise they make . . . I hate this. . . . I don't want to be here. There's this thing. . . . Something here that they put over on top of me. . . . [She gestured to show me where it was.]

Is this machine over your chest?

It's kind of like over my whole middle; maybe it goes down to my knees. I don't think I'm supposed to know all this. But it's a black machine and it's got like these lights coming out of it. And there's lights up there that are, like, I guess it's almost like that

little machine they used on me, and somehow they found something else in there. And it's like a big one. And it's ... vibrating
in my tummy again. It doesn't hurt. It tickles a little bit, but I
guess maybe they're looking inside me. But when you tickle I
touch it ...

Did you touch the machine?

No, I touched the tummy because it tickled. And they put my
thing back down again. But it's okay, they're not mad at me. But
they're just touching buttons up there, and ... blinking something ... I thought maybe they were going to move it up over
my head or something. They kind of talked a little or something,
and then they decided not to ...

Do you hear any sounds from the machine?

Yes. It's kind of like ... the thing I can hear is like a tiny, tiny,
I don't know what it sounds like, it's kind of like a hum. But
it's not a hum. It's a real soft, tiny, tiny noise. It's sort of like
a buzzing ... it's just a tiny, tiny noise. ... I'm tired. I want to
go home.

Are you in the same room as you were before?

Yes.

Do they communicate anything to you while this is going on?

No. They won't tell me anything, just like the grown-ups. But
they come and mumble back and forth ... shake their head or
something, but they don't tell me anything. ...

Does the machine finally stop?

No, but they're still kind of talking now ... they're pointing to
the lights up on top of the machine, and they're kind of talking.
"Come on! I don't like this!" They're moving it away now. "Can
I go home?" This is starting to bug me a whole lot. I don't like
this. Now they're over there talking again or something. Uh-oh,

what's that they're poking into me? It looks like it's kind of shiny. It's kind of, it looks like metal but it doesn't feel like it . . . it's not cold. It looks like one of Mommy's Tupperwares. . . . Something shiny—really orangy-fiery shiny—it looks like a piece of metal, and it's got a whole lot of little dents in it.

Where is this?

It's over my head. It's just glowing . . . and it's warm on my face. Whew, it's bright!

Can you see colors, or can you see just light, or . . . ?

Well, that thing in the center is orange, and it's a silver thing and it's like warm on my face, and then it's like white. It's so bright!

Is it over your face, or over your head?

Well, it's kind of like over my whole head. They want me to stay still. I'm not supposed to . . . and they didn't say it, but they said they wouldn't hurt me. I guess they wouldn't hurt me. I guess I can do that. I guess I'm stuck here. I don't want to be here. I want to go home. It's really warm on my face! It's really warm on my eyes. It's dark up there still. I wish I could see something . . . they just put this thing on my head. This holds my head down.

Is this like a clamp, or is it like a helmet, or something that's lying on top of it?

It's kind of lying across my forehead. It looks like [whisper] because they . . . all three of them up there at my head. I can't see anything because the machine's on my head. Maybe they're looking inside my head! Maybe that's what they were doing! They don't tell me, but I can't understand the words, but they let me know that . . . special . . . just a kid . . . but they said that I can understand them and that's what makes me special.

(Marva Roberts, 8, 1963)

The machine examinations may be quite elaborate, involving the abductee's entire body. One woman was placed on a table, and a group of identical cylindrical machines were arranged around her table. They all went on at the same time and she felt an intense "pressure" inside of her. She bore it for a few minutes until she could not stand it any longer. When she reached that point, the Beings turned the machines off.

While most machine procedures involve the abductee lying down, many also require her to get into a cylindrical device that envelopes her. Abductees have also described procedures in which apparatuses are placed on top of or around their heads. Some of these head devices appear to make major muscle groupings move in the abductee's arms and legs. Others make the abductee see bright colors and geometric shapes, and still others have no noticeable effect on the abductee. Sometimes headgear is even used in gynecological and urological procedures.

VISUALIZATION

Secondary mental procedures consist of having an abductee visualize scenes and objects that evoke an emotional or intellectual response. This allows the aliens to examine human emotions, abilities, thought processes, memory, and perhaps even intelligence. During these procedures, as in Mindscan, an alien stares deeply into the abductee's eyes.

Imaging

In imaging the Beings bring the abductee into a separate room, where she either lies on a table or sits on a chair. A Taller Being comes over to the abductee and stands next to her. She is shown a screenlike apparatus and images begin to appear on it. The scene is often abhorrent and disturbing—death and destruction, calamity and war, atomic explosions, the end of the world, and so forth. She may see familiar people in it, such as her family suffering from the effects of nuclear war. It is extremely frightening and unsettling to the abductee, and she experiences great anxiety as the scene unfolds in front of her.

Conversely, the scene might be sexually charged. It can contain a romantic fantasy with a boyfriend or girlfriend or simply a person to whom the abductee is attracted, and it might contain a sexual encounter. This agreeable scene creates loving and pleasant feelings in the abductee. At other times the images are mundane and commonplace, such as a scene of a pretty garden with a fountain, or a display of routine and normal family life. These scenes generally evoke a neutral response in the abductee.

Frequently, an abductee is required to gaze at an inanimate object. For example, an alien might hold a box of some sort, perhaps eight inches square with a small red light on it. The abductee develops an instant fascination with the box and stares at it steadily. She cannot move her gaze from the box. The box appears to have no intrinsic or apparent function other than to provide something for the abductee to look at.

All the imaging events have one fundamental factor in common: A Taller Being stands to the side of the abductee and stares deeply into her eyes while the procedure is in progress. Once again, he might be only inches away. She observes and he observes. It is this interactive staring that provides the key to these mental procedures. The aliens seem to want to analyze the emotional effects of viewing the images. The scenes themselves do not appear to have any prescient or prophetic value.

Imaging can be profoundly influential on the psychological well-being of abductees, who can have a difficult time dealing with these sometimes anxiety-provoking scenes in their daily lives. Lynn Miller was thirteen years old when she had a profoundly influential imaging experience. A Taller Being took her into a room and picked up a paper lying on a table. The paper contained a list of male names. The alien told her to memorize the list because "There's war and I'll need to know these names." At first this episode seemed incomprehensible until a staring procedure was revealed.

They take me in the chart room.

What's the very first thing you see when you get inside? Is it light, dark?

It's light. I see the table.

And then what happens?

He picks up the chart and tells me to memorize the names.

Do you memorize the names?

I look at them. He told me I'm going to help them.

How are you going to do this, do you know?

I don't know. He says I'll know when the time comes.

What are you thinking as you're looking at these charts? . . .

"Why are they doing this? Why are they picking me?" . . .

Why do they need help?

I don't know.

Does he seem to be very insistent about this, or is he casual about it, or is there some sort of demeanor about him?

He said he would make me remember it.

How long do you look at these names?

A couple of minutes.

Do you try to memorize them, or do you look at them?

I look at them.

Are you actively trying to commit them to memory?

No.

What is he doing while you're doing this?

He seems to be staring at me.

Now as he stares at you, do you have any unusual feelings about it? Is he creating an emotion in you in some way?

He seems to be doing something. . . .

Does he move close to you?

He's close.

While he's holding the chart thing?

Yes.

Does he ever take his eyes off you while you're looking at the names?

No.

Now as you look at this chart he stands there, and he sort of looks you over. Is that right?

He's staring. . . .

Now, how does he know when you're finished?

He takes it away. . . .

And can you tell me what he says again?

That there's war and I'll need to know these names. And then he tells me to memorize them.

Does he say anything about how you'll remember them later or something like that?

No.

(Lynn Miller, 13, 1967)

Although Lynn remembered nothing about the experience after it was over, she became convinced that a war was about to take place. When her parents bought canned goods she would take some of them down to the basement and hoard them in preparation for the impending war. After a while she developed an intense interest in World War II and became a "buff," studying the battles and leaders. This interest lasted throughout high school. Her preoccupation with war was quite unusual for any teenage girl, but it was all the more inexplicable because Lynn had grown up as a Mennonite and was very religious. Mennonites are not known for their interest in war.

Jason Howard was working as an insurance salesman when we first began to explore his experiences. He later went back to college to get his Ph.D. in English literature. During one abduction episode, he was taken into a room and viewed a screen displaying an atomic explosion on earth.

Can you get a sense of what the purpose of showing you this picture is?

That something happens on the picture.

Okay. So it changes while you're watching it? . . .

A white fog that comes out from the upper left side of the earth.

What does that mean?

Something's wrong.

Does this fog envelop the earth, or just stay off to the side?

It grows big fast, but only around maybe a fifth of the diameter.

. . . How does it make you feel when you see this? In other words, does it invoke an emotional reaction?

Not a strong one. I guess it's sad.

. . . Does this Being explain any of this to you?

Well, I understand what it is, and he understands that I understand. . . .

What do you understand?

That something blew.

Something exploded, you mean? . . . What happens next?

We decide to talk about that.

Okay. Does he begin the discussion?

I do. . . . I say that that's what happened in Japan in World War II.

Are you talking about an atomic explosion?

Yes.

And what does he say?

I think he's surprised that I know that because I wasn't born then, and he says that it's not like what happened then because it's much, much more.

I'm sorry, I don't quite understand what you just said.

He said it's not like what happened in Japan.

Oh, the explosion that you saw was greater?

Yes. . . .

What else does he say?

Well, he says when that is.

When this big cloud is?

Yes.

Is it now, or in the past?

No, it's ahead of time.

In the future?

Yes.

Does he give you a date?

No. He doesn't give me years. It's measured by my life span. . . .
So when he said when the first one was, he said that it was a
certain amount of moments before I was born, and the second
one he says is when I'm a month away from when I would be
forty. But he doesn't use years. It's just a measurable amount of
time that I would have lived.

Then how do you know that it's a month away from when you
would be forty?

Because that's the span of time that we understand.

Okay. Is this going to be a cataclysmic event?

Yes.

How do you feel when he tells you this?

I guess relieved that it will be that long.

Now, when you're talking with him, is he close to you?

Yes.

Where is he looking when you're discussing this?

At my face.

Where are you looking?

At his eyes.

Now during this entire discussion, does he ever look away from your face?

I don't think so, no.

Does he move at all?

I think he kind of inches forward a little.

A little bit closer?

Yes.

About how close does he get, then?

Pretty close. . . . A couple of inches.

So he's right there?

Yes.

(Jason Howard, 17, 1976)

Envisioning

Instead of viewing scenes on a screen, or gazing at objects, the abductee is frequently made to envision them in her mind. She may be still lying on the table in the examination room when she begins to "see" the scenes. Often the scene is so realistic that the abductee does not know until careful investigation that it is being played out in her mind. Sometimes the envisioned scene involves seeing a friend or relative. The abductee feels certain that the friend is "up there" with her. But the "friend" is really a Small Being made to appear like the friend in the abductee's mind.

When Karen Morgan was thirty years old, two aliens lifted her up

from the table and held her at an angle so that the envisioning could
begin.

I don't know why they're holding me up because usually I'm
lying down for this. But they lift me up, and he puts his hand on
my head, and he's telling me to look at the picture. And it's not
just like I'm looking at the picture, it's like I'm in the picture. I
can project myself into the picture.

What is this a picture of?

When my mother died. This time, instead of being where I was,
which was at the bed, I'm looking at the picture from, like, a
corner of the room, and I'm watching the whole thing again. It's
such a vivid picture, even now, all these years later I can see. I
forgot what my mother was wearing but now I can see it.

Is this a bedroom, or hospital room, or . . . ?

No, she had cancer and she died at my uncle's house.

Are you there alone, or . . . ?

No . . . there are a lot of [relatives] in the room. And everybody's
standing around the bed, and she wanted us to say the rosary
like when her mother died. And I'm watching the whole thing.
Why do they want me to watch this? He says I have to look at
it. And I say, "No, I don't want to look at it." But he's telling me
to see something. . . . He's telling me that I have to feel the way
I did then. He's telling me that I have to feel that again. Feel that.
And I say, "Why should I feel it? I've already felt . . . why should
I feel it for *you?*" But it's hard not to, because when he puts me
in the picture it's hard not to feel all that again. And I'm really
pissed off at him. It's not horrible, it's emotional. It's very emotional, and he's making me watch it. I'm trying not to pay attention to the picture, but somehow they've got me in the room.
It's like it's just all happening again.

What does he do while you're envisioning this?

Watching me. . . .

Is he causing you to feel a sadness or an emotion?

He's telling me I have to feel it, but I'm fighting it. I'm fighting it because I'm angry. He's telling me not to fight it, and just to feel. But I'm getting so angry that I'm not feeling it, because I can't get as completely involved in it as I would have to be . . . I'm aware that it's a trick and I don't like it. They're telling me that this is happening now, but I know that it's not, even though I feel like I'm in the room again. In my mind, I say, "Did they make a film of this so that they could play it for me?" That's what it feels like. It feels like they were in the room and they made a film of it. But if they pulled it out of my mind, how did they do it . . . ?

Now, is this a static scene, or does it move?

You know what, they tell me that it's a scene of my mother dying, but I don't think it's moved. It's not really moved. It's not going anywhere. It's like it's frozen. I don't see anybody moving. But isn't that odd? I can remember all the clothes that the people were wearing and stuff.

Are you able to see things close up in this scene, or is this sort of a long shot, or . . . ?

It's as if I'm in the corner of a large bedroom and that's how close up the people are.

You see yourself standing there from the back, I assume?

Mm-hmm, from the side. But I'm the one that I can't see very clearly. I can see the other people. I can see the people who are on the left-hand side of the bed the best, because that's the corner I'm looking down off. They want me to look at my mother, but I won't look. And they want me to see her suffering. They're horrible. Horrible.

Do you ask him why he wants you to do this?

No, I'm angry. I might say why, but mostly I say no. "I won't. I won't. I refuse to do it. I won't." They're trying to tell me that somehow or other I'll feel better if I see it. You know, that it's somehow good for me. But I know that's not true.

Now, if he's got his hand on your forehead, and two of the Beings are supporting you, would he be standing next to one of the Beings, in other words . . . ?

No. They're behind me.

Oh, they're behind you, I see.

And he's in front of me.

But is he dead center in front of you, or is he off to the side?

He's directly in front of me.

So then you must be down by the . . .

Right. My legs are hanging. That's why I thought my knees were up at first, because they were. But they were moving me. I'm sitting on the edge of the table.

(Karen Morgan, 30, 1979)

Patti Layne was sixteen years old when she had a profound envisioning experience. It took place after a needle had been inserted into her navel and after she had undergone Mindscan and bonding.

And they said that they needed some parts, some things from me and that it would help everyone on the planet. They said that there are going to be some bad things that are going to happen.

Do they say what's going to happen?

Well, they gave me some pretty vivid images. . . . But they didn't do it in that room, they put me in a little room with a chair. Just one chair in the middle. But it was like across the hall. It was real little. There were two of them in there, two or three. That was a little later. And I sat on the chair and they put this scope on my head. It looked something like what they looked at me in. And it's real bright now. It seems like a bright room, and they told me terrible things would happen to the Earth and that it would just blow up, and cities would crumble and mountains would fall and the sun would be black. And they said that it's bad because people can't stop being greedy and that they were doing something to help us, and I don't know how. I couldn't make the connection how putting something into my stomach would help us. But they were horrible images, the images I still see in nightmares. I have recurring nuclear war dreams.

Why do you think they're telling you this?

I don't know, because I think it's going to happen.

So you're just sitting in a chair and you're getting these images, is that right?

Yeah. They're really bad images.

Now as you're sitting in the chair what are you looking at? What's on the other wall or whatever?

There's like a, it's weird, it's like outer space, stars and . . .

Are you looking at a window?

Well, it's kind of a window, but I don't see the treetops or anything—they're not there. There are like stars and lines, images, geometric things.

Geometric images?

I guess. They're like lines and dots, things like that.

And [the Beings] are sort of putting these images in your mind?

Yeah, they keep putting images in my mind, about the destruction of the planet, and time when people will be starving, and
there won't be energy because we're using up the resources,
and they keep telling me these things. And I see pictures of my
family struggling to survive and being reduced to beggars.

Are you in this room alone, or is there anybody in there?

They're with me, two or three of them.

What are they doing while you're receiving these images?

Well, one was holding the thing on me, on my forehead. That's
where they keep putting stuff is on my forehead.

What does this look like?

Like a telescope, a kiddy telescope, or kaleidoscope, with glass
on one side. It looks a lot like the thing they had on my stomach.
And they, two of them are looking up, behind me. That's kind of
what they were doing, looking up in the air.

Now, this one that's holding this sort of instrument to your
forehead, what's he looking at?

My eyes. My eyes are open. He's bent down looking over at me.

What are you looking at?

Him.

And what is he doing?

Looking, at images in my mind. He looks kind, he really does.
He doesn't look mean. Kind of like a father or a friend, not a
friend, but a wise kind of person you dream about. You just
want to take away all your problems. That's what it's like.

As he looks into your eyes, do you think he's just looking into your eyes, or deeper?

I think he's looking into my soul. Looking into what makes me feel and think and believe things. . . .

Does this go on for a while, while he looks into your eyes and holds this thing to your forehead?

Mm-hmm. Longer than that other thing. That other part, he kept me there for a while. And then he was done and told me to forget about this, and that I was going to have a dream about a nuclear war, and I'd be shaken up the next day, and I was going to think about it most of the day. And I did, I remember that. At school I was disturbed, and I was so afraid that we would blow ourselves up.

(Patti Layne, 16, 1979)

Patti had recurring dreams about nuclear war for many years after this episode.

Staging

Staging is a combination of abductee envisioning and alien "play-acting." A "drama" may be played out in an abductee's mind while she visually sees "characters" standing in a staged manner. The abductee must interact in a prescribed way with the aliens who are participating in the staged situation. As with the other mental procedures, the purpose appears to be intended to elicit information about the abductee's mental reactions.

For example, Karen Morgan was led into an area that contained a couch, a table with a flower pot on it, and a rug. She sat on the couch and noticed that several human "guards" were standing around wearing beige uniforms. Shortly a person to whom she was very attracted was brought into the room, and she was amazed to realize that he was part of the abduction also. He came over to her and was about to kiss her. She distinctly had the feeling that they were going to make love, something that she desired. As she looked around, however, it slowly became clear to her that the "guards" were aliens standing around. Somebody else was sitting on the couch staring into her eyes all the while. Her attractive friend began to dissolve into the alien that he was. As soon as she realized what was happening, the staging was over. The aliens abruptly got her up and took her away from the scene. She had to step down from a platform where the staged scene was being played out. But she remembered that the couch and the table with the flower pot were solid objects.

Patti Layne found herself in an "office" in which her husband's "boss" was sitting behind a "desk." In some way she knew that the boss had unfairly chastised her husband, and Patti became angry about it. She heatedly began to yell at the boss for mistreating her husband. As her anger vented, she began to notice that something was very wrong with this scene. She suddenly perceived that the scene was of several Small Beings standing around a special area of the room that was used for this purpose. She then realized that she had more muscle control than usual, and she turned and ran into another room.

Another time Patti was taken into a room where she watched a frightening devillike face on a screen directly in front of her. Before she knew it, three "soldiers" were shooting "machine guns" at the screen. She was terrified. She could "feel" the glass splinters fall on her upper body. One of the "soldiers" rushed forward to "protect" her. She was then led away and a Taller Being stared into her eyes. He said they were interested in the concept of "rescue."

In one extraordinary staging event that took place seconds *before* a physical abduction, Charles Petrie, a printer living in Florida, was returning home late at night from the local convenience store, when a child ran out in front of his car. Charles could not avoid hitting him and the injured child scampered into some bushes. Extremely distraught, Charles slammed on the brakes and jumped out of the car to help the child. When he looked in the bushes, he found himself staring at an alien. He was immediately floated into a UFO, where a Taller Being performed extended Mindscans on him because, as Charles said, "he's interested in my guilt."

Testing

Testing is an extraordinary event in which the abductee is given a task to perform and carefully watched while she does it. For example, one abductee described an event in which she was required to pick out a single alien whom she had seen before from a group of other aliens, all of whom looked alike. Others have been shown an intricate "control board," or some such apparatus, and told to operate it. The abductee complains that she does not know how to do it, but the aliens insist that she do it anyway. She then goes to "operate" the board and finds that she can in some way do what they want.

Attorney George Kenniston was shown such an apparatus when he was sixteen years old. He felt sure that he had learned to be some sort of a navigator. He carried out the instructions given to him but had no idea about how he knew what to do.

The role I play is navigator.

In other words, is he communicating about himself, or about you?

No, no, I'm saying this is the feeling I get from him. It's in my mind: I'm a navigator. I can get to the place, whatever it is.

Okay.

I am a navigator. [I] can get there. It's a testing. . . .

[George described a staring procedure that was also administered to him. I asked him if the alien stopped this procedure.]

No, but it's like I'm turned over to someone to be tested, and another one leads me over to the panel. Let me see if I can describe it. I look at the panel. It's built in the wall, and it's maybe eighteen to twenty inches coming out from the wall, obliquely down at the end it's four inches thick, and its probably maybe thirty-six inches across, maybe thirty inches high. It is covered with bright lights, and in that sense there are some buttons that are backlit. To my left there's some level of screen. There is some sort of a visual line display, I don't see it clearly. . . . Some sort of a ball built into the tabletop, or the panel, that I don't understand, but it can roll. To my right there's a series of controlling buttons in columns coming down. There are some sort of readouts, because I don't see them clearly, in the panel on the right-hand side. I see two columns, but I get the feeling of extensive definition both in the readouts and in the panel controls. There's a lot of finite control ability here. They're . . . supposed to be able to manipulate the entire panel.

How do you know that?

Because I know. I'm supposed to be able to do this. Your left hand does one thing and your right hand does another thing, and you look at the panel with the readout to your left at one, and you're watching the panel to your right, guiding something over a long haul. We're talking hitting an object far in the distance and keeping on track. This would be like driving a highway 200 miles long the dead straight, and just keep it between the lines—that level of competence in steering.

As you're standing at the panel, where is this other person?

To my right, watching me.

Is he far away from you, or . . . ?

He is just off my right shoulder maybe two feet. Staring Eyes [his name for the Taller Being] is against the wall at the end of the panel table, looking at my face, watching me do this, and I'm very intent doing what I've got to do. My hands are moving, I'm watching the screen, I'm keeping it between the parameters . . . oh, God, don't let me fuck this up.

(George Kenniston, 16, 1965)

The aliens usually follow testing with staring procedures just as they do in the other visualization events.

Many of the inconsistencies in abduction reports might be the result of the visualization procedures. These mental examinations can strongly affect the abductee's initial recollection of the experiences because she feels sure that the images she saw in imaging and envisioning procedures were "real." It is likely that abductees who have reported disturbing prophecies of destruction and doom, religious visions, or any number of other seemingly incomprehensible images were, in fact, subjected to these visualization procedures. The procedures may also account for the variety of aliens that abductees, without skilled investigation, have described in the past.

CHILD PRESENTATION

Secondary reproductive procedures do not involve reproduction itself, but rather the interaction between abductees and what appears to be the product of the alien breeding program. In these strange encounters, the aliens carefully watch as women, men, and children are required either to observe or physically interact with bizarre-looking "offspring."

The Incubatorium

After the primary experiences, the abductee is walked into a special room that I call the incubatorium. Here she sees scores of what appear to be fetuses in the process of incubation. They may be upright in containers floating in a liquid solution, or they may be lying down in either dry or liquid environments. Abductees report as many as fifty to one hundred fetuses gestating in this room. The containers are often attached to an apparatus that is either in the center of the room or off to the side; this apparatus appears to be responsible for the life-support systems. The abductee can hear a whirring or humming sound coming from the apparatus.

James Austino was taken into an incubatorium when he was fourteen years old. As is usual in these situations, the Beings offered no explanation for why they were showing it to him.

Can you get a glimpse into any of them?

There's like all these tubes running straight up to the wall, liquid or something in them.

Is there anything in the tubes, other than the liquid?

Yeah, I think so. It's like a machine with twenty or thirty tubes. The whole room is like round with them.

Are these just all in a clump, or are they lining the walls, or ...?

There's like the machine, and they're all sitting up on the machine, going straight up. And they line the wall. It's like a big fish tank or something, each one of them's a little fish tank.... It's like blue liquid. There's lights underneath each tube, shining up straight into it.

Is this guy still with you when you go into this room?

Yes.

Where is he standing?

Next to me. He looks at me. His hand's on my back.

What happens next?

There's little things in each of these tubes.

What do these little things look like?

Hamsters.

You mean, they're animate?

Bald hamsters, just kind of lying in there with wires and stuff attached to it. Looks like hamsters.

Do you stand to watch this, or does he have you sit down?

He just walks me in the middle, tells me to look around, don't touch anything.

Are all these hamster things the same size?

Yeah, about. But they don't look like hamsters. They've got little black eyes, like curled up, floating in there.

Now you're saying you're looking at little black eyes.

Mm-hmm.

Are you looking at babies?

It looks like little ones.

Fetuses?

Yeah, just floating in these things. The light shines up on them from underneath.

Is it one fetus per tube, or are the tubes filled with them?

One per. But the whole wall's lined up.

How many would you estimate are in there?

Sixty, seventy, maybe more. The room has a blue glow to it from the water.

Do you hear gurgling and bubbling?

Yeah, it sounds like a fish tank.

... Are these fetuses resting on anything?

They're just floating in it.

Is there anything attached to them?

Little wires. They're about hand-sized, each of them.

How close are you to them?

I walk up to one and I look in to get a better look.

What do you see in there?

A little thing; it's curled up.

Does it look like a human fetus?

A little. It's just the eyes are different.

What color are they?

They look blue from the inside, but that could be from the water. . . . They're veiny, though.

You can see veins in them?

Yeah, all over the place.

Are they red veins?

I can't tell, it's blue. They look blue. . . .

Are these tubes made of glass, do you think?

It looks like glass, because I could see my reflection.

Okay, all the tubes are attached to a central machine, you say?

Yeah, like a monitoring unit, like life support or something.

What happens then?

Then he comes up behind me and grabs my shoulders and moves me toward the door.

(James Austino, 14, 1980)

I asked Karen Morgan about an incubatorium that was behind a "glass" panel.

It's like a big bulging pane of glass. The room is like a big womb up there. There seem to be a lot of new babies in it.

Are the babies lying down?

They're lying in ... yeah, they're lying in cradles or something —boxes, boxes.

Can you tell me how many there are in it?

God, it looks like there are fifty maybe, or a hundred, a lot. I mean, well maybe not a hundred. I don't know—a lot. It's really sad, they all look like they're dead.

Do you see any movement coming from the babies?

I don't see any. But I know they're alive.

As you look do you see any ... is this a room just with these boxes, or is there any other kind of ... ?

I think there's some kind of feeding device, but I'm not sure. There's something very strange about the room, but I don't know what it is. By this time I'm just absolutely exhausted, anyway. I'm too tired to even argue. I just want to lie down.

... Do you see any babies that are completely enclosed in something? In closed containers of sorts. Or are they all just open-air boxes?

They seem like they might be in water or something. Possibly.

Are they lying horizontally, or are they ... ?

No, they're curled up. You know, I think they're little embryos, or big embryos, or fetuses, or whatever. The impression that I have is when I was in biology in college, and they used to have all the babies at every stage, in little jars, it was horrible. That's what's going on here.

Now, when you take a look at these jars or whatever, is that what ... ?

No, they're in boxes. It's like the Museum of Natural History. I am reminded, I keep thinking of fish, fish, I keep thinking of fish. And I'm thinking of babies, and the way they have gills, and . . . I'm just so confused and tired, and I don't care.

So, when you look at this nursery, are you seeing a sort of variety of babies, in different stages of development, or are they all sort of the same?

I think that it's graded, sort of. That as you go into different areas there's different stages, past certain areas. Oh, now I see why I didn't want to remember this, too. When you see the kids it's pretty weird. When you see the babies it's weird, but when you see the little fetuses, there's no doubt about what they're doing.

And what do you think they're doing here?

They're breeding us. I mean, but there's no doubt. I mean, as weird as the other stuff might, I mean, as much of the other stuff might seem not to leave any doubt either, this is absolutely clear. These are embryos they're taking from human women, probably, and they've stuck them in there. . . . Some of them may be human babies, as far as I know.

(Karen Morgan, 32, 1981)

Anita Davis had the opportunity to see the Beings placing an embryo that they had just extracted from her into a tank in an incubatorium. A Being had told her that other babies she had created were on board. She wanted to see them, and the Being obliged.

We just go out straight into this big area. . . . It seems to get brightly lit and very large and almost square, like a room, a big room. I think he says it would be impossible to see all of them that I had ever had a part in creating, because I started creating them when I was eleven. That's too many. They're not all there. They're someplace else.

What's in this room? Is this a big empty room?

There's one row of, the whole wall is tanks, the whole wall of tanks, almost like fish tanks. Rectangular. We know what's in them.

There's liquid in them, you mean?

Mm-hmm, and little hybrid whatever-they-ares.

Mm-hmm.

I seem to have approached them with a positive attitude borne of familiarity, that they're not hideous or horrible, because I've been there so much. Just like he [the Taller Being] is not hideous or horrible, it's familiar. . . . I just walk almost up and down the rows looking at all different phases of development, and he points out, "This one's yours." I want to see which ones are mine.

He can tell that?

He can tell me, yeah—unless he's doing it to humor me. It seems he's very adept at pointing out, "This one is from a month ago." There are five or six that are mine, right on that wall.

How are these babies in there? Are they suspended? Are they lying on the top?

I would say suspended and attached to the side, or almost attached by something, but it is not an organic something, like a cord. . . . It is something that sticks out, and they had plugged a little fetus thing onto it, and that's what it's growing on. That's what provides food, and whatever.

Is the fetuslike thing in a little sort of sack?

Mm-mmm [No], just there. Almost inanimate. You can see bubbles, though. I don't know if there's a breathing process, but it's like fish tanks. They're sort of "starey," almost dead-looking. But they're growing.

How many are there?

I would say a hundred.

Do you hear any noises, or not?

I get the impression that I hear a bubbling kind of, maybe the liquid inside moving somewhat, maybe a machine running the whole contraption. It does seem like real sound.

Okay.

It's not water in there. It's waterlike. It's not solid, and it's more solid than liquid.

It's got a different consistency than water?

Yes. It's like Jell-O before it's set. . . . You could say it's solid, but it isn't. Or the stuff that you make from cornstarch and water that has three different consistencies.

Where is he? Is he standing with you while you're observing this?

Mm-hmm.

When you walk into this room, are these tanks covering 360 degrees of the room?

It looks like just one wall, one side. That's it. I don't think they are anywhere else in the room. Just this one wall.

You say you basically see them in different stages of development?

Mm-hmm.

So I'm assuming they go from smaller . . .

Not in any order.

I see. . . .

The little guy comes in another door while they're standing here looking . . . [and] he walks over to a tank. It's right about at his level. And I'm bending over watching this process. It's like almost a spatula kind of thing.

Hmm . . .

How can he get into the tank? That's what I don't understand, because they're all piled up. He reaches into the top, and has this thing in his fingers. He doesn't have as many fingers.

What about the spatula?

It was to lift it [the embryo] up out of this dish, and to put it like this on two fingers. . . . And he attaches it to something around the middle of the tank. Like a little hose that comes out or something. I don't know how he attaches it. There's a sense of "There, there's another one. I'm done with this job." Then he goes away, the little guy.

Uh-huh.

There's some excitement. It's like I've never been allowed to see this before. . . .

So if he puts it into a tank, are there other empty tanks there?

I think a few, not a whole lot. There's some near the top that look just about fully formed, they're bigger. So maybe there's a big turnaround, I don't know.

So when he puts it in, what does he do then?

He turns around and leaves.

(Anita Davis, 32, 1991)

The Nursery

In another child-presentation procedure, the aliens take the abductee into a room either singly or with a group of other abductees and show her a nurserylike area containing as many as a hundred babies. Abductees nearly always say that aliens attending the babies are females. The babies may be lying on a "bed" or on some sort of a holder. There might be many rows of them, with each row containing perhaps ten babies. More often than not, they are lying in hard, transparent boxes. Obviously not fetuses, these babies are old enough to live on their own. However, the babies appear phlegmatic and sickly.

Karen Morgan has seen nurseries on a number of occasions. The aliens usually show them to her with groups of other people. Typically, she is told that some of the babies are hers. She resists this idea and refuses to have her emotions swayed by it.

Then they took you through a hallway and brought you into this other room. . . .

I'm in the nursery this time. . . . There's lots of babies there.

Now, Karen, as you look at these babies can you tell me what they look like in terms of how they're being held? . . .

. . . There's attendants in the room, those creatures. I think they're women creatures. I think of them as nurses. I know why, because I've seen them before. I think they're the nurses.

You've seen them before in this nursery area, or somewhere else?

No, I've seen them in the nursery. . . . I see attendants in a room, and I don't know how many—four, five, I don't know. Sort of like, see, this is confused with our own nurseries because it's not maybe that different. They're kind of bending over them, you know . . . but mostly they're just sort of standing there, like they're standing guard. They're standing. They're just standing.

Now, as you look at the babies, are the babies horizontal, or are they vertical, or . . . ?

Horizontal. But they don't make baby noises like crying and stuff. I mean, it's not like they're crying. They should be crying, that many babies.

How many babies do you think there are there?

Twenty, thirty, I don't know, a lot. Twenty? . . .

Are the babies . . . are their feet toward you, or are their heads toward you?

I wish I could see it better. The room's here, I have this impression that, okay, I'm standing here and it's like they're, what's the word, they're lying like this, here's their head and here's their feet.

So they're sort of horizontal to you.

Perpendicular to me. I think they might go in like a semicircle. I can't see this very well. I don't know why. It's kind of frustrating, because I know I'm there but I can't really see it.

Can you see what's in back of you?

I'm very disoriented. I don't . . . What I'm giving are impressions, they're not really even . . .

That's okay. Why are you observing this?

I don't know! See, they don't give me any reasons. . . . I think the two little things are still with me, but maybe the other one has come too, the thing I thought was a woman. And I say, "It's a big incubator. It's a giant incubator! My God!" She doesn't say

anything. I say that, "Why are you showing me this?" She says I
have to see it. But why? "Why do I have to see it?" "Because
you're involved with it." "No I'm not. Oh no I'm not!" And she
says, "Oh yes you are." And I don't like the way she says that.
And I stand there and I'm staring at them, and I say, "Sorry, but
you picked the wrong person. I don't care about babies. I don't
even like babies." I mean I'm giving it more coherence than I
thought, you know, but I gave her that impression. She says,
"That's all right, you're still involved. You're still involved." And
right then I'm determined that I'm not going to let them use
those babies to get to me, because I didn't have anything to do
with them. And there's like a curtain that comes over me, and I
just won't let them use it.

Does she say anything about the state of the babies?

Yes. They need mothers. They need something. They need their
mothers, they need their mothers. They have to have their
mothers. I say you should have thought about that before you
started them, because I'm not going to get involved. She says,
"Don't you care about them. Don't you care?" And I say, "Don't
you care. Don't *you* care?" And now it seems like there's almost
something approaching anger in her, it's something approaching
anger. And it's like a darkness in her or something, it's like a . . .
something I feel from her. And she says either "They're yours,"
or "It's yours," or, "Some of them are yours," but there's some
of those babies in that room that are mine. Probably just one,
because they're all the same age. And I say, "So what. I don't
care. I don't care." And now it's like she shrugs and says, "It
doesn't matter if you care or not, it doesn't matter. They need
their mothers, they have to have their mothers."

(Karen Morgan, 30, 1979)

While on vacation in Ireland in 1988, Barbara Archer was abducted and taken into a nursery where she also observed babies in
holders.

They lead me to the end of the third row, and then down the
side, back out to the doorway. And then we're in that hallway

that's darker again. And then we go out onto the main corridor. And then we turn right again. I think we continue down that hallway. We walked by a few rooms, subrooms on the side. And after we passed three or four of them, we come to one that they lead me into. And it's still pretty big, but it's not as big as the other room. And instead of tables . . . [I see] something like a bassinet, but that's not what it is. It's small, and it's not deep, but you can fit something into it. . . .

How many of these tables are there?

I think there were probably about twenty. And there's like a nurse in there taking care of all these babies that are there. I feel a little scared when I see these babies at first.

Are these older babies, or younger, or . . . ?

I think that there are a lot of baby babies, but then they get older. There are some that look like they are several months old.

From your vantage point, when you look at this, can you see them all, or are some too far away for you to see?

There are two rows of ten, and I'm sort of standing in the middle of the rows.

I see. Do the babies have diapers on or something?

They have sort of like a diaper thing, but it's not like Pampers or something. Some of the older babies have like a little dress thing, but not a dress, it's just kind of a, it's not real fancy or anything, it's just kind of, maybe like a nightgown is the best description I can come up with.

Like a smock?

Yes.

Does it have arms?

I don't think it does. They're not long-sleeved if it does. I can't really tell from where I am where the older babies are.

Do you get a sense of whether they're boy babies or girl babies?

I guess there's probably both.

But it's not readily apparent, I guess?

You kind of, it sounds strange, but I think that I kind of know the difference.

So you sort of stand there between the two rows of babies. Do the babies look a little bit different, or ... ?

They scared me when I first looked at them because they looked odd. They look kind of old. They don't have much hair. They have some hair, but not much. They kind of scare me a little bit when I first look at their faces.

What's their skin like? Is it normal-looking skin, or ... ?

It's a little bit more, it's like grayish, or it's like lighter than ours. It's not, but it's not the same as theirs either.

Are these babies squirming around, moving?

Some of them are, a lot. Some of them are just more quiet, I guess. They strike me as being very fragile. I feel like maybe they're what I would think of as premature babies, or babies with, they're fragile, they're not, I feel like they're not real strong.

You're saying they don't look healthy and robust?

Well, they don't look healthy to me. They're kind of scrawny or something. But some of the older babies are longer.

Are they also thin?

They're a little bit more, but none of them are by any means chubby. They seem to have longer arms, but not a lot of fat or muscle or anything. They're kind of pretty in a strange way.

Is this just an empty room with the little tables, or . . . ?

I think that there's machines. There's some machines in the back. And there's something like a cabinet or something. It's the best way I can describe it. It looks like it probably contains things. Up like along one wall. There's not a lot of stuff, other than the babies.

Does anyone say anything to you?

Well, they asked me something like, "Do you like the babies?" or "These are the babies," or something like that about the babies. And I said that I felt that they scared me a little bit, that they didn't look right or something.

(Barbara Archer, 21, 1988)

Usually the aliens' communication about the nursery is vague and emotionless, but often they will try to convey the idea that the abductees are viewing a wondrous and triumphant thing. The aliens are often proud and excited. It seems that they want to share their excitement with the abductee. One of the reasons for this might be to make the abductee feel that she has been a part of the grand scheme and should feel proud of herself. She may be told that some of the babies "are hers" and therefore she is made to believe that she has been helpful in their plan. But this might also be to make her more psychologically bonded to the babies so that her state of mind will be optimally in tune with the babies for closer contact.

Touching and Holding

Child presentations involve more than viewing. Abductees are also required to touch, hold, or hug these offspring. Although abductees will see more babies than any other age group of Being, they are also often presented with young children and even adolescents. Apparently it is absolutely essential for the child to have human contact.

Although the aliens prefer that the humans give nurturing, loving contact, any physical contact seems to suffice.

Typically, the aliens bring the abductee into the child-presentation room. It might be the nursery or a different room with bright lights. Beings are already in it. The abductee stands or sits down on a bench or chair. The Beings who brought her in are behind her. Then a "female" Being approaches her. She is holding a baby. The woman senses the communication: "Isn't this a nice baby? Isn't this a beautiful baby? Wouldn't you like to hold the baby? Hold the baby!" The female Being extends her arms with the baby in it toward the woman, and the abductee takes it. She holds the baby to her chest with the baby's head resting on her arm or shoulder. If the abductee resists, she may be given a "reason" to force her to hold the baby. One woman was told that the baby would get sick if she did not hold it, and that it would develop a rash or some other sickness if she held the baby away from her body. Therefore she had to hold the baby against her skin for as long as possible. The baby may be naked, or it may be wrapped in a "blanket." It is usually very small, but it can be an older and larger baby as well. Women describe the small baby as being very light in weight but with a heavy head. The woman sits with the baby, or she may get up and walk around with it. The aliens stare intently at her and the baby.

The woman hears another directive: "Nurse the baby." "Put the baby to your breast and feed the baby." The woman says, "But I do not have any milk." The response is, "Put the baby to your breast and nurse the baby!" Saying "No" is futile. If she resists, the aliens will put the baby to her breast anyway. It cups its mouth on her nipple. It has a very weak sucking reflex. In many instances, the woman may be surprised to find that she is lactating and that her breasts are engorged. When that happens the baby will partially drain the breast. Often, however, nursing the baby is futile but seems to satisfy the watchful aliens nonetheless.

Unlike many women, Jill Pinzarro found the baby-holding experience pleasant, and she did not look closely at the baby's physical features.

I see someone coming toward me with a baby.

And do they say something to you then?

No, they just give it to me.

And what do you want to do with it?

I don't . . . just to hold it.

Is this a big baby, or . . . ?

It's a little baby, about two and a half months old. Yeah, about that. Maybe a little bit older, younger.

Is this baby wearing anything?

It is when they come toward me. It's wrapped in something.

Do you like this baby, is it a nice baby? What is your feeling toward it?

I like this baby.

Is the baby an active baby, or not active?

It's a quiet baby.

Is it asleep, or is it awake?

It's, hmm . . . it's awake. It's just not very, it's kind of dopey. Not dopey, not dumb, but just passive.

Is it responsive to you, or not?

I get the feeling that it kind of likes being held.

Does this look like a healthy baby, or . . . ?

Yeah, it seems like a reasonable baby.

Can you tell me what color hair it has?

Light, not much. Brown, but not dark. Fuzzy. Not much hair.

Can you tell me about its skin?

I'm not experiencing it so much in terms of visual things, because I feel the need to hold it, so I'm not really pulling it away
and looking at it, I'm thinking about it. So I'm having a hard time
with a visual impression.

Can you get a visual impression as it's just handed to you?

Well, then it's kind of covered so it's hard. It's ... I think it's a
male, Caucasian.

Does it have light skin, or dark skin, within the Caucasian range?

Fair. Quite fair. I think it's very fair, as a matter of fact. Almost
like no ultraviolet light for *this* guy. But I'm having a very hard
time seeing it.

Now, do you hold this baby for a while?

Um-hum.

Does it just lie there? Does it put its arms around you?

It's too little for arms-around stuff. . . .

Do you know sort of what the baby is thinking, or do you feel a
bond with the baby in a mental way, in other words?

I feel as if it's very important to the baby that it has this contact,
and I'm very happy to do it for it. I feel that it really needs that.
If you want to call that ... it's like it's soaking up the experience
of being held. That's what I think.

Do you sit there with the baby the whole time, or do you stand
up with it also?

Hmm . . . I carry it around, yes. I feel as if it needs the rhythm.

Is there anybody else in the room with you now?

A couple of little people. There might be somebody else that's not a little person. Not the tall guy either, but maybe, more like the tall guy than the little people. And not a guy, in a way. Has a different aura. I can't see, though. Just a feeling. I'd say it was the nursemaid.

Is this the one who handed you the baby?

Yeah, that's right, and it is a taller person. It's an "it" that approaches a "she," as the tall guy is an "it" that approaches a "he."

How can you tell that?

I don't know. I have a . . . there's some indication of responsible concern. It has . . . it's a nanny, only not . . . but it has that slightly protecting feeling. Not maternal, but that's why I get the impression of femaleness. It has a sort of hovering. Sort of an anxious, hovering quality, slightly. Not like worry, just monitoring carefully. . . .

Can you hear any communication from her?

Hmm . . . I don't know if it's from this person or from the little people.

What are you hearing, or receiving?

"Baby needs to be nurtured." It's very important, and they can't do it. It needs it from me. They can't give it what it needs completely. It's sort of a species-specific need, I guess. I don't know. I don't know why I know this. I don't feel like somebody's standing up there and saying it, I just understand that. . . .

Okay, you hold the baby for a while, you walk around with the baby, and what happens then?

The nursemaid takes the baby, the nanny. I can tell the baby
really [liked it] . . . I don't know why, I don't see what difference
it would make, but it was good. . . .

So they take the baby away, and what happens next?

I feel a loss, in a way, which is funny because I'm not really a
baby person and I only wanted one child, but I feel a connection. I guess it needs so much, I don't know. And I could satisfy
its needs. I guess I feel a little bonded in a way because I have
bonded to a baby. Not anything like the bonding that I had with
my daughter, but that baby got under my skin a little. . . .

(Jill Pinzarro, 32, 1980)

For many abductees, seeing the features of the baby can be traumatic and frightening. Many women do not want to see the baby.
They may claim at first that they only saw the top of the baby's head.
Others say they held the baby so close to them that they did not get
a good look at it. But in fact they do see the baby. It has a very large
head for its body. It has large eyes with some white showing. Even
for a baby it has small ears, a small nose, a small mouth with thin lips,
and a pointed chin. Its body is long and thin. Its hands and fingers
are long and thin. Its pale-white or grayish skin is almost translucent.
Its hair may be within the normal spectrum of hair colors, but very
often it is "white" and is usually described as sparse and thin. The
baby is not chubby with baby fat. It does not look like a baby alien,
nor does it look like a baby human.

Abductees universally state that the baby does not have the normal human reactions of a human infant. It is almost always listless. It
does not respond to touch as a normal baby would. It does not
squirm; it does not have a grasping reflex with its hands. It is lifeless,
yet it is not dead. Most women think that there is something terribly
wrong with the baby. They feel that they must hold the baby to help
it survive. After holding the baby for a while, women report that the
baby seems "better." It appears to have a bit more energy or to be
thriving slightly.

The baby does not communicate with the woman as a normal

baby would. She may speak to the baby as a mother would to her child, but the baby does not respond by vocalization or by movement. Yet the baby's eyes may have a hypnotic quality to them. Some women say that they are unable to stop gazing into the baby's eyes, which hold a fascination for abductees far more than an ordinary infant's eyes. Some women say that the baby appears to be a "wise baby," that it has some sort of "knowledge"—that it can "communicate" on an almost mystical level.

It is so important to the aliens for the woman to touch the baby—and to *want* to touch the baby—that they will do anything to instill a bond between the woman and the baby to facilitate that touch. But child-bonding is difficult. The woman does not have a familiar connection to the baby. The woman does not feel like its mother—she has not carried it for nine months and "given birth" in the conventional sense. Furthermore, the baby does not look fully human, and it might just as easily repel a woman as attract her to it.

The aliens try to facilitate child-bonding in four ways. First, they try to instill in the woman the idea that the baby is a "nice" baby, a "beautiful" baby, a "good" baby. It is as if the very act of saying it can make the woman believe it. In fact, many women, because of the extraordinary qualities of the situation, feel that they *want* to hold the baby. The communication serves to reinforce what they already feel. When they do not want to hold the baby, the message makes them less hesitant.

The second manner in which the aliens encourage women to hold babies is related to envisioning procedures, making the women visually aware that the baby looks "normal." Women report that they were told the baby was beautiful and when they looked at the baby, it was beautiful—at least that is what they were then seeing. They know, however, that the baby is at the very least "different-looking" and perhaps frightening. The fear is bypassed in favor of the aesthetically pleasing and less-frightening image placed in their minds. Sometimes the abductee will be horrified at how the baby looks and will watch it change into another visage before her eyes.

The third way that the aliens bond the woman to the baby is to tell her that the baby is her baby—and there is reason to believe that this may very well be true. Women report that they feel a genuine bond between them and the baby. The baby's hair might be the same color as theirs—red, for instance—or they might instantly recognize in some other way that the baby is theirs. This might be another sort of mind manipulation, but enough evidence exists to suggest that women are being shown babies that are the products of their eggs. Knowing this increases their desire to hold the baby. They want to love it and nurture it. They can become extremely depressed and anxious when the baby is taken away. They want the baby to stay with them, and taking it away can cause severe stress.

The last and even more bizarre method of ensuring the bonding between mother and child is also the rarest: the dummy birth. There have been reports, for example, of aliens arranging a "delivery." The aliens take the abductee into a room and place her on a table. The aliens communicate to her that she is about to have a baby, and she realizes that she has been placed in a "birthing" position. Suddenly she can "see" herself giving birth in a movielike image in her mind. Sometimes she "views" another woman giving birth. She can see the head and shoulders of a baby coming out. It is a neat, uncomplicated, painless, and generally bloodless birth. While she is "seeing" these images, she is puzzled about what is going on. She was not pregnant before and she knows that she is not giving birth now. After the image of the birth stops, the aliens suddenly produce a baby from between her legs. Usually the baby that is "delivered" is not a newborn. The Beings are happy. They say, "Isn't this a beautiful baby? Isn't this a beautiful baby? Here is your baby. Hold your baby." They place the baby in her arms. The woman holds the baby, but she is puzzled about what has just happened. It is as if the aliens think that the form of the act of birth has as powerful a bonding effect on the woman as does an actual birth. (This procedure should not be confused with the primary fetal extraction procedures, wherein abductees report that a fetus has actually been removed. It is also possible that this might be an envisioning procedure.)

The fact that baby presentations do not occur during each abduction suggests that it is not crucial for the offspring to have ongoing contact with their mothers. Any human contact may be sufficient. When Melissa Bucknell refused to hold the baby, instead of forcibly holding her arms up to cradle the baby, the aliens simply gave it to her brother, who had been abducted with her, and he held the baby.

In 1988 Barbara Archer found herself in a baby-presentation situation in which the aliens compelled her to feed the child.

And then they told me that I could hold one. And they sort of pointed me toward this one baby. And I think that it was a girl baby.

Was this one of the more active ones, or less active?

She seemed fairly alert, and she wasn't terribly active. She wasn't kicking or anything. So they asked me if I wanted to pick her up. I felt kind of scared to pick her up at first, but the nurse woman handed her to me. I kind of liked holding her, but I was so afraid, she was so fragile-looking.

Was she heavy?

No, she wasn't very heavy at all.

Do they want you to hold her in a certain way, or just hold her?

Well, at first they let me hold her the way I want to, and just sort of . . . she had big eyes, but they weren't like theirs, they weren't really ugly.

Could you see whites in the eyes?

I think so. I don't really remember, but I think so. I think there are, if any, though, just a little bit. They were sort of shaped like theirs, but not as big and ugly.

Are her eyes open, I guess?

Yes.

Does she just sort of look around?

Yes. She's just kind of hanging out, or whatever.

I guess what I'm asking is whether the baby looks at your eyes also, or . . . ?

Well, she sort of looks at me, I mean, she doesn't . . .

She doesn't focus . . .

No.

So you hold the baby the way you want to?

Yes, just holding her. I felt like I should hold her close to me. This may sound strange, but I felt like I needed to protect her. I felt very, I wanted to take care of her. I was kind of afraid for her.

Maternal?

A little bit. I mean, I didn't really, I sort of felt . . . I can't really explain it, I mean, I felt that way toward her. I don't know if I just felt that way toward her, or if I felt that way toward all these little babies. But I felt worried because she felt so delicate.

I guess you're saying concerned and protective?

Yes, I felt really protective. Then I felt kind of silly because everyone was kind of standing around there watching me with this baby.

You mean the two who brought you in, and . . . ?

The nurse. One of the other two told me to feed her, and I told them that I can't do that. And I think that they encouraged me to try, or something. I remember this happening from before too. It's still as stupid as it was then for me to be doing this. . . . But I just tried for a few seconds. They didn't force me to or anything.

Did the baby have a sucking mechanism?

I think it did. I mean, I think it tried to.

Some babies, normal, healthy babies, have a very strong sucking mechanism, there's no mistaking it.

Right. I felt that this baby knew what it was supposed to do, but it wasn't, it wasn't as strong an instinct . . .

You didn't sense the baby was used to this?

No. No, I didn't. I felt like I didn't want to give her to them.

Did you put the baby up to one breast, or both breasts, or . . .

Just one. Just my left.

You sort of don't want to give the baby up?

No. I'm sort of worried for her a little bit.

Sure.

But then they took her. They said I had to give her to the nurse. I think that I asked them if I could see her again.

What do they say?

I don't think that they gave me an answer at all.

You mean they just took the baby and put it back and that was the end of it?

I think so, yeah. And then I said something like, "I want to see her again," and I don't think they answered me. I feel like maybe I will, but I don't know if they'll let me. I mean, they didn't say yes or no, they didn't say anything. I think that they said "It's time to go."

Do you see them put the baby back . . . ?

Yeah. I feel really bad leaving her there. . . .

(Barbara Archer, 21, 1988)

Karen Morgan's experiences with babies have been quite complex. For example, she was asked to play with a baby. This play period might be in a large room where Karen will see several other naked women engaging in the same activity. The women hold the babies up in the air, tickle them, and make baby sounds to amuse them. The babies do not respond. They do not laugh or smile, and they do not make sounds in return. Sometimes Karen and the other women might be told to "wash" the baby. A baby lies in its holder, and the woman must take a "sponge" and wipe the baby with it. Once again, the object might be to touch the baby as opposed to actually cleaning it.

Frequently the offspring that the aliens tell the woman to hold is a child who appears to be between two and ten years old, or even older. Like the babies, the child is light in weight and listless. He has a larger than usual head, large eyes with small whites, a small nose, a small mouth with thin lips, small ears, and thin hair. His body is unusually long and skinny. He is semiresponsive and appears to be sickly by human standards. His eyes might have a hypnotic quality to them. These offspring are usually dressed in white "smocks" or loose-fitting gowns, but some wear a black, skin-tight garb. They are silent and not very active, although they are sometimes curious about the human.

Sometimes the aliens will bring out one small child for the abductee to see. At first, the child hides behind the alien as if it were shy. Sometimes the child is preoccupied with something. One woman observed a toddler dressed in skin-tight black garb intently manipulating a large toy block. After a short time the offspring interacts with the abductee. The child will sometimes touch the human and quite often stare into her eyes. Both men and women report that when they see the small child they have an instant rapport with it; they "know" that in some way the child is profoundly connected to them.

On other occasions, the abductee will be required to physically interact with six or seven offspring as each child waits its turn to come up to her and be hugged. Or the abductee will play with the children, which entails much touching and holding. The Beings observe the abductee closely while she is holding or hugging the children.

When Janet Demerest was nine years old, she had an experience with a child that included staring procedures and touching. An alien led her through what she perceived to be a large warehouselike room over to where a woman abductee and a young, odd-looking girl were waiting on a "cot."

And then the man told me to play with the little girl.

Now can you describe the little girl? . . .

She doesn't look real, she looks like the man who brought me there.

Does she have small eyes, or medium eyes, or big eyes?

I don't know.

What color is her skin?

She looks like a shadow, like the man, sort of grayish black. . . . She's thin, but you can't see her bones.

Does she have long arms, or short arms, or medium arms?

They look like they're thin, and that makes them look long.

Can you describe her hands and fingers?

Her fingers are long and thin.

Are they tapered at the end—or something else?

They look the same size all the way, just thin.

. . . Can you see normal-looking genitals?

No.

Can you see anything down there?

No.

Now she's sitting there next to this woman.

I can't see any bones in her.

You mean you don't see a big bone structure?

Right.

Does she have knees? Can you see her knees?

No.

How about feet, toes?

Yeah, I can see her feet.

Does she have ankles, you know that little bone that sticks out at your ankle there?

No, everything's straight.

What about toes, does she have toes on her feet?

Yes, they're long.

How old do you think she might be, if you were to make a guess?

Eight.

Now, as you sort of look back up toward her head, can you tell if she has a nose?

A little nose.

And a mouth?

Yes.

How about lips?

No.

Can you describe her chin?

I don't think she has one.

Now, when you look at the girl's hair, is the girl's hair just sort of groomed, or is it styled in any way?

I don't think she has any.

Now, how do you know she's a girl?

The man told me.

Now, the man wants you to play with her, and so what's the first thing that you do then?

We take a couple of steps and then we sit down . . . on the floor. . . . I sat down cross-legged. I think she did too. We were sitting. And then the man and the woman were watching us. But I don't think we did anything, we just sat there.

Do you communicate with her?

I think I asked her what she wanted to play.

And what does she say?

I don't think she wanted to play.

Does she reply to you?

She might have said, "I don't know." . . . I started to say that I would think of a game. I think she said to "just sit there."

Now what is she doing while you're sitting there?

She's just sitting there. . . . She's looking right at me.

Is she looking at your body, or at your head and face, or eyes?

At first she's looking at my eyes, and I can't take my eyes off of her. She can move her eyes around and look at different things.

But your eyes are sort of riveted on her?

Right.

So basically you sit there and you face each other.

Right. I think that she's looking at me because she has to. But that's because I'm looking at her because I have to.

Why do you think that might be the case?

I don't know, but it seems very important, and I can't move my eyes away. . . . She doesn't have any ears. . . .

So now you're sitting there with her, cross-legged, and what happens then, after you are through sort of observing each other?

I think we hug each other and I leave.

Do you stand up to do that or are you still sitting down?

We stand up.

Does she say something to you then? Communicate with you?

"It's time to go." I think she said, "It's time to go now. Say 'good-bye.' "

Do you hug each other then?

Mm-hmm.

Now when you put your arms around her, can you feel her bone structure when you do that?

She's solid. I put my arms around her shoulders, and she puts her arms around my back.

Does she sort of hold you, you sort of hold her for a while, or is this a very quick thing?

It's quick. . . .

And what does she do when she pulls away?

Nothing. She stands back, and I walk toward the man. . . .

(Janet Demerest, 9, 1964)

Andrew Garcia, who was an alcohol rehabilitation counselor, was referred to me by another abductee. We examined an abduction incident that happened to him just a few months before our hypnotic regression. After several Mindscan preparations in which he was told that he was about to be shown something, he was presented with a five-year-old girl.

There's some little girl . . . she looks like, I call her Maria.

Have you seen her before, do you think, or is Maria somebody you know?

It's not her, it's not Maria.

Who is Maria then?

I thought it was my niece, but her eyes were different, so she wasn't Maria, but I called her Maria.

Does she respond?

I look into her eyes and they are so peaceful, so unspoiled.

When you look into her eyes where is she?

She's like right next to me, coming right up to me. . . .

How close does she get to you?

Close, very close, and she looks right into my eyes and I'm calling her name and I'm so happy to see her. I'm really happy to see her.

Does she communicate with you at all?

No. I don't get the sense that she is, but I get the sense that she is receiving everything that I'm saying in my head.

The communication is one-way then?

Uh-huh. As if all these emotions and thoughts are coming through.

What kind of emotions?

Excitement, anticipation, and love. I want to hold her. She comes closer. Her eyes are so watery.

Do you see any whites in her eyes?

No, they just seem watery, black as marble.

Does she have any hair?

She appeared to have some when I first saw her, she had this black hair, but when she came closer I was transfixed on her eyes.

Okay.

I can't seem to focus on other things.

Is she still coming closer?

Yes. She's like at my face.

I see.

I'm drawn into her. . . .

Does she touch you at all?

Yes, she does.

How does that happen?

Very lightly, very careful, not like someone walking up and touching you.

Where does she touch you?

On my cheek, like a little poke. Did you ever watch a kid that wants to touch something and just pokes it?

Right.

There's a sense of joining, yeah, and it's not long.

What's happening now?

She's like pulling back. I'm like screaming in my head.

Screaming for her?

Not to leave. I'm like upset, I'm calling her. I'm very upset.

Does she respond to that?

They don't understand why I'm upset. No sense of compassion, or no real understanding of the separation. I'm very upset, crying. The one [Taller Being] comes up to me, the one at my side, he stares at me.

Does he communicate to you at that time?

Yes. I have a sense of calming down. "This is how it has to be." I asked him if she will be back. He says, "Yes, another time."

(Andrew Garcia, 34, 1989)

Once in a while an older child is brought out. This Being appears to be an adolescent. Here again the central purpose of this encounter is for the abductee to hug the child. The aliens once asked Karen Morgan to embrace an adolescent female. When she refused, the aliens put the girl next to her, placed Karen's arms around her, and the adolescent embraced Karen. When Karen attempted to put her arms down, the aliens immediately wrapped her arms around the teenager again, and held them there with their hands. The girl off-spring remained motionless, hugging Karen, for a long time. Then when she was finished, Karen's arms were let go and the adolescent, now a little more active than before, turned to Karen and silently said, "Thank you."

Abductees almost never encounter adult offspring in a controlled physical contact situation as with the younger ones, but some abduc-tees have reported that they have seen what might be adolescent and adult offspring helping the aliens in their procedures, especially sperm collection. But the purpose of the production of offspring remains one of the great mysteries of abduction research.

Chapter 6

Sexual Activity and Other Irregular Procedures

"YOU MUST NOW BREED."

Some of the more sensational material in abduction accounts, including a variety of specifically sexual activities, comes out of the abductee's ancillary experiences. These specialized procedures performed by aliens may recur many times to an individual abductee although other abductees may never experience them. The reasons for their existence remain obscure. Yet their compatibility with the overall structure of abductions strongly suggests that they are an integral part of the abduction experience and not just anomalies.

The ancillary experiences usually come after the primary experiences, but it is not necessary for secondary experiences to have taken place beforehand.

The Breathing Pool

In one common ancillary procedure, the aliens bring the abductee into a room with a large tank or even a small "swimming pool" in it. The aliens tell her to get into the tank. The liquid is clear and at first glance looks like water, but it is not water. The abductee is told to submerge herself in the liquid and stay there. She may be scared that she will drown, but the aliens reassure her that she will be all right. She gets in over her head and then is told to breathe. She finds that she is able to breathe normally even though her head is under "water." After a short time she is told to get out. Sometimes the aliens dry her off, but most of the time they do not. The purpose of the pool procedure is unknown.

James Austino had a breathing pool procedure in 1988. During his hypnotic regression he described seeing an adolescent offspring wearing a white smock and helping the aliens. James found himself looking at a large, oval pool of water, and the adolescent urged him to get into it.

It's like, "We've got to go in the water." I'm like, "No, no, no. . . ." She says, "It's not so bad," that's the impression I get. And then she gets in. The water's green.

Green?

Yeah, it's almost like it's luminescent. When I look at her, you can see the silhouette of her body. She's just standing in it.

In the water?

And she says, "Come on, it's not so bad."

Okay. Does she just jump in herself first?

She just kind of eases herself in.

When she says, "We have to go into the water," does she use specifically that word?

No, but that's the impression I'm getting.

So now you see her in there, is her hair getting wet?

No, she's standing in it. That's why she's not sinking.

Oh, I see. How far into the water is she?

About up to her chest.

Is her dress straight down, or is it sort of floating out?

It's kind of floating a little bit, but not straight out. And I just jump in.

And then you just go straight down past her?

Mm-mmm.

Oh, you don't.

I'm in and I look at her, like, "Okay, I'm in." And I look back, and the five or so things look pleased.

Okay.

And then she comes over to me and says, "Just lay back, and just relax." That's when I sit back down. That's when I feel like I'm going down.

But you're not being supported by anything, then?

Mm-mmm. I just sink down to the bottom, and I start to breathe.

How far is it down to the bottom?

About four, five feet.

So it's not a very deep tank, then?

No, it's about four feet. And I start to breathe, that's the neat thing.

Now, when you look at the sides of this thing, can you see the walls? Is it transparent?

It's just walls. It's pretty big, though. I see her getting out, because I see her legs leaving.

How does she get out? Does she go over to the side and pull herself out?

She pulls herself out. That's when I start to feel blacking out and stuff.

Did you taste the stuff?

No. It makes you numb, though. It feels body-temperature, too.

Okay. So you go down, you're about four or five feet down.

Mm-hmm.

You feel numb, and then you're sort of blacking out a little bit.

But I'm breathing, which is really strange.

Yes, it sounds strange. What happens next, then?

I hear sounds under water, like mechanical sounds.

You mean, like something is going on while you're in there?

Mm-hmm.

Can you look around and see what's up?

Yeah, they're just sounds. It's light in here, but there are no lights. I'm just kind of floating, though.

Are you actually touching the bottom, though?

A little bit. I'm moving around, though.

Can you look up? Are they up there looking down at you?

Yeah, a couple of them are.

Do you see the girl up there?

Mm-mmm.

Okay, what happens next, then?

I feel like it's time to come out. So I push myself up.

Can you kind of swim up in some way?

Mm-hmm. I paddle myself up a little bit, and I get up along the walls and I stand up. There's like two of them kneeling down.

On the edge of the pools, you mean?

Mm-hmm.

Why are they kneeling down?

To grab my arms.

Is it hard to get out of there?

The water feels slimy almost, now. When I come out it's still on my body, it doesn't run off like water. You have to take your hands and slop it off.

So it doesn't have the same . . .

Consistency.

It sounds like you're saying it's almost viscous.

Yeah. I get out of the water. And they just kind of walk me into another room.

(James Austino, 23, 1988)

Cures and Specialized Internal Procedures

In extremely rare cases, the aliens will undertake a cure of some ailment troubling the abductee. This is not in any way related to the contactee Space Brother concepts of benevolent aliens coming to Earth to cure cancer. Rather, in special circumstances it appears that the aliens feel obliged to preserve the specimen for their own purposes. As one abductee said, "It's equipment maintenance."

At least two abductees have reported that their cases of pneumonia were cured during their abductions. Lynn Miller feels certain that the aliens were responsible for curing her diphtheria. Lynn's Mennonite background precluded her from getting vaccinations, and when she was six years old she became desperately ill. Even though the physician had told her mother that the disease could be fatal, her religious beliefs did not allow Lynn to be taken to the hospital. She steadily deteriorated over a two-week period, and the doctor came daily to do what he could. Finally the physician told her mother he did not expect Lynn to live through the night.

That night Lynn experienced an abduction, during which the aliens told her that they were going to cure her. They passed a portable, rodlike device around her body and then made her stand in a vertical cylindrical machine that had a small window. The aliens sat in chairs and watched as a blue light slowly came down toward her from the top of the machine. When the light was about eight inches from her it began to go back up. It reached its highest point and shut off. The Beings then told her to get out. They informed her in a matter-of-fact manner that she was now cured and "cleansed." They then performed other procedures on her and took her back home.

The next morning her mother was astounded to find Lynn playing on the floor. She cheerily told her mother that she felt fine. Her mother ordered her into bed at once and called the doctor. Her temperature was normal. The astonished and puzzled physician told Lynn to stay in bed for another week, but she wanted to get up that day and play more. Her diphtheria seemed to be completely gone.

Sometimes an abductee reports that the aliens appear to be doing surgery on her, either at the base of her rib cage, near her gall bladder, or behind her eye. This is often a fairly long procedure involving several Beings. The abductee feels no pain during the operation; when it is over, no scar is evident. It is not clear what the aliens are trying to accomplish with this procedure.

In another procedure a tube is inserted into the abductee's mouth and then down her throat and at the same time a catheter is introduced into her urethra, as if the aliens were flushing out her digestive system. After a while the aliens remove the two tubes at the same time. Sometimes the aliens force the abductee to drink a liquid or pour it down her throat, which might result in vomiting. At other times the aliens wait a while after the ingestion of the liquid and then take a urine sample. One woman woke up at night and felt a powerful urge to eat something, even though she was not hungry. An abduction followed in which the aliens examined her intestines and required her to regurgitate her food. With other abductees, the aliens inject a needle into the person's head to remove either fluid or tissue; one abductee was told that they were removing "just a few" brain cells. The reasons for all these procedures are unclear.

Pain Threshold

Some of the most distressing of the ancillary experiences are those that elicit physical pain. Creating pain might enable the aliens to examine the neural pathways in a human that allow for the transmission and perception of pain. One man has been the victim of numerous pain experiments ever since he was a child. The aliens touch various parts of his body with a special tool that causes excruciating and unremitting localized pain. Sometimes they place a metallic plate around sections of his body. When energized, the plate creates agonizing pain wherever it touches his body. The pain grows in intensity until the man mentally screams for them to stop—but to no avail. During the pain procedures, an alien stares deeply into his eyes. In one of Steve Thompson's abductions, the aliens placed a machine on his head that caused such unbearable pain that he lost consciousness. After the procedure, a Being told him, "It had to be done."

Proto-Beings

I have received extremely bizarre accounts from two abductees who describe "Proto-Beings" in the process of manufacture. One abductee was fitted on several different occasions with "suits" that covered different parts of her body, as if molds were being made. Then on other occasions she saw obviously manufactured Beings who looked like rough imprints of humans—tall, with featureless faces. The aliens were in control of these "robots." The figures had wires attached to their "proto" backs and heads that seemed instrumental in making them walk and move like humans. Until more is known about this, these reports remain as tantalizing hints about possible other aspects of the abduction scenario.

Media Displays

Media displays are different from other mental-visual procedures because they do not involve staring by the aliens. They can be presented in a large room with "screens," or played out as an objective reality in the abductee's mind, as in the envisioning procedures. The purpose of these displays is unknown, but one abductee had the feeling that they might have something to do with making her more psychologically receptive to the aliens' reproductive procedures.

For Karen Morgan, media presentations began when she was nine years old. She was made to observe a screen from a table she was lying on just after the examination. Later, when she was grown, she was taken into a special media room with other people. The room is large and circular, with Small Beings standing at regularly spaced intervals watching the abductees. Groups of five to ten naked humans are made to stand in roped-off areas within the room. They are compelled to look up, and a series of "screens" appear toward the top of the wall around the room. The lights darken and the show begins.

The actual pictures are always puzzling and sometimes very difficult to remember. Usually they are moving pictures of beautiful and idyllic landscapes. A majestic mountain might appear in one scene, while another might show a flowing river, a hawklike bird, fields of grain, and so forth. The scenes are always sunny, cloudless, devoid of rain, snow, or any other inclement weather. Abductees do not report seeing any cities or evidence of civilization or of artificiality. No humans or aliens are depicted in the media displays.

The entire scene has a slightly unreal quality to it. The colors are a little "off," not quite natural. A voice then enters the abductee's mind. Karen describes this as a "telepathic public address system," assuming that the rest of the humans in the room are hearing the same thing as she is. The voice starts out by saying "Behold!" or something like that.

Although Karen finds it difficult to recall, she gets the impression that the scenes being shown to her are of a wonderful new world that the aliens are, in some way, developing. This is a beautiful place that will some day become very important for all people. She also has the distinct impression that this place is connected with the babies. Sometimes she thinks that the place is another planet, and sometimes she thinks that the planet is Earth, after alien intervention —and this scares her.

On three occasions between April and June 1987, Karen was taken to a display room where she was forced to observe idyllic scenes. In

April she also felt certain that the room that she was being led into with the other humans had something to do with babies.

They're going to show us something.... It's, I saw a light, and it's, the light's going to show us something. They're going to show us an image or something but I'm so bored and pissed off that I just want to get this over with.... They're showing us a place. I don't know if it's on a projector or what.

You mean a geographic location?

Yes.

Is this inside, or outside?

Okay, let me describe it.... I think it's meant to look like it's outside. And it's a place, it's a place. I can't see the place.

This is an outside scene?

Yeah. I think the impression we're meant to have is, "This is where we're taking the babies." I think this is the impression they're trying to give us. But what is the light? I can't see it. Why can't I see it? I can't ...

Is this a city scene?

No, it looks more parklike.

Is there grass.

... It's green and brown and blue, maybe there's a stream in it, maybe not. It's meant to look very idyllic, but still symmetrical. ... I think the deal is that we're supposed to believe that that's where they're taking the kids, or that's what we're helping them prepare the kids for ...

Are you just observing this in your mind's eye, or are you actually looking at this through your eyes?

No one's touched me. I think we're all seeing this, kind of. I think. I could be wrong.

Does it have an Earthly quality to it, as opposed to an alien quality?

Definitely Earthlike. . . .

Now, as you look at this scene, is this a static scene, or is this a changing scene?

No, it's a panorama. It holds on one thing, then it kind of goes around. I don't like this because they know that this is what I think is beautiful. Maybe everybody *is* seeing something different. And I know that they never show you anything unless they're trying to manipulate you, so I'm trying to stay detached from it. It's . . . I can see it better. There's fir trees. There's a river. We've moved from sort of where the trees were and the grass. Now there's a river, there's a canyon, it's like the Colorado River. It's cut into the ground. It's moving fast, but not so fast that it's scary. I mean, you could still raft on it. And there's a beautiful fir tree standing next to it. It's not exactly like our aerial photos. This is different. I don't want to look at it, because I know if I look at it then they'll be able to do something to me. So I'm trying not to look at it.

Are you trying not to look at it by averting your eyes, or by . . . ?

I can't avert my eyes. I don't know why. No, I'm looking at it with my eyes open, but I'm thinking, "I will not be involved in this."

One month later Karen once again was shown the display room during an abduction. This time she was more apprehensive about the message that was imparted to her.

Your attention is directed upward, you can't help but look up, and then there's a message that comes through the PA system. . . . And I think, "They're showing us something about the world," and the message, even at the time, is . . . see, I'm as awake as I've ever been in this room, and the message even at the time isn't clear. There are words being broadcast like, "Look at this, here's a picture of . . ." and then you can't put your finger on what they're saying. It's a female voice doing the narration. But, David, the message is that this is the way, all of these beautiful things that they keep showing us, this is the way the world will be. It's just like Big Brother. There's no difference.

This is the way *our* world will be?

Yes. This is the way the world will be. . . . I'm really depressed by this. It's one thing to have eggs taken out of you and feel like a lab rat; it's another thing to think that they might be really up to something that involves the world.

(Karen Morgan, 38, 1987)

Information Transfer

After an abduction, an abductee may have the distinct and frustrating feeling that the aliens have injected some sort of special "knowledge" into her. She usually cannot recognize or recover the knowledge, but she thinks she could if she knew how. To date no specialized information has been recovered from an abductee, but a few have displayed isolated factual knowledge about scientific topics that they have never studied, and others have shown inexplicable interest in physics or astronomy. This might be related to alien testing procedures or to the fact that for most of her life, before undergoing hypnotic regression sessions, the abductee unconsciously "knew" that she was being abducted.

A corollary to this comes in a puzzling situation when an abductee reports that some sort of headgear is placed on her while an alien wearing headgear stands nearby. A wire is run from her headgear to the alien's headgear. She is then required either to remember something or emotionally feel something. Envisioning might be used in this endeavor. The abductee feels that the mental processes going on in her mind are being transferred to the alien. In some cases, the abductee will be attached to several other Beings either at once or one after the other.

Sexual Activity

Sexual episodes, despite how lurid and unbelievable they might appear, seem to be an important, albeit confusing, part of the abduction experience. Alien involvement in human sexual activity represents one of the few direct interventions into a person's life. There are indications that the aliens think sexual intercourse and orgasm promote conception. Evidence also exists that the aliens can intervene in normal sexual activity.

From time to time an abductee will report a sexual experience with someone that seemed in some way related to her abductions. She might be making love to her partner and realize that they are being watched by aliens in the room, yet be unable to stop. In other situations, abductees might feel compelled to masturbate seconds before an abduction takes place. They are certain that their actions are directly related to the impending abduction.

Far more commonly reported is alien control of sexual activity between two humans aboard their craft. The aliens bring the abductee into a room, and there on a table is another human of the opposite sex. Abductees report that the other person seems "out of it." The aliens make it clear that they want the abductee to have intercourse with the other person, so the abductee either duly climbs up on top of the other person and intercourse ensues or she lies on the table and intercourse is performed on her. If an orgasm is created, the Beings often stare into the abductee's eyes during it. It must be emphasized that this is not a sexual fantasy situation, and most men and women feel that it is an uncontrollable and traumatic event. One man tearfully said that he felt like he was raping a woman when he was forced into having intercourse with her.

In July 1988 a young woman was brought over to a man in his thirties who was lying on a table near her. The man's eyes were closed, and he appeared to be unconscious. The aliens wanted her to get on top of him and in some way become sexually excited. She resisted this but could do little about it. The woman recalled the incident without the aid of hypnosis.

It seems like I climb up [on him].

Does he move or anything? Does he respond?

He doesn't do anything, it doesn't seem like . . .

Does he respond genitally?

He doesn't seem to, really. He doesn't. I don't do anything, after I get there. Then it's like they don't even know what's going on, what to tell me to do or something.

So you're lying there.

Well, I sit up. I kind of straddle him. . . .

What happens next?

It seems like the one on the left side comes around, comes near me, like around to the front. And then, I don't know if he tells me to kiss him or something. It seems strange, I didn't think they would know that word, or whatever. I don't really want to. . . . Then I think I could fool them because they don't really know what they're talking about.

Do you kiss him . . . ?

I try to trick them. . . . I just thought that maybe I could trick him by some way, by doing another thing and saying I was kissing him. I put my hand on his chest one time, and I said, "There, that's it."

How did they respond to that?

Well, they didn't seem to mind.

You mean they accepted it?

Yeah, because I acted like it was a big deal. But I wasn't sure. . . . But they didn't seem to want to force me to do things. . . . It wasn't like before when they were forcing me to look at him. It seemed like they told me they wanted me to touch his penis, but I didn't want to. . . . Like I was supposed to scoot down below, you know? Down low on the table. I didn't want to, but it didn't seem like I had to.

So you could resist it more?

Yes. And I was saying, well, that's not what we would do. We don't do that.

You tried to deflect it?

Yes.

How did they respond to that?

They didn't seem as bad as before, they wouldn't force me. They weren't controlling my body so much, so I didn't have to go down to the bottom of the table or anything like that. . . . I just said that I didn't like him, that nothing could happen because I didn't like him. I didn't like this guy. . . .

Do they argue with you? Do they try to urge you to?

They don't argue back, but I was trying to come up with all sorts of excuses to them. I said, "He's just lying there." I was just coming up with stupid things . . . if they're just lying there, and there's people watching you, I don't know, it just seemed really . . . sad.

It is sad, of course it is.

It was just really bad. And I was just getting exhausted again, too. I just remember being tired during it, and I just kind of was hanging my head down.

So you don't scoot down there?

Mm-mmm.

What happens next, then? . . .

Maybe he gets an erection, but he doesn't have any other signs, and I'm just sitting on top of the guy, I don't even know how he could breathe, I'm just sitting on his stomach. But he's not really excited. . . . It seems like I know that he does have an erection at some point. . . . There's no other part of his body that responds, so it's not even like an erection, do you know what I mean?

Now, after he does have an erection, what happens then?

Now they want me to have intercourse with him. It's really bad. I tell them I don't want to. It's just starting to seem like something really terrible that they're doing. It just seems really immoral. I just think it's really bad. . . . I just feel like it's really bad. . . .

Do you find yourself doing this?

Yes. It's totally mechanical, it's really bad. I don't think I have feelings or anything.

Does he have a normal ejaculation . . . ?

Yes, I guess he does.

After he ejaculates, what happens directly after that, within a few seconds?

I have the black feeling [Mindscan?]. It seems like I get kind of stimulated for the first time. . . . I wasn't before, but then I feel, I don't know. It's not like he just kind of winds down. I don't remember much.

You mean, he just stays erect?

It's so weird because it's not like any normal pattern that I've ever been through. It's like they're lying there. I get a little worried because I think, "God, I could get pregnant by this guy." I remember thinking that.

Where are you in your cycle . . . ?

Right in the middle.

(1988)

A fifteen-year-old girl had the traumatic experience of being forced into intercourse with an older man. The aliens attached headgear to her and began Mindscan procedures.

Two things happen next. One is they bring somebody over to look at me.

You mean, another one of them?

First. And then they do things to me.

Who is it that comes over first?

It's another one of them, but he's bigger.

He's bigger?

He's bigger. He's dark, and he's bigger. He's much more power-ful than they are. He's much more powerful. The word that comes into my mind . . . is that he's much more advanced than they are. It's like he's the senior one. . . . I was extremely frightened. . . . He's looking in my eyes and I can't see. I can't see. I can't see anything because he's in my eyes. How can he be in my eyes? He's in my eyes. This is making me crazy. I can't stand this. How can he be in my eyes?

You mean, he's staring into your eyes?

He's in my eyes. He's flooding my eyes. He's completely pene-trating me, every bit of me is in my eyes. He's in my eyes . . . I can't do anything about it. . . . He's spreading into my brain. He's spreading into my brain . . . totally, he is invading me. He's in my brain. Oh, God. He's in my mind. He's everywhere. He's absolutely everywhere. I can't stand it. I can't stand it. I can't stand it.

Does this go on for a long time, or for a short time?

It feels like a horribly long time.

How does he withdraw? Does he do it gradually, or does he just break away?

He finds a place that he wants to be for a while and then it's not so complete. It's not so black. I can see a little bit. I can see sort of a shadowy gray. And he's making me feel things. He's making me feel things. He's making me feel things in my body that I don't feel. He's making me feel feelings, sexual feelings. He's making me feel things. It must be that he's making me feel them because I don't feel them. And he's in my brain. I wouldn't feel them. He's making me feel them. He's making me feel things. . . . And he's there. He's everywhere. He's in my brain, and he's everywhere in my body too somehow. That's very confusing. But it's not so black. But my body is changing. My body is getting tense in a different way. He's making my body do things and then they take the thing off my head. Somebody takes the thing off my head. That's good, because it was uncomfortable and heavy. I didn't like that. And I can see more now. And he's still there, but it's not everywhere. But my body is, I have funny feelings. I'm not used to these feelings. I don't understand, between my legs. I don't understand why this is feeling this way. And he tells me, oh no. Oh no.

What is it?

Oh no. Oh no. Oh God, no, no, no, no. No . . . oh God, no.

What's happening?

There's, he's standing there looking in my eyes, and the others are standing around, and there's a man standing at the foot of the table.

A regular man?

Yes. There's a man standing at the foot of the table, and his eyes are sort of cloudy, and he's erect, and he's just standing there, and I'm afraid.

Is this an older guy, or a younger guy?

It's an older man. It's a grown-up man, and I'm afraid. I'm so afraid. I'm afraid of what's going to happen. I'm so afraid.

[I comforted her and reminded her that this happened many years ago, that she was frightened at the time, but need not be frightened now.]

Was this guy small, thin . . . ?

He's sort of a big guy. He's got a little bit of a paunch.

Does he have a full head of hair, is he bald?

Middle-aged guy. He's got receding hair. He's dark, and . . .

Is he sort of out of it, or is he . . . ?

He's absolutely out of it. His mouth is hanging slack, and his hands are loose at his side, kind of like an ape. And his eyes are glazed over, cloudy, unfocused.

So he doesn't make eye contact with you?

He doesn't make eye contact with anybody.

Okay.

And the guy who's looking in my eyes is still looking at me, but he kind of moves aside so I can see this guy. And then he comes back, and he's making my body respond sexually. I mean, I didn't know what it was at that time, what a sexual response was. I knew it was very strange. It had pleasurable parts to it, but it wasn't a pleasurable situation, obviously.

Of course not.

And the guy . . . the inevitable followed.

Do they say anything to you while this is going on?

No.

Do they explain to you what's about to happen?

I have the idea that I've just ovulated, or I'm about to ovulate or something. And that's connected. I don't want this to happen. But it does. . . .

Now, does this guy just stand at the end of the table and do his business, or does he climb on top of you?

Climbs on top of me. Oh, before he moves away, the guy who was looking in my eyes sort of zaps me. There's a sort of jolt of power or something, and all of a sudden I'm really sexually excited. Overwhelmingly sexually excited. And this guy climbs on top of me, and he's moving and it . . . doesn't make any sense, but it feels like he starts to climax and doesn't finish, or he gets to the point of coming, but what's the point of that? What's the point of that? . . . They just pull him off, and they stick something up where he was, a metal thing it feels like. And then they're moving very fast. Oh, I know from other times what's about to happen.

(1959)

She described how the Beings apparently took an egg from her at this point and they then walked the man away.

Sometimes the aliens display a great interest in promoting human sexual activity, especially for young girls. From time to time a woman will report that when she was going through puberty, the aliens examined her and said something to the effect of, "You are now 'ripe.' You must now breed. Go and breed!" When one woman was thirteen, the aliens told her this, and then, as if to show her how it is done, they brought in a teenage boy who seemed to be "out of it" and put him on top of her so that intercourse could be accomplished. Afterward, she felt pain and noticed blood on her legs. Her hymen had been ruptured. This was done at least one other time to her when she was a teenager. Both times the aliens couched the event in terms advising "breeding." Obviously, these embarrassing and distressing moments can have a disastrous effect on the abductee's sexual development and subsequent social life.

A final variation on sexual activity is an alleged sexual encounter between an abductee and an alien or a hybrid. Sexual imagery is often an important part of this event. In an envisioning procedure, the abductee is made to believe that either her husband or loved one is with her. Abductees sometimes say that the face of the husband, for instance, tends to "phase" in and out of the face of the alien. Intercourse takes place without much preliminary stimulation. The insertion of the "penis" is quick, and the penis does not feel normal; it is usually very thin and very short. The normal thrusting movement does not take place, but the woman feels a sudden "pulse." Then it is all over. We have no clear evidence that the aliens have genitals, but hybrids sometimes do. Therefore, actual intercourse may not be taking place with an alien. Three possibilities come to mind. Either the abductee is having intercourse with an offspring who does have genitals, or the aliens are inserting something inside the woman to make her think that intercourse is taking place, or the entire affair is a part of envisioning and no physical event is occurring.

Women who report early sexual contact during an abduction experience also invariably report that their hymens were not intact at their first normal intercourse. Women also report that they feel there was some sort of "strange" and disturbing "intervention" during it. Some have the distinct feeling that they were not in the room alone with their partners. Others become uncharacteristically confused when they try to recall what happened during that initial sexual experience, as if something were blocking their ability to remember.

The ancillary experiences are still a mystery to abduction researchers. We do not know why they take place. The surgical and

physical procedures seem related to the aliens' desire for more information about the body. But how the mental and sexual experiences
relate to mental examinations or the breeding program is not clear.
What is clear is that the ancillary experiences can be the most traumatic and the most negatively influential on people's lives. During
hypnosis, abductees have screamed in agony as they relived pain
procedures. They have tearfully reexperienced the profound trauma
and humiliation of being forced to have sexual intercourse with a
stranger or a hybrid. And through it all the Beings seem clinically
detached—either because they can do nothing about it, they do not
understand, or they do not care.

Chapter 7

Going Home

"IT WAS A REALLY NICE EXPERIENCE."

When the abductee's time on board the craft is over, the aliens unceremoniously tell her, "It is time to go now." If the event took place in a larger object, Small Beings quickly take her out of the main room and hustle her down the hall to where her clothes are. If she is walking too slowly for them, they might impatiently say, "Hurry up! Hurry up!" as they push and pull her along. If they are on a smaller object, the aliens get the abductee off the table and either help her dress or watch while she puts her clothes on. Once she is dressed, she begins the trip back home.

The abductee is still very much under alien control during the return and cannot physically affect her situation with any degree of forcefulness. The exit from the object is often difficult for her to remember. Some abductees step on a specific round plate in the floor and the next thing they know they are either floating down or are already on the ground. Others enter a small room where an alien makes them lose consciousness. When an abductee awakes she may find herself in transit. If she is coming from an object in the sky, she feels herself "floating" down, much as she did in the original transit and entrance.

If the abduction took place from her home, the abductee usually goes directly through the window (wall or ceiling, in some cases) and "rematerializes" in her room. If at night, an alien accompanies her to her bedroom and watches carefully as she gets into bed. He might even put the covers over her and tell her to go to sleep, and then he leaves. If the abductee is in an object on the ground, she may float back to an area near her house or apartment and then walk in the darkness to the door, an alien accompanying her. She then floats up and into the window, or she might simply walk into the house through the back or front door. Once in a while an abductee meets a member of the family while coming back into the house. Inexplicably the family member seems not in the least disturbed or puzzled at seeing the abductee come in wearing her nightclothes and says nothing about it at the time or even later. The abductee walks to her bedroom, gets into bed, and goes to sleep.

Patti was still exhibiting strong bonding feelings for the Taller Being when she was told it was time to go home.

And he said, "That's it for now. That's it for now." He helps me off the table, and those other ones, they picked up my clothes from the floor, and they helped me put them on, and he stood watching, staring.

Do you have your nightgown there?

They helped me put my nightgown on.

And your underpants?

Uh-huh. They helped me put them on. I think they put that nightgown on backward. Not backward, inside out. I think that's what they did, because I remember the next morning thinking that I was stupid, I must have been awfully tired because I put my nightgown on inside out. I think that's what they did.

Did they put your underpants on in the correct way?

Um-hmm. They did that all right. The nightgown was on inside out, like it was taken off. And he waited patiently, watching, and I think I didn't want to leave because I knew it was time to go. He held out his hand, and I was happy to take it.

As they're putting your clothes on, do you get a chance to look around the room?

Not really. I'm still looking at him because I keep getting this image of looking down at him. I thought, "Isn't this funny. I'm looking down at him, but yet I feel like he's really in control of everything," but I didn't mind it. I don't really want to go back. I liked him. It was a really nice experience. I'm interested in this kind of thing, but I wasn't asking him any questions, it's like I just understood everything. You know, I didn't feel like there was a need to be curious about his ship and what he was really doing.

Well, while you are out there, though, do you happen to notice if there are other tables in the room?

No, there was just one, and I didn't go in any other rooms. [Out back] there's this little tiny hallway, I don't know, corridor or something. And he held my hand and he walked down the steps with me. We walked out into the woods and into the field. You know, I think we walked pretty far, just slowly. And I don't think we said anything, but I was really enjoying the feelings, like I was taking a midnight stroll with a lover.

Do you feel the ground underneath?

Um-hmm. I had socks on.

You took the socks off, though, or . . . ?

I can't remember that, but I know I had socks on, I always had socks. But I could feel the ground, the trees, the nuts all over, rotting nuts on the ground. And I know I walked down the road with him now, it was real vivid. We walked down the right side of the road. And I think I was telling him about how my grandmother and I would walk along here just for a walk, and she would get paranoid that I would get into the poison ivy, and he wanted to know what that was, and there wasn't any to show him, but I said it grows on trees right around here, this creek here, that the road goes by. And it makes you itch. And he seemed to know what that meant. And we walked across the bridge, this little bridge, went over the creek, and we walked up the road a little ways and up the steps.... And I remember standing at the top of the steps and walking up the sidewalk, and there was some green ivy, but there wasn't many leaves growing up the side of the house, and I said, "Ivy grows up there but it's not poison." And there were roots and little things attached to the bricks. And that's the last thing I remember because then I just kind of felt like I floated up through the window and back into my room, and in bed with Roy [her husband]. And I woke up and I felt like I had to go to the bathroom.... And I shook Roy and I did wake him up, and I said ... "I just had a nightmare," or, "I just had a really weird dream." He just mumbled something and turned over and went back to sleep.

Was Roy in the same position as when ... ?

No, he was taking up the whole bed. I lay there for a minute and I got up and went to the bathroom, and I came back in. I had to fight with him to get him to lie so I could get back in. And he wrapped himself around me and said, "Where did you go?" And I said, "I was in the bathroom."

So when you got up, though, you noticed that your nightgown was on inside out?

Inside out, yeah. And the little strings weren't tied around the neck. They were open, and I usually tie them because I am afraid they'll get wrapped around my neck in the middle of the night, and they weren't tied. And I kept thinking, "Boy, I must have had a restless night."

(Patti Layne, 23, 1985)

Like many other abductees, George Kenniston floated down from the object and then walked directly in the back door of his house.

I'm moving from the field over the trees over the back alley of Green Street, and the houses, now I see myself, I'm going over the street, and I'm going over the other houses . . . then the convent, then I'm coming over Third Street, and I'm kind of spiraling down and I land on the hill. It's a little higher on the alley side of the houses behind Third, and you go down the hill, and that's where I come down. I come down the hill and I climb up. And I go over, we had a kind of a wicker-weave fence, and I go right up over it and I'm down, I'm in my backyard, I go in the back kitchen door, I put myself to bed.

Is anybody up when you come in?

No.

They're asleep?

. . . I see my father at the door in a tee-shirt and baggy shorts, and that's how he used to sleep. Did he say anything? He might have said something, but it doesn't seem to go anywhere. And I made some excuse like I went and got a glass of water or something. And I went back to bed.

(George Kenniston, 15, 1964)

Janet Demerest remembered, without the aid of hypnosis, an incident in which she was lying in bed with her six-year-old daughter when an abduction began. She saw something that looked like a "laundry basket" come seemingly from nowhere and hover over her and her child. At the same time a gray Small Being appeared on the side of her bed. She was paralyzed and could not scream. Suddenly the basket and her daughter disappeared and then the empty basket reappeared. Now she felt nauseated and confused, but she had the feeling that *she* was in some way inside the basket and moving. After the abduction was over, she returned first in the basket to an empty bed and lay on her back, and then she could see the basket disappear and reappear and her daughter was again lying beside her.

If the abductee was taken from a car, she walks back to the car, gets in, closes the door, and starts driving. If there were others in the car who were "switched off" during her abduction, they suddenly become animated. The driver starts the car and they resume the trip. None of the people in the car are aware of what just happened, nor are they yet aware of a time lapse. They might remember that they saw a "flying saucer" and they might even talk excitedly about it, but that memory soon fades as well. The next day the abductee might have the sense that something strange transpired, but the others are completely unaware of anything unusual.

If the abduction occurs during the day, the abductee may simply walk out of the ship and back to the area from which she was taken. If it is a child who is abducted from within a group, the remaining children, after being "switched on," usually do not make an issue of the abductee's absence. When Janet was nine years old, she left the wooded area where she was playing with her friends to walk over a hill. She was abducted and gone for over an hour. When she returned, her friends asked her where she had been. She told them that she had gone exploring, and that answer appeared to satisfy them.

Very often with daytime abductions, however, the period of time in which the abductee is missing is noticed by someone. When nine-year-old Jill Pinzarro returned from her experience (which began while she was reading a book in the park in Rochester, Minnesota), her parents were frantic with worry.

What was the next thing that you can remember?

Sitting on the bench. . . . And I'm scared because it's dark.

Do you have a book in your hand?

Yes, but it doesn't feel like I've been reading it. It's just sitting there on my lap. But it's like I've suddenly awakened.

And what do you do?

I'm really upset and frightened. It's so late. And I don't know how I could have lost track of the time. When they put me to sleep it was just like ether. There's a moment when you realize that something's happening, and then you're just gone. You just feel yourself getting smaller, no consciousness.

And yet when you're on the park bench your clothes are on?

Oh, yeah. It's just like nothing's happened.

Do you go home quickly then?

Oh, yeah. I throw my books on the bike, and I hurry because the park gets dark too, and that's scary. I'm scared of the dark, being that I have to go through the edge of the woods and over a little bridge, up a hill, and all the houses are lit and I can smell the dinners. All up the block you could smell that food's been there, but it's late. It's dark. And I get to the corner two blocks away, and a car turns. That's my parents. . . . They're driving the car. They take my bike in the car.

They see you from the car.

Yeah, they found me. They were out looking for me.

And what do you say to them? What do they say to you?

"Jill, is that you, Jill?" And they're so relieved they're not even mad. And I say, I tell them that I didn't know it was so late, I didn't know how it got to be so late. I was just reading in the park. And they say, "We've got the police out looking for you. We've been worried sick." And they take me in the car. But they're not really mad, they're just so glad. And it sort of amuses them in a way, not immediately, it amuses them that I would get so lost in a book as to lose track of the time.

(Jill Pinzarro, 9, 1957)

Nine-year-old Karen Morgan was abducted with her brother Robby when they wandered off from a group of friends. The time was dusk, and when they missed dinner her parents were concerned.

I can remember floating down. I came from very far away. We were very high up in the sky, it seemed to me. And when I was put down they put me down gently.

You were with somebody?

I think it was the little ones. I wish I could remember how I got back down. I wish I could remember how they did that.... It seems like ... it seems like you're in a room, and the floor ... I feel like I'm right on the open sky, you know? Like, on a stretcher.

Are you lying, or are you standing in this situation?

I'm lying down. I don't know how they keep you so that you're not cold. It's a beautiful, beautiful starry night. And before I go I think, "Where's Robby? Where's Robby? Where is he? Where is he? What if they keep him? Where is he?" But then as I'm lowered down I forget it. I have this feeling of being rocked to sleep, and of being ... and then they gently put me down. Here's the trick, I guess—they put me down not where I remember having been, they put me in the wrong place, sort of. I mean, at the other end. But when they put me down, there was a period when they left, I guess. And then I really was asleep for a minute. Because when I woke up I was staring up at the stars, thinking, "Wow! That's what it's like to be unconscious!" Not remembering all this stuff, but just staring at the stars and not being able to take my eyes off them.

Do you stand up then?

No. I didn't. It's funny the way you remember something, but it didn't really happen that way. At first I would have said yes, I stood up, but when I think about it I didn't stand up. I just lay there staring at the stars. I couldn't take my eyes off them, really. It was very cold. And then I did a very funny thing. I started feeling my body to see if I was paralyzed. And then I thought, "That's ridiculous. You fell down and hit your head."

Did you go home then?

I went right home.

And what happened when you walked in the door.

I was confused. I was confused.

Did your mother say something to you?

She said, "Where have you been? You missed dinner." I said, "No, no, no, no. I was playing at the Murphys' and then I hit my head, Mom, and I was unconscious. I never was unconscious before." I said, "I really saw stars!" And she said, "Oh, that's ridiculous. I've been calling and calling you. How could you have been unconscious?" I said, "But I was. I was!" I had a terrible temper as a kid. I was getting very agitated. My father came out. He said, "Where have you been? Was Robby with you?" I said, "Robby wasn't even playing with us." I said, "I fell and hit my head and I became unconscious. I never was unconscious before. Don't you care? Isn't that interesting?" I was all excited. And my father said, "When did that happen?" And then my mother took her finger and she went like that in front of my eyes to see if I could follow it [she gestures]. Because with all the kids everyone was always hitting their heads. And she said, "You don't seem to have a concussion." And my father said, "Do you have a bump on your head?" And I said, "No, it doesn't even hurt. I think I slipped on the ice." And he said, "No, I don't think so, Karen. You don't just fall down and hit your head and get unconscious and jump up usually, especially if you've been lying outside." I said, "But Dad, I was!" He said, "Well, if you left the Murphys', what time did you leave the Murphys'? They've been in for hours!" And I said, "At dinner time, around five-thirty, five o'clock." He said, "Well, you couldn't have been out this long. It wouldn't have been possible." He said. "We've been so worried about you and Robby. Where is he? Where has he been?" I said, "I don't know. He wasn't with me–I was all alone." I said, "Well, I really *was* unconscious." That's all I remember.

(Karen Morgan, 9, 1958)

Aside from being missed by people, there are sometimes odd inaccuracies about the return trip that alert the abductee to the idea that something might have happened to her, although she has no idea what that might be. From time to time the abductee does not return to exactly the same place. It may be a matter of a few feet or some miles. When Patti Layne was floated back to her college dorm, she landed in her roommate's bed. The startled roomie woke up with a jump, and a confused Patti made up a story on the spur of the moment, saying that she had received a crank call against her life and she was scared. After a later abduction in the same dorm room, she woke up on the bathroom floor. All her toiletry articles were scattered around the floor. What had happened was a mystery to her.

Others have come to consciousness driving their cars miles away from where they should have been—not just down the road but on a completely different highway. Steve Thompson had a far more frightening return with a friend of his while on a trip across Texas. They were sleeping in a car on a small street near a main highway outside of Dallas when they were both abducted. The next thing they knew, Steve, who had been in the back seat, was driving on the wrong side of the highway with oncoming traffic. His friend yelled, "What the hell are you doing?" and Steve, suddenly aware of where he was, quickly got back over to the right side of the road.

Lynn Miller came to consciousness many miles away from where her car had been stopped. She was outside of her car on a strange road in an area of New Jersey that she had never been to before. She got back in the car, started it up, and drove down the road for a few miles, not knowing where she was. When she approached a small town, she instinctively made a left turn at a flashing yellow light. That road got her back to a main highway, and she was able to eventually get home two hours later than she should have.

Many abductees have returned to find oddities about their clothes and bodies. It is not unusual for people to notice that their pajamas or nightgowns are on inside out when they felt certain that they had put them on the correct way the night before. Others have woken up to find their underpants folded on the foot of their bed after they had gone to bed wearing them. Some abductees have reported that their clothes were draped around a chair when they woke up in the morning.

Lynn was abducted from a tent outside of Los Angeles in 1988. The aliens took her right through the screen window inside the tent. When she returned she walked through the underbrush to get to the tent and then floated back through the screen window. She got into her sleeping bag and then took off her socks because they had picked up ground material from the walk. When she awoke in the morning, she was puzzled and surprised to find her socks outside of the sleeping bag and leaves and twigs inside it.

Karen had to wear a bite plate on the palate of her mouth for her teeth each night. She put it in with pressure, creating a vacuum on the roof of her mouth, then attached it to rubber bands hooked to her braces to keep it in place. One night she had an abduction experience and the focus of the abduction was the bite plate. The aliens took it out without too much difficulty, but when it came time for Karen to go, they were not able to put it back into her mouth. They tried and tried but could not achieve the suction necessary to hold it in place. Eventually they gave up. When Karen woke up in the morning, her bite plate was on her stomach. It was puzzling because she had never had it come out of her mouth before or since; one would expect that if it were to come out, it would fall onto her tongue, or into her throat, most probably waking her up, or it simply would fall on the pillow. But finding it resting on her stomach was disconcerting.

Sometimes abductees wake up in odd positions. They might come to consciousness sitting up in bed or slumped forward over their knees. They might regain full consciousness standing next to their bed and wonder how they got there. They might find themselves on top of the covers when they never sleep outside the covers.

Often abductees notice strange marks on their bodies the morning after an abduction. They find bruises, black-and-blue marks, and rashes, and they have no idea how they got there. One woman woke up in the morning after an event with fourteen black-and-blue marks on her legs. Nosebleeds in the middle of the night are another common occurrence after returning. With no discernible trauma, the abductee wakes up in the morning and the bed and pillows are covered with blood. This happens to both children and adults.

Sometimes women wake up with a sticky, clear substance running from their genitals down their legs. They are at a loss to explain this; the substance quickly dries. Other men and women have discovered unusual stains on their bedclothes. They were absolutely certain that the stains were not there when they went to bed the previous night. Almost all abductees wake up feeling tired, restless, agitated. They feel that they have not had a good night's sleep and that they have been "through the mill."

When the episode is over, amnesia sets in. Abductees might remember something for a few seconds or, in some cases, for a few hours, and, of course, some experiences are fully remembered, but generally the memory is blocked immediately afterward. We do not know how this is accomplished. It might be a function of the alteration in consciousness that all abductees experience as part of the abduction itself. There is little evidence to suggest that the aliens specifically tell the abductee not to remember something as if with a posthypnotic suggestion. Yet when abductees first begin to relate their stories to an investigator, it is often with a sense of guilt and betrayal. They feel that they should not be telling anyone about these experiences. This sense of guilt can occasionally be so deep that it effectively prevents an abductee from talking about his or her experiences.

The return is the end of the physical abduction itself. But the abduction experience does not end there. Whether the abductees remember the abduction or not, their lives can be profoundly affected.

Chapter 8

The Abductors

Ever since the beginning of the UFO phenomenon, witnesses have claimed to have seen alien beings near UFOs. The majority described small aliens with large heads and eyes, although a variety of sizes and shapes of Beings were reported. It was nearly impossible for researchers to learn anything about the Beings simply on the basis of these sightings. Writing in 1969, a UFO research team could say only that the aliens appeared to be curious and cautious. Very little was known about the details of their appearance and still less about their behavior.[1] However, the vast accumulation of abduction reports has now provided a wealth of detailed information about these aliens. At last we know enough about their activities and appearance to paint a preliminary portrait of these enigmatic Beings.

Aliens do things that seem like magic to us. They make humans and their clothes go through solid matter like windows, walls, and ceilings. They cause themselves, humans, and other matter to be invisible when they are outside the confines of the UFO. By using light beams, they transport victims and even their automobiles to their destination. They seem to have a monitoring ability that enables them not only to find their victims but also to determine the biologically appropriate time for an abduction.

Some of their greatest abilities come in the area of human mind manipulation. They alter consciousness and affect people's anticipatory powers. They modify visual perceptions so that people have difficulty seeing objects close to them or discerning spatial relationships well. They interfere with people's volition and force them to do things against their will—and they can do this from afar. They mitigate fear and stop physical pain. They institute selective amnesia, communicate telepathically, and create complex images and scenarios in people's minds. They generate at will sexual arousal and emotions such as love, fear, and anxiety. They produce orgasm with mind manipulation. They make people love them. The ability of humans to control the situation and force their own wills upon their abductors is severely limited. In many ways the aliens seem all-powerful.

Yet they display an awareness of limitations. It appears that the aliens cannot proceed with their breeding program without the involvement of human beings. For whatever reasons, they are fearful of being detected—hence they use clandestine methods of abduction. They seem to be afraid of human power. They treat humans gingerly, as if they were zookeepers handling sleeping gorillas, fearful that they might wake and become uncontrollable. They often assign two or more Small Beings to handle an individual human, and they are very cautious. They keep careful mental and physical control. They sometimes put restraints on their victims' arms and legs.

The aliens are highly routinized. They seldom change their pattern of activity to suit the abductee. They are focused on their tasks, regardless of momentary circumstances. Some abductees have speculated that the general behavior of the aliens suggests they have difficulty doing several things at once.

Who—or what—are these aliens? No solid evidence exists to indicate whether they are living beings, manufactured beings that act as sentient physical beings, a combination of the two, or something entirely different. But they do have a physical being.

ANATOMY OF AN ALIEN

By far the most common types of aliens reported are the Small and Taller Beings. The Small Beings are from two to four and one-half feet tall, thin, slight, and even "delicate" in appearance. They have a head, a body, two arms, two hands, fingers, two legs, two feet. They stand and walk like humans. The Small Beings are light in weight.

Taller Beings stand from two to six inches above the Small Beings and have most of the same gross physical characteristics.

Abductees are often vague about what the aliens wear. In many cases it is difficult to detect whether or not they are actually wearing clothes. Sometimes the color of their skin and the color of their clothes are reported to be exactly the same. Many abductees cannot see where the clothes end and the skin begins. They feel quite certain that the aliens are wearing something, but it is difficult to describe the "fabric" that the clothes are made of. Other abductees have described alien "garments" that fit so tightly that they look "spray painted." They are able to describe the end of the "fabric," the beginning of the skin on the hand and the neck, and so forth. On occasion the Small Beings are wearing robes or garments that are loose-fitting. Sometimes abductees report a belt around the aliens' midsections, but this is unusual.

Abductees rarely describe bodily adornment. The Beings' clothing has no personal touches, no expressions of individuality. Some Beings might have an insignia on their clothes that seems to resemble "serpents" or some sort of elongated shape. Sometimes it is simply a jagged line. In general, however, abductees see little or no diversity in the garments the aliens wear.

Descriptions of the aliens' skin color vary from dark gray to gray to light gray to tan to tannish-gray to white (not Caucasian) to pale white. If an abductee reports another color (like yellow, green, or blue), it is almost always in conjunction with gray. The skin color is uniform, without darker and lighter spots or areas (often the lighting in the room will change the way the aliens' color appears). By and large, most witnesses report the Small Beings' skin as just "gray." There is no visual evidence of a vascular system that might add streaks of other colors.

When abductees touch alien skin or are touched by the aliens (usually when being escorted down a hallway or into a room), they report it to range from a rough, leathery feel (for the Taller Being) to a soft rubbery or plastic quality (for Small Beings). The skin is extremely smooth, without the pores, hair, freckles, bumps, ridges, discolorations, warts, moles, scratches, wrinkles, and other common elements found on human skin.

It is difficult to tell whether aliens grow older. The abductees are unable to discern the slightest change over time in alien facial features or physical demeanor. When abductees have had experiences for thirty or forty years with presumably the same group of aliens, they report that the aliens look the same during the last experience as they did during the first.

The Small Beings all look basically the same. Their faces do not betray a readily detectable uniqueness that might distinguish one from another. Nor do they seem to have any sort of emotional characteristics that can be seen on their faces. For instance, one does not look "happy" while another looks "sad." Although abductees cannot tell one Small Being from another, they commonly report that they in some way "know" that they are dealing with the same Taller Being during all their abductions.

The physical frames of both the Taller Beings and the Small Beings do not reveal any boniness. Most of the contours on their bodies are smooth and rounded, with no hard angles. Witnesses do not report bones, such as the clavicle or sternum, apparent under their skin. They do not see evidence of ribs or wrist bones or the like. Nor do they see any form of apparent musculature.

The heads of the aliens are, in human terms, disproportionately large for their bodies. Their craniums are bulbous, especially above the eyes. There is no indication of cranial, facial, or neck hair, or hair anywhere else on the body. The neck and face are smooth with no wrinkles. The Small Beings' heads are also smooth, with no indication whatever of any external markings.

The aliens' faces somewhat resemble humans'. They have eyes approximately halfway down the face, an area where a nose might be, a small mouthlike slit, an area where one might envision "cheeks" (although none can be seen), and a chin. Using humans or higher primates as a model, all of the features are in the correct position. But the resemblance is merely in the general effect, and each organ and feature differs markedly from that of humans.

The huge eyes are the single most striking feature of the aliens. They span the entire width of the broad forehead. They are largest in the center and taper off to a tip on the side of the head. They contain no pupils, irises, or corneas. When people look into their eyes during Mindscan or other staring procedures, they see black, usually opaque organs. The eyes have no gradation in color, and they do not move from side to side as would a human's. At times abductees see some hint of liquidy "movement" inside the eyes. A few witnesses have reported a "sparkle" or "light" inside the eyes. Some aliens' eyes can "move": They can squint, and turn on their axes so that the outside tip can be raised or lowered. This is done mainly in Mindscan procedures. Other aliens have eyes that are more rounded and not as almond-shaped as the others. A few abductees have thought that the external eye might be a covering for an eye inside.

Witnesses generally do not report eyelids. Although some abductees have said that they have seen the Beings blink in unison, this may be confabulation; blinking is usually not reported. The aliens do not have eyebrows, although it is commonly reported that they have a ridge that might be caused by a "bone" around their eyes.

A few abductees report noses on the Small Beings, but the overwhelming majority of the reports indicate that the Small Beings have a slight raised bump but no nostrils or openings that might be interpreted as nasal passages.

The aliens' slitlike mouth does not have lips. Witnesses are ambivalent about an opening for the mouth. Most do not see one, but some have mentioned seeing a "membrane" over an opening. (A small number of abductees report that the mouth is perfectly round, forming an "O".) Abductees do not see teeth, a tongue, or saliva. The aliens do not use their mouths for communication.

A small and pointed chin lies below their mouths. Sometimes the mouth is so low that there is the appearance of no chin at all. The aliens do not appear to have a jaw or jaw hinge below where the ears would be. They seem to have no muscles attached from anywhere on the face to the top of the head for mastication. The overall look of the face, then, is that of a large forehead leading down to a tiny pointed chin. When they look at the face, some witnesses are reminded of a light bulb, a skeleton head, or a parking meter.

Aliens sometimes may have a small raised feature where human ears would be, but without an opening. Abductees can find no evidence of a device for collecting sound waves on alien heads.

Aliens do not have a thick neck with the head fitting on it in a human fashion. Instead, the head is attached to an extremely narrow, tubelike neck that seems too thin to support the head's weight. The head does not fit into the neck as human heads would. The neck is short and sticks into the bottom of the head much like, as one abductee put it, "a pumpkin on a stick." Witnesses see no throat movement denoting a tongue or a swallowing mechanism. The aliens do not appear to have an epiglottis. When Ken Rogers was twelve years old, he was able to reach up during the Mindscan procedure and grab a Taller Being by the throat. He reported that the neck seemed solid, as if it contained material inside, but it did not have the feel of moving muscles. No Adam's apple is evident in their throats, and there is no indication of vocal cords since communication is telepathic and abductees usually do not hear sounds coming from the aliens.

The alien's chest is small and narrow, with no noticeable bony structure in it. No sternum or clavicle is discernible. Abductees report no ribs protruding from under the skin. Nor is the chest bifurcated like a human's chest. Witnesses see no breasts or nipples. The normal human triangular configuration of the shoulders leading down to the waist is not present. The overall outline of the upper and lower body is one of rectangular straightness down to the legs, with no waist. The aliens do not appear to have a pelvis or prominent hip bones.

The area where the stomach would be is flat. The aliens have no rounded paunch or line of demarcation for a food-processing mechanism like upper and lower intestines. Witnesses do not see a navel. Nor do they see genitals. If the "male" Being is wearing tight-fitting clothes, no bulge is evident where human male genitals would be. If he is not wearing clothes, then abductees specifically state that he does not have genitals. Similarly, in the "female" alien, abductees can see no hint of a pubic arch, which is consistent with a lack of pelvis. There is no apparent method for the elimination of liquid waste.

The aliens' backs are consistent with what witnesses describe on the front of the Beings. There is no triangular shape to the back. It is smooth, with no discernible "bumps" of vertebrae. Most abductees do not see shoulder blades. If witnesses see the buttocks area, it is not fleshy and padded as on humans. While abductees do not see individual buttocks per se, they often describe a horizontal oblong ridge at the base of the alien's back that does not protrude.

Aliens' arms are long and very thin, with no apparent musculature. They bend at the "elbows" and can be used the way humans use their arms, with a free range of motion. Their arms and elbows do not display any boniness and are apparently the same diameter from the shoulder to where the hands join. They have no wrists.

Their hands and fingers also resemble humans' although they are thin and long. Their fingers are most often said to have rounded "pads" at the ends, although sometimes they are described as being tapered at the end. They have no fingernails. Frequently abductees see only three fingers. They have an opposable "thumb" or at least an appendage that acts as a thumb. Occasionally abductees report that the thumb is in a lower position on the hand than humans have. They have no small, curved ridges or swirls on their hands or finger-tips that might denote fingerprints.

Their two legs are short and thin, and they bend at the "knees." The limbs have no evident muscle development. Their legs go straight down, with no sense of a thigh, calf, or ankle. The legs are the same diameter from the top of the thigh to the bottom of the calf, and flow smoothly into the feet. Little is known about the feet and toes. Abductees describe the feet as being either rounded or elongated, and toes are not usually noticed.

When a female alien is described, it is generally in vague terms. The abductee knows that the alien is female, but the physical de-scription is not unique enough to suggest significant anatomical dif-ferences. The female is often the same size as the Taller Being. She has no mammary glands and no hair, cranial, facial, or pubic. When asked to describe the differences between the male and female, the abductees say that the female alien is thinner, more "graceful," more "sensitive," and "kinder." Even with these vague descriptions, the abductees are quite clear about whether they are being tended by a male or female.

The aliens' small motor dexterity is excellent. They are able to conduct physical examinations with great speed—touching, poking, prodding, lifting, and feeling. They can maneuver instruments with precision, for example in performing tissue-sampling procedures. They generally do not drop instruments or have accidents where things spill or are knocked over. They remove abductees' clothes without much fumbling or clumsiness.[2]

Abductees have the impression that the aliens are weak and frail, and they are often surprised at the strength the Beings can display. The aliens can maneuver humans through hallways and rooms and onto tables. They can push and pull abductees. Working together, two or three of them can carry an abductee to a table and then lift the abductee up onto it. They can grip abductees' arms and legs with strong hand pressure. In spite of the aliens' abilities, abductees usu-ally think that the Beings can be swept aside, pushed over, or hurt, if only the abductees had the muscle control to do it.

The Taller Being is very similar to the Small Beings. He can be a few inches to a head taller. His skin is often more leathery and striated. Because of the nature of his tasks—egg and sperm harvesting, Mindscan, etc.—the abductees usually have stronger reactions to him than to the Small Beings. The abductees who hate and fear him tend to describe him as being "uglier." Others, especially those who are more "bonded" to him, think that he is friendly and kind and tend to describe him as not being any uglier than the Small Beings. Both groups, however, describe his specific features in similar ways. He has enormous, liquid, black eyes. He usually does not have a nose although sometimes abductees do report seeing a nose. His head is not as smoothly rounded as the Small Beings'; it is more angular. He seems to have more "character" in his face. Abductees sometimes report striations and indentations in the Taller Being's forehead or on top and in back of the head. He also has no hair anywhere on his head. He frequently wears distinguishable covering, such as a white, gray, or black "lab coat," smock, or robe. Sometimes abductees report that is he wearing something on his head like a hat or a surgeon's cap.

Although we know little about the physiology of the aliens, speculation often leads to interesting hypotheses. For instance, if we ask, "Do aliens breathe?" the speculative answer can lead in surprising directions. To answer this question we must put together bits of information. In virtually all abduction accounts, the communication between the aliens and the abductees is done through "telepathy," and not aurally through their ears. Words are not sent through the air in the form of aspirated sound waves formed by lungs expelling air through a set of vibrating vocal cords. The same phenomenon is reported when aliens talk among themselves: Abductees report that they can also nonaurally understand what the aliens are saying to each other. Also, open mouths are rarely reported, and neither are mouths assuming various shapes as if in word formation. In fact, mouth animation does not appear to be a function.

Humans use the nose, in part, to inhale and perhaps to heat air for breathing, to sense gases, and to trap particulates floating in the atmosphere for odor registration. The lack of a nose on an alien suggests no need for these functions and is therefore consistent with the speculation that they do not use the atmosphere as we do. The same is true for their lack of eyelids. They apparently have no need to keep the outside of their eyes free from dust and other particulates.

In addition, abductees do not report seeing an expansion and contraction of the chest as if the aliens were inhaling and exhaling air. Nor do they feel the rush of air on their faces from exhalation during the extremely close Mindscan procedures. All this leads to the possibility that the Beings do not breathe air, at least not in the manner that we are aware of, and do not interact with the atmosphere as we do.

"Do aliens eat or drink?" The evidence seems to suggest that they do not. Abductees never see aliens eat. The aliens do not appear to have a moveable mouth, teeth, saliva, or tongue. The throat is a narrow tube with no indication that it contains a complex apparatus for swallowing or ingestion. The lack of a jaw further supports the notion that if the aliens eat, it is not accomplished through mastication. Lack of a nose suggests that the sense of smell is not involved with the important (human) function of taste. If that is the case, the ingestion of "food" might be very different, if it exists at all.

There is no evidence of a stomach. Also, all the Beings appear to have the same bodily frame, with no evidence in weight differentiation as if one were eating more or less than the other. There are no discernible buttocks or solid and liquid waste elimination apparatuses. In fact, abductees do not report water as part of the experience. They see no water basins, no spouts or faucets, no cups or glasses for drinking water. The aliens never offer food or drink to the victims other than a liquid for some specific physical procedure. They never wash their hands, at least within sight of the abductees.

A cursory examination of alien morphology, then, leads to the conclusion that these Beings are very different from humans. They do not appear to breathe or to ingest food and water, which means that at least two major human physiological systems are missing or are organized completely differently.

ALIEN BEHAVIOR AND COMMUNICATION

The technology and science that the aliens possess suggest that they have logical thought processes with a great capacity to learn and understand. The achievements they have demonstrated depend on cooperation among the aliens, and this would probably entail a hierarchy of work and divisions of labor; the differentiation of tasks that abductees report suggests this as well. Furthermore, the Taller Being's behavior lends evidence to a hierarchical structure not only of work but of command and knowledge.

The Taller Being appears to be in control of the abduction. He usually makes his appearance after the abductee has been examined. He directs the operations of the Small Beings. He conducts what might be considered the more specialized procedures—Mindscan, gynecological procedures, and sperm collection—rather than the more general ones, such as the physical examination.

In addition to executing the Taller Being's orders, the Small Beings have their own specific tasks to perform. They retrieve abductees, oversee clothes removal, situate the abductee on the table, and help perform the physical examination. They often maneuver machinery and take the abductee to various stations. Yet they are not simply "robots" with no independence. Most of the time they act in concert to carry out their assignments. On occasion they will discuss a problem and agree upon a solution. For example, one time when Karen Morgan was taken on board the UFO, she felt extremely "out of it" as she lay on a table in an entrance room. The Small Beings apparently saw this, and Karen could "hear" them communicating about the fact that she was not ready for the examination. They decided that the best course of action was to wait. So they waited until Karen began to feel a little less groggy. Then they took her into the room for the examination.

The "female" Being usually looks more like the Taller Being and performs many of his duties along with other tasks. She interacts with both men and women, but she more often reassures males, performs Mindscan and bonding, and extracts sperm. The "female" Beings attend to the babies and nurseries. They bring the children out to be held, hugged, and nursed, and then take them back after the abductees are finished with them.

The aliens are generally cooperative with one another, and abductees report no instances of conflict among them, although there may be differences of opinion about how to proceed when something unusual occurs. The Taller Being may be irritated when the Small Beings have not done something to his liking, such as not taking an abductee's clothes off fast enough.

He told me that I had to get undressed. He seemed kind of annoyed that I wasn't already.

You mean, annoyed with you?

Well, annoyed at them. I felt like he was mad at them. He said something to them; he just was unhappy.

Did he turn around and say something?

Yes, sort of off to the side.

Did you happen to pick up a little particle of that discussion?

For some reason I think he said something like, "This isn't the way this is supposed to be done." And then he said something about me supposed to be undressed already, or why wasn't I undressed already, or something like that.

What happens then?

He turned back to me, and he looked at me again, and I knew that he'd be back, and he went out of the room again. . . . I guess they just took my clothes off when I was lying there. . . . He came back after a few minutes. . . . He looked at me again, and he said, "This will be over in a minute." I started to feel scared again, too.

(Barbara Archer, 21, 1988)

The aliens' demeanor is businesslike. They do not waste time; all their actions are deliberate and economical. Abductees get the impression that they are part of an assembly-line process. They are received, processed, and returned as fast as possible so that the aliens can move on to the next victim.

The aliens seem to respond to human needs with a certain amount of compassion. The reassuring nature of their conversation suggests that they appear to understand human fear and aversion to pain (although they sometimes conduct pain procedures). They comfort the abductees by telling them that they will not be hurt, that there will be no pain, that they should not be frightened, that it will not last long. They may have evolved this line of communication because human fear is a constant factor in nearly all abductions.

On the other hand, telling newly pubescent young girls that they should "breed" or "mate," as if they were animals in a biological experiment, suggests that the aliens are either unaware of or indifferent to human emotions and psychological responses. The aliens act as if the process of making babies involves only the physical uniting of sperm and egg.

They do not seem to understand why humans resist them. The Taller Beings often seem puzzled when someone tries to resist. When an abductee attempts a modicum of physical resistance, the aliens simply enforce their wishes. When the abductee does not mentally cooperate or when she silently cries out against the aliens, they disregard it. They ignore accusations that they are hurting the abductee or ruining her life. If she pleads with them to stop, they answer, "We can't stop." If she threatens them with finding a way to put a stop to it, they answer, "You can't stop us. We won't stop," or something similar. Patti Layne reported a very short but typical exchange with the Taller Being.

He looks in my eyes and says, "How do you feel?" And I say, "Not good, why did you bother me?" And he didn't answer. He just stared at me too. "I'm going to get rid of you guys somehow." And he said, "Okay, you do that." But that's all I remember.

(Patti Layne, 17, 1980)

When resistance occurs, the aliens do not seem to become angry. In fact, anger does not emerge as a significant feature of their psychological makeup. They may seem perturbed, exasperated, stern, or annoyed, but they do not manifest anger, even when pushed. They have no outbursts, and they display no uncontrollable behavior. Similarly, abductees report no violent or aggressive physical behavior.

In their efforts to try to get abductees to do what they want, the aliens display a curious substitution of form for content. During child presentations, for example, the aliens sometimes insist that the baby is "beautiful" even though the woman might be repelled by the sight of it. They insist that a woman hold a baby to her breast even though she might not be lactating.

In general, the aliens are evasive in their communications. When asked direct questions not relating to the experience at the moment, they often ignore the question. In fact, most abductions take place with little or no communication whatsoever between alien and abductee. If a telepathic dialogue does take place, it is usually with the Taller Being and it has limits. The Taller Being will ask a question of the abductee related to her physical state, especially if he has found something about her that he has not seen before. She replies and then he might ask a few more questions. Or the Taller Being may sometimes ask a casual question, such as "How are you?" Instead of answering, often the abductee will ask the Taller Being why he is doing something. His answer is evasive. If the abductee persists, the Taller Being will remark about how the victim is asking too many questions and tell her to relax.

The Taller Being and the Small Beings silently communicate among themselves. Usually the Taller Being initiates the conversation and the Small Beings respond. Once in a while abductees report a situation in which the Taller Being explains something about human physiology to the Small Beings, as if he were a teacher and they were students. He will point his finger at various areas of the abductee's body, the Small Beings will look at the areas, and the Taller Being will communicate with them about it. Abductees often report that they are able to "tap" into communications between Small and Taller Beings. Invariably they are discussing something about the abductee's body or the procedure they are about to perform on it. Sometimes the Small Beings stand around and communicate with one another, but idle conversations between aliens and abductees are rarely reported. At times the Beings seem pleased or almost happy, especially when the victims have cooperated fully with them in all their procedures.

Abductees rarely describe humor or lightheartedness in any of the aliens, although we do have one reported episode. The Beings had just cut off a lock of a young girl's hair. The Taller Being then put the hair up to his head and showed it to the other Beings. This apparently was amusing. In the main, however, abductees say that the Beings do not express a sense of fun.

Virtually all conversation revolves around the experiences that are taking place. There is no discussion about the lives of the abductees or of the aliens apart from the abduction scenario. (It must be remembered that the telepathic and nonsyntactical quality of most conversations means that abductees must interpret the correct meaning from the impressions that they receive.) The Beings express absolutely no interest in anything about the abductee's daily life apart from physiology. They express no interest in her personal, social, or family relationships, except as they bear upon the breeding program. They express no interest in politics, culture, economics, or the rich and extraordinarily complex tapestry that makes up human relationships and societies. They do not ask even idle questions about this. They do, however, express interest in birth control, smoking, and health problems that might directly relate to childbearing for women.

For example, when Barbara Archer was sixteen, she suffered from anorexia and had lost a considerable amount of weight. This greatly concerned the aliens.

I feel nervous now because he's angry with me for something.

At this time, were you in the middle of your anorexia problem, or at the end of it, or just beginning?

Toward the end.

So you were sort of at a lower weight, then?

Yeah. But I don't think that that's the problem. I don't know. I feel that he's concerned about the weight, but he's more concerned about other stuff, too.

What do you think he might be concerned about?

Well, I think that's he's concerned about what losing the weight has done. He's concerned about the problem, but I think that it's not really the fact that I'm real skinny, it's just that I think that he knows that my period stopped.

Did your period stop for a long time, or ...?

I guess it was about eight months. Maybe a little bit more than that. Not fully a year, I don't think, but kind of a long time. . . . And [the Taller Being and the Small Beings] sort of talk or something. They sort of are in the corner of the room, and I know they're talking about me.

Can you sort of get a sense of what they're saying . . . ?

Well, I think that they're saying, this is the feeling that I got, I feel that they know that I stopped menstruating, and they think that . . . I'm also so skinny they think that I'm sick or something. The taller guy seems annoyed again because I've lost weight. They keep saying I've lost weight. They don't know why because they can't see anything wrong. I'm not sick as far as . . . I don't have any sickness, you know. They don't understand why I lost all this weight. But all they do know is that I lost all this weight and it stopped my period. . . . They kind of left, I think, and it was just the taller guy.

What does he do?

Well, he comes over to me, and he wants me to, he wants to know why I lost all this weight. And I just said, "Because I want to be thin."

How does he respond to that?

He says something like, "But you made yourself sick" or, "Now you're sick," or something like that. And I said that I just wanted to be thin, that's all. I didn't want to do anything else. But I feel like he's kind of annoyed with me. And he tells me that I have to start eating because my body doesn't function right if I don't.

Okay, does he tell you this in a nice manner, or . . . ?

Sort of, but not really nice.

Is there an edge to it?

Yes. I feel like I'm messing things up. I feel like he's not going to be nice to me the way he usually is unless I do. . . . He comes over, and he looks at me again. I feel so upset. I mean, I'm sorry that things are messed up but I can't eat more. I don't want to eat more. . . . I think that he's sort of annoyed with me now. I get the feeling that I've ruined . . . things can't be done now or something. But after he says that, he just starts looking at me again. And everything is pretty okay. I get those same feelings again, and I get the feeling he's not really mad at me.

(Barbara Archer, 16, 1982)

We have no direct knowledge about the aliens' lives—either on board the craft or elsewhere. Abductees have not only never seen food or water, but they have also never seen beds, or other "creature comforts." They see no magazines or apparent entertainment devices like radios and televisions. Abductees do not report seeing aliens at rest. Witnesses see no art on the walls, and the rooms have no furniture, benches, tables, or chairs, other than those used for the abduction procedures. The rooms lack decoration. The wall colors are metallic gray, black, and white. Basically abductees cannot find any apparent indication of alien life or society outside of the confines of the craft on which the abduction is taking place.

When abductees have the presence of mind to ask direct questions about the workings of alien society, the aliens evade the questions. When abductees ask the aliens where they are from, the aliens usually either do not answer or say that this information is not for the abductee to know. Karen Morgan had a discussion with a Taller Being just as he was about to begin Mindscan.

And then I say, "Are you taking me with you? Where are we going? Where are you from?" And he says, it says, "We're from . . ." I can't remember—something like "very far away," or "you wouldn't understand," or "it doesn't matter," but he's not giving me a straight answer, and I'm really mad because I want to know.

(Karen Morgan, 30, 1979)

In 1983 a frightened and confused Patti Layne asked them if she were in hell:

I just go into this room, and I was just sitting there in this chair, more like a bench, sitting on this bench in this room and there's this guy in there, he had these same eyes. And he said, "I have something to show you." And I said, "Am I in hell?" Because that's what I thought was happening, that I was dying in my sleep, and he said, "What's that?" "That's a lot of fire and stuff like that." He didn't say anything and just went away. I was just sitting there.

(Patti Layne, 20, 1983)

The composite picture that emerges from the many abductee accounts is of rational, logical, goal-oriented aliens who perform a variety of clearly outlined tasks with maximum efficiency in a detached, clinical manner. There is a hierarchical structure and a differentiation of labor. They are focused on human physiology, neurology, and reproduction. The aliens display very little sense of individuality. Their outward appearance is almost always the same, given the range of clothing types found. They volunteer no information about themselves. Although once in a while more complicated dialogue takes place, the consistency of their communication behavior suggests that they are carrying out a systematic policy of noninformation.

Finally, we should address the question of whether the aliens have more intelligence than we do. Although they have an extremely advanced technology, we have no indication that aliens have a higher or greater capacity than humans to learn or to solve problems. Nor have we yet uncovered evidence of creative, intuitive, or aesthetic abilities. Given the right amount of information, human beings appear to be capable of understanding everything that the aliens are doing. Alien activities that at first seemed incomprehensible have become logical and rational as we have accumulated more information from abductees. We have not found a situation where our ability to understand and to learn is clearly on a lower level than theirs as if we were a lower form of animal.

But one thing is clear—the Beings are not human. Their mental abilities and their physiology are very different from ours. They are, in the profoundest sense of the word, "alien."

PART III
LIVING
WITH THE
SECRET

Chapter 9

Exploring the Evidence

Many abductees have adjusted well to the abduction phenomenon and are able to lead their lives free from the disruption that these experiences can cause. A few abductees feel that in some way they have been enlightened and even prepared for some future benevolent purpose. Some, who have not investigated their experiences, have successfully integrated the barely remembered events into their daily belief structure whether it is religious, New Age, or pragmatic ("Don't strange things happen to all people?"), and the experiences become little more than a psychological irritant.

For other abductees, however, the effects of abductions can be terribly traumatic and destructive. Once these victims bring the memories to consciousness through hypnosis or unaided recall, and once they understand what has happened to them, they find little positive in the events. The experience does not improve their lives, give them mystical powers, or put them in touch with Universal Truth. They wish their abductions had never happened and are fearful that they will occur again. Their problems are compounded because few people will believe them when they confide their stories to them. They can produce no hard evidence to prove their contentions.

So far, the strongest evidence presented is the myriad of abduction reports that have surfaced, with the congruence of narrative and the richness of exact detail. "Hard" evidence has been slow in coming, but it is increasing. Now that we know what to look for, the eventual discovery of evidence constituting irrefutable proof might be much closer than ever. In the long run, the hard evidence may be the most important supportive evidence, but currently it is the physiological and psychological effects of abductions that provide many of our strongest clues to the abduction mystery.

RESIDUE FROM THE OBJECT

Physical evidence for abductions is difficult to come by. Returning home with an artifact from the UFO is virtually impossible. It would mean having the physical ability and mental acumen to take something surreptitiously, hiding it while naked, keeping the theft a secret from the aliens, and then remembering where the artifact came from after the abduction. In spite of this predicament, UFO researchers have found some physical signs to support abduction claims. For example, from time to time people will say that they were abducted into an object resting in their backyard. When the area is investigated, a flattened or burned circle can be seen where the UFO rested. Budd Hopkins reported in *Intruders* that he found a circular ring and a forty-foot streak in the backyard in which the soil had been altered to such a degree that for several years nothing grew there.

Even stranger, someone might expel a tiny metallic ball from their nasal passage, although this has not happened to the abductees I have worked with. In all but a few of the cases the artifact has been lost or discarded. In the cases where they have been recovered, analyses have so far been inconclusive about their origin, or the analysis has not yet been completed. CAT scans, MRIs, and X-rays have been employed to detect supposed implants. In a few of these, a small, unusual mass has been detected in the upper nasal passages where abductees have indicated that an implant might be lodged. To date, no operations have been performed to remove the suspicious masses because the risks and problems inherent in surgery outweigh recovery considerations, or the object mysteriously disappears.

Stains

In early 1987 Melissa Bucknell called to say she thought something may have happened the night before because she found marks on her back and "blood" on her nightshirt. But, when examined, the stain on her nightshirt did not appear to be blood: It was not encrusted or oxidized, and it did not have the familiar dark-brown color; rather, it was a dark orange. Its location on her garment did not correspond to the area of her body that she said had been touched. The marks on her shoulder were not puncture or scratch marks, and there was no scab or apparent blood on her skin. Soon afterward Karen Morgan also came forward with a nightshirt that had a puzzling dark-orange stain on it. The stain had not come out in the wash, and she had even gone to the trouble of smearing makeup, coffee, and other substances near the stain to try to duplicate it, but with no success.

Sometimes the stains are not on a garment. For instance, Janet Demerest sleeps in the same bed with her six-year-old daughter, Hillary. One night when they woke up after an apparent abduction experience, the little girl complained about pains in her arm and elsewhere. When Janet examined her daughter, she was horrified to find that Hillary's genitals were red, swollen, and leaking a clear fluid. She had a brown substance painted between her thighs. Janet went into a panic and frantically began to wipe the substance off. As she did, she noticed that the substance simply dried up, turned white, and then "evaporated" until none was left. She found some flakes and a possible stain on the sheet. She stored the flakes in an airtight jar in the freezer, but within a few days they also had evaporated.

A month later the same thing happened again to Hillary. Once again she woke up with the brown liquid painted between her legs. This time Janet peeled off all the material that she could and put it in the freezer. Then she took some toilet paper and wiped the rest of it off. Once again, however, the substance simply evaporated within a few days, but some of it adhered to the toilet paper and is presently in storage.

Another woman had an abduction one night while she was taking a nap clutching a favorite teddy bear. She remembered without hypnosis that when she was about to return from the abduction, she was lying on a table and an alien came up to her with the teddy bear. He placed it on her chest, but it fell on the floor. He picked it up and "dabbed" at it a little bit as if he was cleaning it. After the abduction, when the woman remembered what had happened, she looked at the little shirt that the teddy bear was wearing and found orange-brown stains on it.

Karen offered a glimpse into the function of the stain substance. She reported that during an event the aliens made her lie on a table and then a small alien came along with a "brush" of some sort and painted the brown liquid in wide swaths on her body. Next, they placed electrodelike devices on her elbows and thighs, and she was required to move her arms and legs one at a time while the aliens either observed or measured something. When I asked her if the aliens wiped the fluid off her when the procedure was completed, she reported that they did not.

We do not know what the stain substance is made of. It either sublimes or evaporates extremely quickly. We do not have enough of the stain substance to mount a viable chemical analysis. Crippen Laboratories of Wilmington, Delaware, attempted a Fourier Transfer Infrared analysis on three of the stains. For two, the analyses showed that they were not common substances such as iodine or caffeine. No analysis was possible for the third stain (from Janet's sheet) because it had evaporated from the surface.

In 1988 the American Standards Testing Bureau of New York City attempted an analysis. It used a fresh stain from a shirt that Janet had been wearing during an abduction. A small team was assembled to attack the problem. The chief chemist decided that the best way to go about a more in-depth analysis would be through the use of High Pressure Liquid Chromatography (HPLC). The laboratory obtained an HPLC apparatus especially for the analysis, but the team members immediately began to encounter problems. The solvent needed to remove the substance from the garment had to be exactly right so that it would not dissolve the stain completely or alter it chemically. After employing different solvents, they decided that water, after all, would be safest, but the minute traces that they were able to obtain were not enough for anything approaching a complete analysis, even with HPLC. After eight months of sporadic trying, they gave up, unable to go further. Soon after that, a chemist at a Pennsylvania university attempted to analyze an abduction-related stain, with help from his graduate students. After trying for six months they, too, gave up. And there the matter stands. Until a complete analysis is possible, all we have is tantalizing but incomplete evidence. In the meantime the number of stain samples has increased.

PHYSICAL AFTEREFFECTS

The abductees suffer a variety of physical problems caused by abductions whether or not they have recovered the memories of their experiences.

Scars and Bruises

Many abductees notice mysterious scars on their bodies that they later realize are associated with abduction experiences. The scar may appear at any age, young or old. Abductees report no pain associated with such scars, nor do they describe blood, bandages, or a healing period. The scars range in shape from small "scoop" marks to elongated, thin scars. These scars are permanent records of abduction experiences and can be anxiety-provoking reminders for the victim.

Scarring is found not only on the body's surface. It may occur internally as well. Abductees have reported anomalous scar tissue in their vaginas, bladders, gall bladders, nasal passages, and sinuses. None of the scar tissue found in these areas has been associated with conscious trauma.

A less harmful but disconcerting physical effect is the anomalous bruise. It is common for abductees to wake up with black-and-blue marks on their bodies. Men discover large bruises around their genitals. Both sexes find numerous black-and-blue marks on their arms and legs right after an abduction.

Vision Problems

Eye problems are also typical. Abductees often report red, stinging eyes, blurred vision, or swollen eyes after an abduction event. These difficulties can last for a few hours or linger for as long as three months and even, if there is nerve damage, be permanent. As part of a machine examination, Lynn was forced to look for an extended period of time into an apparatus that contained an extremely bright blue light. She could not blink her eyes, and they quickly became quite painful. When the abduction was over, her eyes were red and tearing, and the next day they were swollen. She had difficulty seeing printed material, and it became impossible for her to concentrate on reading. This condition was acute for about three months, and it then slowly subsided.

Abduction victims report other neurological problems associated with sight. Seeing brightly lit colors, "lights," or even "figures" at inappropriate times is a disturbing consequence of abductions. The visions may be large and disruptive to the normal course of the day's activities, but more often than not they are seen through the corner of one's eyes and are a constant annoyance. We have not discovered the stimulus for this condition within the abduction scenario. Melissa Bucknell went to an ophthalmologist for this problem and was told that it was a common and somewhat normal neurological condition for an elderly person—but she was twenty-six years old at the time.

Muscle Pain

Temporary muscle aches throughout the body are often associated with events done during an abduction. The pain might be severe and last for a few days. In one instance, Janet was on a table while two Beings had their hands on her shoulders; her head was bent back at a sharp angle as if she was trying to look directly behind her. The Beings stared intently at her as she lay in this position with her body rigid, and one Being performed a gynecological procedure at the same time. The next day she had severe cramps in her neck and shoulders, and the pain persisted for twenty-four hours.

Nosebleeds and Earaches

Nosebleeds, "holes" in the nasal passages, and ruptures in the eardrums are also common ailments associated with abductions. The nosebleeds occur in both children and adults. People wake up with their pillows soaked with blood. Physicians have examined the holes but have found no readily explainable causative factor. Abductees frequently complain of blocked nasal passages that make breathing difficult. Similarly, people with ear punctures find blood on the pillow in the morning, and some abductees endure a form of tinnitus, an irregular ringing in the ear.

Discharges and Vaginal Problems

Unusual discharges sometimes occur following an abduction. A woman might notice a brownish substance coming from her vagina or her navel. A frightened fifteen-year-old Patti Layne went to the school nurse the day after having an abduction experience because a brown liquid was coming out of her bellybutton. The nurse was unable to identify the substance or explain why it was leaking from her navel.

Abductees' unusual vaginal problems can indicate recent abduction experiences. After being abducted, one woman woke to find that the interior wall of her vagina was hemorrhaging. She was unaccountably fearful of going to her gynecologist, and she soaked through twenty tampons in one day before the bleeding finally stopped. After another abduction she discovered perforations in her vagina.

It is not unusual for a woman to have her hymen ruptured during an experience. One abductee reported that at her first regular inter-course her hymen was not intact, and she experienced no pain or blood associated with the sexual activity. During hypnosis she re-membered that her hymen had been torn during an abduction when she was seven years old.

Then he looked between my legs. And I said, "That's not nice; you shouldn't do that." He said, "I'm not going to hurt you, I just want to look inside." So this light came on somewhere. . . . There's this big light between my legs. And I could just see this big light kind of burn my eyes.

The light was not focused on your eyes, though, is that correct?

The light was focused between my legs. Then he stuck some-thing in it, and it really hurt. It just really hurt, and I couldn't move.

Was this an instrument of some sort, do you think?

Mm-hmm.

Can you get a sense of the shape of it?

Whatever it was it fit, but it hurt. It just ripped right through in there. It just ripped me right, it felt like I was ripping. I know there was some blood there. It felt kind of dripping and wet.

(Name omitted upon request, 1970)

Later she stated that she felt they had torn her hymen.

Pregnancy

The problem of unplanned or inexplicable pregnancy is one of the most frequent physical aftereffects of abduction experiences. Usually the woman feels pregnant and has all the outward signs of being pregnant. She is puzzled and disturbed because she has either not engaged in sex or has been very careful with proper birth control. She has blood tests and the gynecologist positively verifies the pregnancy. Typically, between the discovery of the pregnancy and the end of the first trimester, the woman suddenly finds herself not pregnant. She has no miscarriage, no extra-heavy bleeding or discharge. The fetus is simply gone, with no evidence of the rare phenomenon of non-twin "absorption," in which physicians theorize that a nonviable fetus can be absorbed into the woman's body.

During the first trimester the woman may decide to terminate the pregnancy. At the appointment, the physician begins the procedure and is stunned to find that there is no fetus in the uterus. In Janet Demerest's case, the physician was so surprised to find the fetus gone that he became angry at the attending nurse for in some way causing the mix-up. The nurse had to gesture to him to be quiet lest Janet hear his anger and confusion. The "Missing Fetus Syndrome" has happened to abductees enough times that it is now considered one of the more common effects of the abduction experience.

PSYCHOLOGICAL TRAUMA: POST-ABDUCTION SYNDROME

Many abductees, whether they are aware or unaware of their abductions, suffer from what Dr. Ronald Westrum first identified in 1986 as Post-Abduction Syndrome (PAS).[1] PAS involves a multiplicity of psychological symptoms that are caused by abduction experiences and has its greatest effect on unaware abductees. While similar to Post-Traumatic Stress Disorder, it differs in that the external forces compel the abductee to repress the memories of traumatic events, even though the abductee may want to remember them. Furthermore, the abduction episodes are repressed even though many do not have the classic violent traumatic content of Post-Traumatic Stress Disorder. Finally, PAS is generated not only by past experiences, but by ongoing events as well.

The severity of PAS varies greatly from person to person, ranging from mild to debilitating. Many unaware abductees act or think in ways that are inexplicable to them; they wonder about the origins of their unusual thoughts and behavior, but they are unable to discover them. Some PAS victims operate normally in society; others are so anxiety-ridden that they have great difficulties functioning in everyday life.

It is very important to note that many symptoms similar to those of PAS also occur in people who have not had abductions. *Having one or a number of the symptoms does not necessarily mean that the person has been abducted.*

Sleep Disturbances

The most common of all PAS problems are sleep disturbances. For the average adult, sleep can be something to look forward to for relief from the anxieties and tensions of the day. Abductees often view sleep very differently. It can be a time of terror and distress. They desperately need sleep, but an irrational fear makes them afraid to close their eyes. They may be scared that "someone" will come into their room, or that "something" will happen to them while they sleep. To reduce the fear, these abductees often sleep with lights, the radio, or the television on. Some sleep with all three on. Their spouses have to check the house to make sure that no intruders are around. The doors to the bedroom and to the closet have to be closed. Even after this ritual, abductees still have terrible bouts of insomnia. When they close their eyes, their minds become flooded with terrifying images of hideous Beings staring at them with large horrible eyes. These images are so frightening that many abductees will stay awake as long as possible rather than chance seeing them.

When they do fall asleep, frightened abductees often have difficulty staying asleep and wake up many times during the night. Their dreams can be vivid and disturbing. They have visions of lying on a table, of being surrounded by small, large-eyed creatures, of "operations" being performed on them, of seeing strange-looking babies; and there may be a horrifying sexual component to these dreams.

Both ongoing and past abductions can be half-remembered as very frightening, lifelike dreams. When the victims wake up in the morning after having an abduction experience that is now relegated to a "dream," they are shaky and nervous—a feeling that might last for a few days. They feel exhausted, even though they presumably got their normal amount of sleep. Then, inexplicably, they may be seized with the desire to rearrange the furniture in their bedroom in the unconscious belief that their fears will disappear if their room is different from before.

Abductees may develop strong fears of their bedroom and sleep in another room from then on, all the while telling themselves that they are foolish or stupid to act this way. They sometimes find that they can go to another person's house and sleep soundly, but when they return to their own room the sleep disturbances begin again. Often boys and girls and even young men and women living at home prefer to sleep on the floor next to their parents' bed, even though they may be embarrassed to do so, but being in the room with their parents gives them a feeling of safety that they cannot get in their own bedrooms.

Fears, Anxieties, Depression

Fears, anxieties, and sometimes serious depression are frequent symptoms of PAS. Sometimes the fears are minor annoyances that do not have any great effect on the abductee's life; at other times they may be serious, life-changing problems that the abductee wrestles with. The fears that grip adults and children alike seemingly have no basis in reality. The abductees cannot point to a specific traumatic event in their childhood that might have provoked the phobia. They understand that their fears are completely inappropriate, but they are unable to control their illogical and perplexing feelings.

Abductees may be extremely afraid of being alone. They find that they must be with someone at all times and particularly at night. This is not because of loneliness, but because they are scared that "something will happen" if they are alone, although they are not overly frightened of burglars.

Some abductees suddenly develop seemingly irrational fears of stretches of road or of fields. They may have traveled the same route for years without giving it a thought, but one day they become inordinately afraid of it. They stop traveling on that stretch of road, and go miles out of their way to avoid it. Child abductees who have played in a nearby park every day suddenly are afraid to go there and never want to play there again. They may have suffered strange missing-time episodes at these places, and they will agonize over what happened to them for many years. Other abductees develop strong fears of their basement, their bedroom, or their backyard. Riding on escalators or elevators can provoke anxiety.

Visiting physicians can be extremely stressful. Although most women find a routine visit to the gynecologist an uncomfortable but necessary event, many abductees are seized with panic when they must go. Some women abductees never visit gynecologists. They dread the thought of a doctor performing an internal examination on them, and even though they tell themselves that their fears are silly, they become hysterical when the procedure is begun. As a result they forgo yearly checkups, which can endanger their health. One twenty-seven-year-old abductee had gone to a gynecologist only three times in her life, and the last time she cried uncontrollably throughout the examination.

When anxiety becomes acute, panic can plague the victim. Abductees may be seized with a panic attack at any time with no recognizable stimulus. As fear overcomes them, their hearts "race," they breathe rapidly, they become flushed, and they may hyperventilate. A life-threatening fear overwhelms them. These attacks may become so severe and debilitating that they can prompt agoraphobia: Abductees become so consumed with worry about suffering a panic attack that they are unable to leave their homes to carry out their daily routine. One abductee sometimes suffered attacks while she was teaching her high school class. They became so frequent that she was afraid to go to the market because she once experienced an attack there and had to abandon her cart and run home. This type of panic can interfere with work, and with social and family relationships. Panic attack victims find that they cannot drive alone or even be alone at home at night. When the attack starts, even being with someone does not diminish the fears.

Abductees commonly suffer from moderate to severe depression. They may break out in tears for no apparent reason, or have episodes of withdrawal. They may even contemplate suicide to alleviate the pain. If they are unaware of the origin of their malady, the depression is usually not amenable to normal psychological treatment.

Unaware abductees can have inexplicably exaggerated emotional reactions to normal activities. For instance, they might wake up in the morning with intense feelings of euphoria. They ride the crest of an emotional high that seems to have no cause and that may last for several days. One young woman woke up feeling extremely euphoric. When she rode her bicycle into town she had the inexplicable feeling that she was falling in love with every man who looked into her eyes. Conversely, abductees might feel an almost overpowering rage at someone for simply staring at them, while this might not have ever bothered them in the past. Animals with large eyes might provoke great anxiety in abductees, who sometimes inexplicably develop aversions to deer, rabbits, monkeys, cows, and even inanimate objects. Ken Rogers was a small child when his mother brought him a souvenir "tiki god" from a trip she had taken; the face and eyes of the souvenir so frightened him that he threw it out after having it for one day. One unaware abductee had several abductions from his car. After the last one, he sold his car and gave up driving for several years but did not know the reason why.

Obsessions and phobias relating to "borderland science" are also a common symptom of PAS. For example, after an abduction, some unaware abductees suddenly become obsessed with unidentified flying objects. They buy every book they can get on the subject, compulsively talk about it, and seem unable to concentrate on much else. Yet a few days or weeks before, they had little or no interest in UFOs. Others go to the opposite extreme and are inordinately repelled by the subject of UFOs. They refuse to entertain the notion that there "might be something to it." They dislike talking or even thinking about it. They become extremely angry when the topic is raised and may leave the room so that they do not have to participate in a discussion. Their attitude is so negative that it assumes the dimensions of a phobia.

Some abductees experience extreme emotional reactions when they see illustrations of aliens in a book about UFOs. The pictures rivet the abductee as she stares at them in stunned horror, unable to take her eyes off them, all the while wondering why she is reacting in this manner. Others will pick up a book on abductees and have a powerful yet puzzling reaction to it, becoming extraordinarily emotionally involved with its contents. They might break into tears and sob for no apparent reason. Still others become inordinately frightened by such books and are unable to read them through to the end.

Memories or dreams can become an obsession as the unaware abductee desperately tries to understand their meaning. It is common for abductees to feel that in some way they left their bodies, usually during the night. When they floated out of bed they were often accompanied by someone they believe to be a deceased relative or an angel.

A few unaware abductees claim not only that they have had out-of-body experiences but that they have also experienced what they call astral travel. They know that they have in some mysterious way experienced a strange displacement in location. One minute they were in one spot and then seemingly the next instant they found themselves in another place. They might be aware of this occurring several times during their lives. The only way that they can reconcile what has happened to them is through the only available cultural explanation—astral travel—no matter how ill-defined that might be.

Other PAS anxieties are related to babies. Some women develop "avoidance" postures toward babies. Even though they may have already had children, they find that they do not like babies very much or claim to be "not a baby person." Sometimes babies generate not only anxiety in them but even fear or dread. Others react in a completely opposite fashion and become convinced that they once had a baby that has since been taken from them. They have the inexplicable feeling that they were once pregnant and actually gave birth. Some women can become so obsessed with the "missing baby" that they may even substitute a doll for it to assuage their baffling feelings of desire and guilt.

Missing Time

Missing-time episodes are common in abductees' lives. They are unable to account for a "lost" period of time, which might be as short as an hour or two or as long as a day—and sometimes even longer. Trying to understand the origin of the missing time can torture the victims. It makes no sense. They have no explanation, and yet they know it happened.

Psychosexual Dysfunction

The basic reproductive procedures that occur during an abduction experience can fundamentally influence the psychosexual development of the individual. This is especially true for young abductees, who are most vulnerable and impressionable.

Consider this scenario. A young girl is taken on board a UFO occupied by strange-looking creatures. She is stripped naked and cannot physically resist. Every inch of her body is examined and touched. Her genitals are probed and manipulated. By the time she has reached sixteen years old, she might already have had a number of traumatic internal examinations that have been stored in her unconscious mind. As a boy, the events surrounding the taking of sperm can be just as traumatic and humiliating.

To complicate matters, while the aliens are performing their procedures, young boys and girls sometimes see naked adults being examined and probed on other tables. Children watch as the aliens perform procedures on sometimes-erect male genitals. They see naked women enduring internal gynecological procedures. Children see their parents being subjected to gynecological and urological examinations. These events can induce a profound sense of shame and guilt in children, both for having seen them and for thinking that perhaps they caused these events to occur to their family members. Furthermore, the children learn that adults have no control over the situation and their roles as protectors cannot be fulfilled. Adults are powerless. Only the aliens have power, and the children are wholly and totally dependent upon them. This can lead to a deep sense of distrust and suspicion in young people.

The problems are made incalculably worse by the bonding and sexual-arousal procedures performed on all abductees. When the alien performs bonding on a young child who is lying naked on a table, the rush of pleasurable emotions in her is irresistible. She is completely defenseless. This is even more injurious when the Taller Being ("male" or "female") elicits intense sexual arousal feelings, and even orgasm. Then, while bonding and/or sexual feelings are at a peak, the Being begins the gynecological or urological procedures and physically intrudes into her genitals or mechanically extracts his sperm.

These procedures can have devastating effects on the child's psychosexual development. The sexually bizarre nature of the event is retained deep within the unconscious mind. Abductees are forced to have sexual feelings while they are focused on a nonhuman creature in a strange setting, and then they are made to forget these feelings so that they are unable to come to terms with them. When the alien is finished with a young girl, he coldly turns around and walks out of the room while she is lying there with the residue of sexual feelings. In other less-frequent scenarios, the aliens might urge the teenage girl to "breed": They might conjure up mental pictures in her mind of humans having sexual intercourse, or they might flood her mind with clinical images of the physical details of intercourse to instruct her; they might bring in a man or boy to have intercourse with her for demonstration purposes. The psychological ramifications of all this can be profound—leading to guilt, shame, distrust, and other psychosexual development disturbances, as well as resulting sexual dysfunction.

These abduction events can influence sexual attraction and behavior. Some women abductees report that they prefer men who are small and dark, or they like powerful, dominant men who make love to them and then "just walk away." Sexual fantasies for women may include odd science fiction themes. Some men and women who are psychologically accustomed to frequent violation, pain mixed with "pleasure," and the inability to move on a table report fantasies involving masochism and bondage.

As a result of these procedures, some abductees lose interest in sexual relations completely. They might go for years without a sexual relationship. Any sexual contact is unconsciously viewed as another assault; therefore it is to be avoided. In one extreme case, an abductee's avoidance behavior was so profound that not only was it impossible for her to have normal sexual function, but she was unable even to talk about her reproductive organs, refusing to admit that she knew their clinical names.

For men, impotence and difficulties with ejaculation are common. Some become obsessed with control. They try to control every aspect of their bodies, including ejaculation. Some men masturbate excessively, unconsciously trying to keep the aliens from having their sperm. Others have a feeling of shame and guilt when they are sexually active, unknowingly rekindling feelings that they may have had during the abduction experience.

The problems engendered by PAS lead both men and women to question their own mental stability. They are often extremely introspective, having continually ruminated about their odd behavior—both sexual and otherwise—for most of their lives. These problems can be so severe that thoughts of, and even attempts at, suicide are not rare for adults and even young children.

SEARCHING FOR ANSWERS

Many abductees engage in a lifelong search for answers to questions they cannot fully formulate. For some, the New Age movement (wherein spiritual and humanistic values are achieved through alternative pathways to conventional learning) provides an answer. In some way they know they are in contact with a "higher" or "cosmic" consciousness. They feel sure that they can communicate with other people by mental telepathy. They know that they have been in touch with another realm of existence.

Some unaware abductees become attracted to channeling and might even become channelers themselves. The personal, benevolent, channeled messages they receive from "alien spirits" give them a secure feeling that the ill-defined events they have been undergoing are benign, and they feel enriched and emotionally rewarded by the messages.

It is not unusual for a person to seek answers to the disturbing qualities of their lives through organized religion—usually evangelical Christian groups. When the abductee tells the minister that strange things have been happening to him, the minister frequently invokes "demons" or demonic possession. It is the devil's work. Prayer and faith will vanquish the demons and allow the victim to lead a life free from harassment. For some abductees this explanation and prescription are satisfying because they give meaning to the experiences and dictate a course of action to control them. But for many others the demonic analysis does not quite ring true. When prayer fails, they look elsewhere for answers.

It must be emphasized that unaware abductees are trying to deal with the phenomenon as best they can. The internal pressure to discover the origin of their experiences can be tremendous. In New Age and psychic societies they find kinship with others who claim to have had the same type of experiences. They discover meaning in their half-memories that satisfies the "cosmic" implications for which they were searching. In religion they find solace and seek to master the events through faith and prayer. Often their quest is primarily to reinforce their hope that they are not mentally ill. They anxiously want to prove to themselves that their feelings and bleed-through memories are "legitimate," and that they are not just fantasizing. They desperately want to exert intellectual and emotional control over fundamentally uncontrollable events in their lives.

Rather than joining New Age groups or religious sects, many abductees turn to mental health professionals for help. They know that there must be something "wrong." A few abductees have even checked themselves into hospitals because they think that mental problems are causing them to imagine the bizarre events in their lives. Others seek conventional psychological or psychiatric help.

The vast majority of professional therapists are not trained to help abductees. "Standard" therapy not grounded in the knowledge of what actually happened to the abductee rarely dissipates anxieties, and the problems continue unabated. Well-meaning therapists try to convince abductees that their problems stem from familial relationships in childhood, or that their vivid dreams originate in repressed sexuality or in childhood sexual abuse. When the abductee says that her problems might have something to do with seeing a strange object in the sky, a "monster" in her bedroom, or an unexplainable lapse in time, the psychologist or psychiatrist tries to convince her that these are just fantasies and the problems are psychological. Some less conventional therapists who have attempted to deal with the residual effects of the problems regardless of their cause have had the best success. A few have referred abductees to competent abduction researchers.

Hypnotic regression—and special counseling by an individual familiar with hypnosis, psychological techniques, and the abduction phenomenon—affords the best opportunity for the abductee to come to terms successfully with the predicament that she finds herself in. Few people are trained for this work.

Recognition that a PAS symptom is related to UFOs often starts with a memory that suddenly wells up. Casual reading about abductions might trigger a memory. Glancing at a book with a representation of an alien in it might cause the terror and anxiety of forgotten incidents to come rushing back. The same anxiety might be triggered by viewing a television show on abductions or even just engaging in idle conversation about the topic with a friend. Or one day an abductee simply remembers a piece of an incident with no obvious activating mechanism.

For some abductees, knowledge of the abductions finally gives them the answers they were seeking, and they let go of previously held belief structures that were never fully satisfactory. But, for many others, awareness of their involvement in the abduction phenomenon brings about a new set of problems.

The first problem is emotional isolation. Although the abductee desperately wants to discuss the phenomenon with friends and relatives, she finds it very difficult to tell anyone about her experiences. The person that the abductee confides in may think she is "having a breakdown" or is mentally unstable. She may be ridiculed outright. It is not uncommon for an abductee's spouse (particularly a husband) to disbelieve her. The same is true for parents of children-abductees; these parents tend to think that it is a phase the child will outgrow. (Yet most abductees manage to find at least one friend or relative to believe them or to take them seriously.) If an abductee is not married, then she wonders if she can ever get married. Will she put her spouse in danger? Can she lead a normal married life? Does she have a responsibility to her future spouse to warn him of the danger?

Knowledge can also bring a new round of nighttime fears. The abductee becomes extremely anxious when she goes to bed. Any unusual sound in her house or apartment sends her into extreme fear. Driving at night can be frightening, especially in isolated areas. She is constantly aware that an abduction can take place at any time.

Abductee parents are concerned for the safety of their children. They fear that they can do nothing to protect them. They may even have seen their children during an abduction, and they suffer intense guilt feelings because they were powerless to help them.

For some abductees, the idea of being taken against one's will by nonhumans and undergoing a variety of physical and mental procedures is overwhelming. They prefer to think of their experiences as fantasies or dreams. They want the phenomenon to be benevolent and insist, against all evidence, that it is. This is why many abductees, after discovering what is happening to them, continue to embrace channeling. The thought that they might be victims of abductions rather than "chosen people" who are looked after by Space Brothers is difficult to cope with. They willingly retreat into the comfortable scenario of channeled information from kindly and benevolent aliens, in which, instead of being victims, they are cooperative participants who have some measure of control over their destinies. Other abductees face the facts squarely. They know what has happened, and after wrestling with the fear and the terror and coming to terms with their predicament, they want to get on with their lives.

It must be emphasized, finally, that PAS does not occur in all abductees. In fact, most people find a way to cope with these incredible experiences. Whether they know what has happened to them or not, they find a way to lead normal lives with only minor repercussions from the events that have occurred to them. The fact that a person has had abduction experiences does not automatically mean that she is suffering from the most psychologically destructive aspects of them.

No matter how they handle the experience, all abductees have one thing in common: They are victims. Just as surely as women who are raped are victims of sexual abuse or soldiers can be victims of Post-Traumatic Stress Disorder, abductees are victims who require sensitivity and, if needed, help in understanding what has happened to them and the possible consequences that abductions have had for their lives.

Chapter 10

The Struggle for Control

Abductees desperately want the abduction experience to stop. They have tried by pleading with the aliens, threatening them, and being willfully uncooperative. They have moved to another house, to another city, to another state, trying to get away from them. They sleep with a knife or a gun. They stay up all night—fearfully waiting, hoping that they can defend themselves. But the abductions continue.

Even biology has no effect. Physiological changes in a woman's reproductive cycle do not prevent abductions. Women who have had tubal ligations and hysterectomies and who have had their ovaries removed continue to be the victims of abductions, although they are spared the typical gynecological procedures. We have not had enough experience with men who have a low sperm count or who have had vasectomies to know whether these conditions forestall abductions.

PREVENTION AND INTERVENTION

Little headway has been made in preventing abductions, although we have had some success with the use of a video camera. The camera makes it impossible for the aliens to maintain secrecy during an abduction, and in some cases it is able to effectively forestall the experience. For example, Melissa Bucknell began to have abduction experiences almost on a daily basis. We decided to use a video camera to try to "catch" the aliens in the act. We set up a camera and a VCR on a dresser top pointed at her bed. Melissa had been abducted the night before we set up the equipment. But after we installed it, days went by with no activity. We viewed all the tapes and she was sleeping at all times. Then one day she reported that she thought "something might have happened" to her that morning. She had gone to sleep very late the night before and had slept until noon. The tape had run out at 6:00 A.M. Investigation revealed that the abduction took place sometime between 6:00 and 12:00. I thought this was a near miss and the taping continued. Weeks later she had another abduction episode. This time she had slept on the living room couch to get away from the noise of her neighbors arguing upstairs—once again it was impossible for the camera to record the abduction.

A few months later Karen Morgan agreed to use a video camera and a similar pattern began to emerge. As long as the camera was trained on her, no abductions took place. But when Karen was away from the camera her problems began. When she went out of town to visit friends or relatives, she would be abducted. When she went to Michigan for a wedding and to Virginia to spend a night on a friend's yacht and to New York to visit relatives, she had abduction experiences. When she "forgot" to set up the camera or VCR for the night, there was a good possibility that she would be abducted.

More abductees wanted to use the camera, and, as we gained experience with it, we began to notice that the video equipment would sometimes mysteriously malfunction or be turned off—and an abduction would follow. Unusual power outages that affected only the immediate surroundings (sometimes not even other rooms) would cause the VCR to go off and an abduction would take place. After one abduction Karen noticed that the camera wires had been pulled from the back of her VCR. Another time she noticed in the morning after an abduction that the video camera was off when she had specifically remembered turning it on and seeing the red light indicating that it was in the "record" mode.

The problem that the camera was generating for the abduction was overcome in other ways as well. For example, an abductee felt the urge at 5:30 A.M. (her camera put a time stamp on the tape) to get out of bed, walk over to the VCR, and turn it off—all of which was duly recorded on tape. She later remembered seeing Small Beings who were standing just outside of camera range directing her to do it. In another case, a young woman abductee felt very nervous one night and had the irresistible urge to get out of bed (and out of the camera's field of view) and sleep in her parents' room. As soon as she was away from the camera, she was abducted. One woman had the urge to go to bed three hours before she normally did. An abduction took place before the VCR was programmed to go on.

Six people have used a video camera and all have had similar experiences. The video camera does not stop abductions from happening; it only forestalls them. Nevertheless, the video camera is the only mechanism known that brings relief to the abductee at night. It helps to alleviate feelings of helplessness and gives the abductee a sense of fighting back and a slight measure of control over her life. It is a form of intervention that forces the Beings to contend with a detection device—something that they do not want to do.

A video camera has its drawbacks, however. It quickly becomes a crutch, and abductees feel that they cannot sleep without it. If they go on a trip and do not have the video camera with them, they can become beset by fears that an abduction will occur. Furthermore, sleeping for long periods of time under a video camera is something that no one looks forward to.

There are other methods of intervention that can be employed during the abduction itself. These appear to be able to affect the course of the procedure, and to switch control of the situation, if only for a moment, to the abductee. For example, several abductees have planned in advance to ask the aliens a question. It does not matter what the question is; the act of asking is most important. During the actual episode, the question is often extremely difficult to remember because of the changes in the abductees' consciousness, but some abductees have managed to do it. The aliens' answers have been vague and singularly lacking in information, but the important thing is that they seem to be caught off guard. This has given the abductee a sense of control, no matter how small. For a few minutes the abductee calls the shots and might even slightly change the course of the abduction.

During one abduction Karen Morgan was able to ask her question as the Taller Being was beginning Mindscan. As usual, the situation is more revealing for the way in which the alien dealt with the question than for the information imparted to Karen.

And then I ask it the question, "How long have you been doing this?" And it says, "That knowledge isn't given to you." And I say, "Jesus Christ, will you answer a question for the love of God? How long have you been doing this, and stop with those stupid answers." I'm so pissed off at it. And it sort of just smiles and doesn't answer. And I say, "Have you been doing this forever?" I don't think it understands forever. And then I ask what it's doing. "What are you doing?" It wants me to give it my mind, and then it will show me what it's doing. I say, "No dice, I don't care that much. No thanks, I'm not that interested." It says, "Why are you afraid? Why are you worried? Don't be afraid." All the same bullshit that it always wants to give you.

(Karen Morgan, 38, 1987)

Ken Rogers had intended to ask a predetermined question in several abductions but found it was too difficult to remember. Based on the idea that the aliens appear to be attracted to anything unusual on a person's body, he decided to put dots on his chest with a washable marker. He hoped that the aliens would be drawn to the marks on his chest, and that their interest would in turn prompt his memory, and he would ask the question. The question he was to ask was similar to Karen's: "How long are you going to continue to do this?" Nothing happened for a period of weeks. Then he was abducted. As predicted, the aliens immediately focused their attention on the dots. After the examination, they sat him up on the edge of the table and, while the Small Beings watched, the Taller Being pointed to the dots and asked him what the marks were. Instead of asking the question, however, Ken became a little bit frightened and simply stated, "They are dots." The aliens tapped his chest and looked a little more. When he was leaving, several more Taller Beings approached and he had to lift up his shirt while they carefully surveyed the dots.

Determined to gain enough control to ask the question, Ken decided to try again with a new query, "Do you sleep?" Once again he had an abduction experience, and once again the aliens were drawn to the marks on his chest. This time he asked the question. The answer was evasive. "We are always sleeping." After this event, however, Ken was led into a special room off to the side of a large examining room where several Taller Beings carefully examined his chest and performed Mindscan procedures on him. Ken was convinced that the mental activity was related to the marks.

Other abductees have attached various objects to their bodies in the hope of causing the aliens to depart from their routine and contend with the new object. One abductee wrapped a piece of masking tape around her arm and went to bed. That night she woke up and had the strong urge to take the tape off, which she did. An abduction event followed. At another time she wore a special bracelet that a friend had made for her that had battery-powered flashing lights on it. When the abduction event began, she could see the aliens carefully detaching the bracelet from her arm before they took her. Later she had an extremely "penetrating" Mindscan that she felt was directly related to finding out what the bracelet was for.

Will Parker decided to write a letter to the aliens telling them, in essence, to leave him alone. He folded the letter up; on the outside he drew a picture of a smiling alien's head and wrote, "Have a nice day." He taped the letter to his lower leg on and off for several months, but he had no abduction events. Then one day he woke up and the letter was gone from his leg. He frantically searched the room and his apartment for more than two hours for the missing letter but could not find it. Two days later, he awoke and was stunned to find that the letter was taped to his leg again in exactly the same place as before.

We conducted a regression session about these two episodes. The first abduction event was odd. Instead of the characteristic sense of rising up out of bed, Will distinctly felt as if he was sinking down. He found himself lying on a table, with a Taller Being looking into his eyes, but this Taller Being did not have the sense of familiarity to him that was usual. He could see two others doing something to his legs. Suddenly one of the Beings abruptly and painfully pulled the letter off his leg. Another Taller Being put the letter right up to his face and stared at the picture of the smiling alien as if he were doing Mindscan on it. The aliens said nothing and asked him nothing about it, but, according to Will, the Mindscan procedure was particularly "deep."

The second abduction was with the familiar aliens, ones with whom Will had been involved for some time. In this episode, the Taller Being communicated something to the effect that a mistake had been made and that "everything was going to be put right, the way it was before." Then when Will woke up he was dumbfounded to find the letter taped to his leg again. The letter appeared not to have been opened and the seal was intact.

Some adventurous people have used more direct methods of intervention. Risking the possibility of injury, Janet Demerest tied herself to the lamp one night; the only thing that happened was that she succeeded in turning around in her sleep and knocking the lamp off the table and breaking it. Ken Rogers tied his ankle loosely with a bathrobe cord to his bedpost, and although we are not sure if any abduction occurred, he received the distinct impression that for a while the aliens were annoyed at what he had done and then simply slipped the cord off his ankle and continued with the abduction.

Resistance

Resistance to the aliens' procedures occurs infrequently because most abductees are so closely controlled, both physically and mentally, but when it does happen it offers us an unusual opportunity to observe the aliens when all is not going according to plan. The most common type of resistance is simply to try to get away. Although all abductees sometimes think that they should run, few have the opportunity to do so. Nevertheless, once in a while an abductee bolts. Generally, the Small Beings run after the abductee and retrieve her. Evelyn Livingston was being taken on board the UFO when she managed to run down a hall a little way before she was stopped.

I get up, and I look, and I start to try to run, I think. Down there's a hall or something, there's a passageway, and I start to run away. I'm trying to get away, and I thought I'd see something they wouldn't want me to see, and then I'd be able to do something. They would take me out, they would let me get out if I did something that I wasn't supposed to do. I could get away. So I was running.

So you have enough muscle control to do that?

Yes. I get a little way.

Is this off to your right, or ...?

It's like on the right.

Is this a passageway . . . ?

Kind of something like that.

This is directly off the room, then, or the area that you kind of came in on your knees?

It's right in the middle of that part. And it was like we were in a passage.

How far do you get?

I don't get that far. I get a little ways. . . . I'm trying to run, and I can't. . . . Then I'm up against the wall, because I can't move. I'm pressing against something. They say, "Don't be afraid." And then . . .

Do they run after you?

Just the one is walking toward me, but he doesn't even look at me; he says, "Don't be afraid," but there's not any expression on his face. He just is walking toward me. . . .

How many steps did you get, do you think?

Maybe twelve, fifteen.

So you got quite a ways, actually.

I got a little ways down the hall. It felt really good to get away. . . .

What happens next?

He's walking beside me, in front of me a little bit, and I try the other thing, to go backward, instead of running forward to resist it backward, but it's even harder to do that. And I push, kind of kick backward. And kicking against it, I can't do that either. Just with my right foot, I tried to kick.

Kick the . . . ?

Kick the force, or whatever it is. It's like I'm on a . . . moving along, and I can't even control it.

(Evelyn Livingston, 19, 1980)

Patti Layne was in the process of being examined when she discovered that she could resist physically more than usual. She used the opportunity to jump off the table and run. Before the regression she had wondered about where she had gotten several "burn" marks on her back and arm.

It seems to me that at some point I got a second wind, then I got up, and I don't think they wanted me to do that.

While they're doing the examination?

Mm-hmm, like it took every ounce of will that I had. I got up off the table. I just kind of pushed past them. They're not physically strong, but there's some other kind of control they have to use, and I think I was really fighting it.

What was he doing when you got up?

I think he was preparing to look up inside of me, but I think I decided I had had just about enough of it.

Do you see yourself actually getting up off the table?

Mm-hmm. I had to push past a couple of little ones.

Do you swing your legs around and stand up?

Mm-hmm. It was kind of wobbly, but I just had to put forth all of my energy and my will to move.

You pushed past them, then?

Mm-hmm.

Are they heavy?

No, they're very light. If you punched one you could probably send it flying.

When you push past them, do they fall off balance, or do they just move aside?

They don't really attack you that much. They just kind of backed off a little. They tried to stand in my way, then they backed off.

. . . So how far do you go?

Not very far, I start walking across the room. I think I walked out the door and into another area.

Alone?

Well, they were close on my heels, but I was trying to move fast.

You were calling the shots, though?

Pretty much. And I was in another area, another control kind of area where they had the window and the machinery. And there was something in the middle of the room. It was like a big round thing sticking up that was luminous, it was lit up. And there was a little bar that went around it, but I found myself being cornered into it. A couple of ones had left their areas in this room, and they started cornering me, like you corner a cat or a rabbit. . . . But I got my back against it. . . . And I just got my shoulders pinned up against it.

You say it had a rail around it.

Yeah, but that wasn't far away from it, and that pressed into the small of my back, kind of like it was drawing me toward it, pulling me back. Maybe it's magnetic or something, but I guess there wasn't any metal on me. But I pulled away from it, I felt like it shocked me or burnt me or something. I kept inching around the rail, but they kept moving in. . . . I kept inching around and around this rail because they were coming at me initially from one side, but then they just surrounded the thing. They came up, and somehow I felt like something just came over me and I was sitting down on the ground by it. I wasn't touching it, but my head was where the rail was. And there was one of them doing something to my head again.

How do you mean?

I don't know, I felt like he was sticking something into my head, like up in here.

And he was touching your head with something?

Yes, he was poking something into it. It didn't really hurt. It wasn't like somebody was trying to drill something into your head, but you could feel something sticking in and the initial sting.

This is over up above your ear, or . . . ?

Up in here [she points to a spot above her left ear]. Come to think of it, I had a bump up here too that I didn't know where I got it. It was sore for a couple of days.

How does that make you feel, or does it at all?

It felt like there was a flash of light in my head, but then I started to feel kind of soothed and tingling all over, like I had just been drugged. I couldn't really tighten any of my muscles. . . . Then they put their hands over me and I just started floating again. They floated me up, and back into the examining room. I couldn't move really, I felt like Jell-O. . . .

What happens next?

I couldn't move then, and they were busy putting my feet up in stirrups, little raised areas. And he [the Taller Being] starting doing a very intense pelvic procedure.

(Patti Layne, 26, 1988)

Similarly, Will, during an abduction with his wife, also found himself with more muscle control than usual. He was able to run down a hallway with his wife in tow.

I just grabbed Nancy, turned, and went out the door.

Does Nancy say anything to you?

No, she's not saying anything to me. She's not talking to me. But I say, "Come on," and I'm pulling her and she's going with me. . . . I turn to my right, I pull her behind me, and we go out the door opening. . . . There's a wall on the right, and then that wall bends back and we're in the big room now. But I keep bending right, like I'm going along the wall there. And there's another opening, we go in there. That's where it's like another room like the first one but there's no bed in it, no counter. . . .

Are you holding on to Nancy?

I've got her by the wrist.

She's cooperating?

Yes, she's coming with me. I mean, if I pull, she comes. But she's still not saying anything, it's like she's in a trance still. . . . I keep having the sense that all of this is staged. It's like they want me to think I'm getting away. Like it's, it's like I'm thinking I want to get out of here, and so they're going to let me think that I can get loose.

Okay.

I don't know why I'm thinking that, because I keep thinking I'm going to get into this damned room. I don't even know how the hell to get out of here. They're going to get me anyway, but it's like you've got to do something. I've got to get the hell out of here. . . .

You go through the big room into . . .

Well, I go along the edge of the big room, alongside the wall, and I go into the first door I find.

What's in that room?

Nothing. It's like the room that they had the bed counter in, but there's no bed in it. It's just empty. But there's the same rectangles on the wall and everything. It's the same thing except for no bed in it.

Is there anybody in this room?

No, I don't see anybody. But there's an opening there. I keep thinking it's like a cellar, it's all dark inside. It's real dark. I remember turning to Nancy and saying, "That's not a very good idea. I don't think we can get out of there."

Does Nancy respond?

No, she doesn't. She's not saying anything. . . .

Do you walk into the room, or do you just look into the room?

I ran into the room.

[Will said he had the sense that aliens were following them. Then two Taller Beings caught up with them in this room and immediately began to exercise control over Will.]

Yeah, there are two tall ones, just two tall ones, that's all.

Okay. Do they come over to you?

Yeah. They, it's like I feel myself getting limp, like I'm losing mobility. It feels like, it just feels shitty. I'm losing the ability to move out of there. I have the sense that they're not amused.

Do they communicate with you?

I have the sense that they were telling me that I could have caused serious problems if I had gone the wrong way. I'm thinking, "What do you mean? This is serious enough." But they're saying it was very serious if I had not stopped.

Okay.

They said, "Highly serious." They said, "You would be no more if you had not stopped." And they are not happy at all. They are definitely not very happy about it.

What happens next?

They're up in each of our faces, both of them. And I can't fight it. They might as well do what they're going to do. . . .

Do you get a sense of what happens next? Do you just sort of stay there near the edge of this big room?

I don't really remember that. I just remember kind of drifting off. They told me, "You're going to sleep." It's like they put emphasis on "You're going to sleep. You're going." I'm thinking, "Yeah, but where?" They said, "To sleep." Now I feel real drained. I feel like I'm a battery that's been completely discharged, extremely weak. I feel like I'm shutting down.

(Will Parker, 33, 1988)

Another common form of resistance is for the abductee to try to get up from the table when she is lying on it. Barbara Archer tried it, and the aliens handled it by calling over the Taller Being.

I sat up. I don't want to be there anymore. They kind of looked upset when I did that.

When you sat up?

Yes. And the other one came in.

How do you know they were upset?

Well, they sort of rushed over, and then in a few minutes I guess they told the other one or something, because he was there. I just have this feeling like I wasn't supposed to sit up.

Do you continue to sit up, though?

I sat up until the other one came in. . . . The other one came in, and I felt a little bit better. He came over. He touched me.

Where does he touch you?

Well, at first he touched my hand, but then he moved his hand to my head.

Are you still sitting up, then?

Well, when he came over and touched my hand, I lay back down again.

(Barbara Archer, 22, 1988)

One of the most bizarre episodes of resistance during an abduction occurred when Jason Howard was drunk. He had gone to bed having had too much to drink, and then was abducted. The aliens were performing procedures on him when he simply decided to get up off the table. They tried to calm him down and asked him questions such as "How do you feel," but he would have none of it. He laughed, swung his arms around wildly in mock karate chops, and managed to stand in the middle of the room. The Small Beings immediately backed up against the wall. The Taller Being tried to reason with him, but to no avail. Then the Taller Being came up to him, stared in his eyes, and the next thing he knew he was standing in his underpants on the grass of his college campus about a mile from where he had been abducted.

Jason's experience was typical of how the Beings act when the abductee gets out of control: The Small Beings immediately back off and allow the Taller Beings to deal with the situation; they do not try to intervene, nor do they try countermeasures; it is up to the Taller Being to remedy the situation.

Unquestionably the greatest opportunity for resistance comes when the Beings force the abductee to hold a baby. Many women and men want nothing to do with the baby. The baby looks strange, and they may be reacting negatively to the suggestion that it is their baby. In any case, many women simply refuse to hold the baby. When Lynn refused, they put the baby in her arms; one Being pushed the baby toward her chest, while another Being stood behind her with his arms in her back preventing her from backing up.

Melissa wanted nothing to do with the baby, but this time the Beings did nothing.

It's a baby. Little baby. It's ugly. . . . It's not mine.

Is it a little baby or a big baby?

I don't want this thing. I don't want anything to do with this species.

Is this baby a human baby?

Gross baby.

Does it have normal eyes?

No. It's . . . an ugly one like the little creatures. I don't want anything to do with this species, nothing at all. I'll kill it. I swear to God I'll kill it if you bring it near me. I hate you. I hate it. I hate this. It's so fucking unnatural. Fucking stupid. Disgusting thing. I'll kill it if you bring it near me, I swear. Move it away.

They just stand there with it. I'm not looking at it. I'm not going to look at it. I hate it. . . .

Do they take it away?

They try to put it in my arms. I push it away. I'm getting really pissed off. If they keep doing this I swear I'll smash it. I hate it already. I get really angry. I hate you when you do this. Don't you ever listen to me? Don't you ever listen to me? Don't you ever listen to what I'm saying to you?

Do they respond?

No.

(Melissa Bucknell, 27, 1987)

Karen Morgan has been perhaps the most resistant to the aliens. She rarely misses an opportunity to exert her own individuality by refusing to do what they want. She has, at various times, walked too slowly down the hall, with the Small Beings frantically urging her to move faster while they pushed and pulled her. Once when two small aliens walked her down the hallway, she stopped suddenly and the alien behind her bumped into her. She dropped to the ground, forcing them to carry her to the table. In one remarkable event, as two small aliens were leading her into a large examining room, she hooked her left arm into a panel on the doorway, and she could not be easily dislodged.

I came in from the little anteroom, maybe it's a big anteroom, but there's a room where they undress you. . . . I'm really putting up as much of a fight as you can under the circumstances, and I'm refusing to do anything at all because I have more muscle tone than I usually do. . . . I remember coming in through a door and grabbing onto the panel, and they can't get me away from it. And I've got my arms sort of locked around the panel. I just want to see how far I can push them.

What do you mean by panel?

There's a panel, a door, except I don't see the door, and I think they open it somehow, but I don't see that part either. It's just not like a normal door. And you walk into this big examination room from this area, and usually they lead you right through the middle of it, but this time there's one on my side, leading me, and [one is pulling me by my arm].

One is leading you, and one is pulling your arm?

Right, and the one who's on my side has my arm like this, and there's one sort of in front of me. . . . The one gets ahead of me. . . . I have enough muscle tone to pull my arm away from him and lock my arm like this into the panel. So I put my arm like that and it's surprised. It sort of turns around like, "What just happened?" And so I have my arm like that, and I sort of look at it [the Being]. And the other one is pulling my other arm, but I won't let go and I'm stronger than they are. They must be very weak. . . . I've got my arm hooked in such a way that I've got more leverage than they do, and so there's creatures in the room. . . .

Do they say anything to you?

They're impatient. They say, "Come on! Come on!" sort of. I'm not really sure those are the words. And I say, "No, I'm not going anywhere." Then there's these other Beings in the room that are doing the . . . examinations, and they sort of look up like, "What is going on?" And I just look at them and smile. And they look at the two little ones and say, "What's happening here?" And now it's not so funny anymore because it looks like the little ones are getting scared, and I wonder what they're going to do if they're scared. But then I say, "So what? Who cares? Let's find out." I just won't let go of the door. So they come back to me, and one is still pulling on my arm, and the other comes around behind me and pulls my arm like that, which explains, I think, why I have such a sore shoulder for a couple of days after. He pulls my arm away like that. But they got scared for a minute, they got frightened. I think they thought that they really messed up. And then they bring me into the room, and there's two other creatures, the ones that have the big eyes, and they're sort of looking at each other like, "What was this disturbance?" And then they put me up on the table, and they tie me down real fast.

You mean, your whole body or your arms . . . ?

My arms and my legs, real fast. They do everything so fast that I can't respond. . . . Ever since the door thing it was like . . . right into the table. And they tie me down, and I don't know how I know this but I think they drug me more. . . . I'm getting woozier and woozier, and I think they drugged me. I think that they just hadn't given me enough. That's why I was able to do that. Maybe not, but most of the time you don't get to do those kinds of things because you don't have that kind of muscle tone. . . .

So they get you down on the table, and you feel yourself getting a little bit woozy. Do they then begin the examination, or do they wait a while?

I lie there for a while, then the creature comes over and he puts his hand on my chest, and he says through my mind, "Well, that was quite a little scene," or something like that. But . . . he says it in such a condescending voice, like he's talking to a three-year-old. And I say, "I'd like to kill you guys, every one of you." He says, "I know, you don't like us," or something like that, "but just relax, but just relax." And I say, "I don't want to relax. I don't want to be relaxed when I'm here." And he says, "It's much easier if you relax, it's much easier." And I say, "It's much easier for you, but it's not easier for me." And he says, "Now, now, you know there's nothing to be afraid of." And I say, "There's a lot to be afraid of, and you had better stop doing this to me." And he says, "Don't resist, there's no point in resisting." And I say, "Yes there is, there's every point in resisting. I don't believe you, I don't trust you, I know that nothing you say is true." And then I say something I've forgotten. All those years I've forgotten about it. And I say, "You're a shapeshifter." And he looks puzzled. And I say, "You're a shapeshifter. You can take any shape that you want, and you can make us think you're anything that we want to believe that you are, but I know what you are." And then he sort of shrugs and takes his hand away. He's indifferent really. But when I said he was a shapeshifter he looked puzzled, and then when I sort of explained what it was, there was just sort of a flash of recognition. . . . For all these years in literature people have been writing about the shapeshifters. Maybe that's where they got it from. And somehow I feel better knowing what he is. Being able to put a name on it. And now I think he puts his hand on my head, they're always doing this. And he looks into my eyes, and because they drugged me they think they can do this now, and he tries to suck me, pull me into his eyes. And he says, "Look at me, look at me." And I say, "No, you can't give me enough drugs to make me go along with this, you'll have to kill me." And he says, "We don't want to hurt you. This can feel very good, this can feel good." And I say, "No it won't because I won't let it happen. It won't work with me." And then I say, because they always say to me, "Why do you resist," I say, "Why do you keep doing this? You know it's not going to work," in the same way that he always does it to me. And then he looks at me like he's wondering something, and somewhere in the back of my mind I think, "Maybe I really have him thinking for once," and then I think, "No, they're not capable of that." But that's good because now I'm really not in any danger of having him be able to pull me into his mind. But he keeps his hand on my forehead and the pressure gets more and more intense. Starts to hurt.

(Karen Morgan, 38, 1987)

Karen has consistently balked at holding a baby. She invariably does hold it, but not without a mental struggle. Her thoughts and actions have pushed the aliens further than most. In one episode, the Beings took her into an incubatorium and then wanted her to hold a baby.

And that's when we go to that place with the bench. And she's fighting with me about taking this baby. I say, "I don't want the baby." And sometime during the discussion, which really isn't a discussion because she's going to win, but sometime during this she's trying to make an illusion, she's trying to create an illusion in my mind. She's trying to make me feel something that I'm not going to feel. And I say, "No, sorry. But we're not all alike, and you're not going to get to me through a baby because I don't care." And I'm so angry, and I hate them so much, that I think for a minute that I'll take the baby and I'll throw it down on the floor. And then what are they going to do to me? But she knows I'm thinking that. You can't think anything because they know it.

Does she do something now?

Mm-hmm. She says, "You won't hurt the baby. You won't do that." And I wouldn't. She's right, I wouldn't. But I never feel anything for it.

(Karen Morgan, 30, 1979)

Karen has continually upset the aliens by her constant refusal to hold the babies. They become exasperated. But no matter how irritated they become, their exasperation does not escalate into more than that. Abductees do not report aliens using violence or threats of violence to get their way, and they usually get their way. On one occasion when Karen refused to hold the baby, they forced her hand onto the baby's lower abdomen.

And she says, "All right now, touch, rub the baby. Touch the baby." And I say, "Oh, come on, will you? This is ridiculous." And she picks up my hand and she puts it on the baby's skin. Ugh! It's creepy.

Does it feel like skin?

Ugh! No! Ugh! I can't stand to touch it. I pull my hand away. I probably don't move it that fast because I'm drugged, but ugh! It was on my lap but I don't remember feeling it that way . . . ugh.

How did it feel?

Soft. I mean, it has no tone.

It wasn't firm like a baby's tone is firm?

No. No. They're so thin, their skin is like paper. I don't like it. She says, "Oh, you mustn't do that," or something like that, some stupid thing. "Oh, no, no, no, no," and she puts my hand back and I don't like the way the baby feels at all.

Does the baby respond at all when you touch it?

A little bit. It does. It sort of, I can feel it respond. I can feel it respond. . . . I don't really like what they're doing to me. I don't care about this baby. I don't like what they're doing to me. They're putting my hand on it. She's putting my hand on it. She's forcing me to touch it. Their hands are very strong when they want them to be. . . . And this one holds my hand down and I can't move my hand. . . . I'm really mad now. I'm really pissed off because she won't let go of my hand. And I say, "Let go. How dare you touch my hand?" And she says, "You have to touch the baby." She's very stern. "The baby needs you, you have to touch it." I say, "No I don't. You can make me touch it, but I don't have to touch it." She says, "You've got to touch the baby." And then I say, "If you keep pressing like that you're going to kill the baby." And she says, "It won't hurt the baby." And I think, "These people, things, don't know what they're doing. She's got my hand pressed into the kid's stomach." But maybe they do, I don't know. And I say, "Fine, go ahead. Keep pressing it." But you know what, maybe she really does know what she's doing. If you pressed a human baby this hard it would scream. It would scream. But what she's doing is, I've got it now. I've figured it out. She's pressing my hand into its stomach . . . because they wanted to get energy from us. So she's pressing my hand really hard into its stomach. Real low on its stomach, almost by its genitals. She's pressing my hand there really hard so that it will get energy. . . . But at the time I thought, "Boy, she's sure pressing hard. A human kid would cry." And I'm really mad that she's pressing that hard. Then she takes her hand away and she says, "There, there. The baby needs you."

(Karen Morgan, 38, 1987)

In all, the abductees' ability to resist during the abduction episode is limited. The aliens meet resistance with either patience or exasperation. Because they can physically and mentally control humans, they treat resistance as a nuisance. If the abductee gets out of control, the Small Beings usually back off and let the Taller Being deal with the situation, and the proper procedures for regaining control are instituted. Yet some abductees have learned the areas where defiance and self-assertion are possible. When they do resist or at least throw the aliens off their routine, they briefly enjoy a sense of control and mastery of the situation that allows them to feel they are fighting back and are therefore less victimized.

PART IV

THE
SEARCH
FOR
MEANING

Chapter 11

Answers

Suppose that all of the abduction accounts have their origin in the minds of the people relating the stories and not in objective reality. They must, therefore, be explainable in conventional terms. In fact, a great variety of explanations have been proposed, all of which attribute the abduction phenomenon to subjective rather than objective causes. An analysis of these conventional explanations for abductions—psychological, psychiatric, cultural, and exotic—might be helpful in evaluating whether or not any of them can truly solve the mystery.

PSYCHOLOGICAL EXPLANATIONS

Psychological explanations suggest that abductions are generated in people's minds for a variety of emotional reasons. These explanations do not come from people who suffer from organic brain problems or mental illness.

Fabrication

Fabrication is, of course, the first explanation that must be addressed. Debunkers have routinely said that people who claim to be abductees lead "humdrum lives," and their fabricated abduction stories generate publicity, excitement, and maybe even money. The contactees in the 1950s set the precedent for this theory, with their tall tales of ongoing contact with benevolent, cancer-curing, war-stopping Space Brothers.[1]

Contactees provide the model for what is not legitimate, but their claims serve as a convenient touchstone for deciding which abduction reports are probably bogus and which may not be. Major differences exist between the contactees and the abductees. Contactee claims were deeply rooted in the popular science fiction of the period, and their tales were bounded by their knowledge of science. However, abductee claims contain events that include exact and minute details of procedures known only to a few UFO researchers. It is virtually impossible that nearly all abductees would chance upon these details at random and lie en masse to make their claims seem valid. Whereas most major contactees knew and supported each other's claims, most abductees do not know each other, do not know much about UFOs, and are not familiar with abduction literature. Furthermore, while contactees talked of utopian worlds and compassionate Space Brothers, abductees describe aliens who use them as specimens. They feel violated and victimized. They fear the abduction phenomenon, they do not want it to happen again, and they wish that they could lead their lives free from it.

Contactees actively sought money and publicity, and devoted a tremendous amount of energy to getting both. Most abductees have sought neither. Rather, they are extremely concerned that their identities might be revealed and that they might lose their standing in the community and in their work. Only a few of the abductees that Budd Hopkins and I have worked with over the years have gone to the media to tell what has happened to them, and this was at our request and only after they engaged in considerable soul-searching. To the best of my knowledge, none has profited monetarily from these media appearances.

There have been instances in which a person has fabricated an abduction event. One woman who wanted to write an article about her experiences went to an abduction researcher for hypnosis. From the beginning, her story was unlike other abduction accounts. The aliens were tall monsters, all of the primary, secondary, and ancillary experiences were missing, and nothing else resembled known abduction reports. The investigator found her out very quickly. In another case, a person who was fabricating an account went to an abduction researcher who accepts *all* accounts as valid regardless of whether they are channeled information, dreams, abductions, and so forth. This well-meaning but unsystematic researcher simply accepted the woman's story as true even though it also did not match any of the known abduction events. Thus, lying can fool an inexperienced researcher, but not one who is familiar with the abduction experience that has been confirmed so many times over.

Repression of Abuse

One of the most popular explanations for abductions in recent years has been that the accounts are "screen" memories masking the repression of sexual and/or physical abuse. This theory postulates that the victims are so traumatized by abuse they suffered as children that they forced the incidents out of their conscious memory; now, years later, the painful memories have resurfaced in disguised form.

Therapists have seized upon this explanation more than any other to get at the root of the abduction memories for two reasons. First, memories of abuse will suddenly be triggered in adulthood in much the same way as abduction memories. Second, abuse victims suffer many of the symptoms found in Post-Abduction Syndrome.

But there are serious problems with this explanation. Most abductees do not claim to have been sexually or physically abused as children (at least not by humans). If indeed they have repressed the abuse from their conscious memory, one would assume that they might spontaneously remember it at some point during hypnosis. However, this does not appear to be the case. No abduction screen memories have ever been stripped away to reveal a past history of abuse.

Those abductees who have been victims of sexual and physical abuse clearly remember the instances of abuse and have either come to terms with them or are working with a therapist to that end. They explicitly differentiate between the abuse that they suffered and the abduction memories. They have no psychological need for screen memories to convert their abuse into fantasy situations.

Furthermore, because the abduction phenomenon is ongoing, the memories are of events that happened in the very recent past, not screen memories of childhood when the abuse would have taken place. I have talked with abductees who have experienced abductions from a few days to only a short while before our meetings. They do not remember what happened to them, but they know something occurred. For example, one woman abductee took a nap on her couch in the afternoon and "woke up" standing in her backyard. She groggily walked into the kitchen and called me about eight minutes later. Jason Howard was in the process of getting ready to come to my house for a support group meeting. He was putting on his shoes by the front door a few seconds prior to going out, when he had the irresistible urge to lie down on his couch and go to sleep. When he woke up two and a half hours later, he knew something had happened. His shoes were off and he was lying on his bed upstairs. Within three minutes he called to tell me about it. A subsequent hypnosis session confirmed his suspicions and he related a complex abduction.

Although I have purposely not conducted hypnosis with children —not enough is known about how their knowledge of being abducted would affect their personal development—from time to time worried parents will either tell me about what is happening to their children or bring them to talk to me. I find this to be the most heartrending and frustrating aspect of the abduction phenomenon. Although the parents usually do not discuss abductions in front of them, children as young as two years old will talk about "egg-men" coming in through their windows at night and taking them places. "Bad doctors" come into their rooms and "hurt" them. When given a series of drawings of popular children's storybook and television characters, the children readily point to a picture of an alien as the culprit.

Older children will sometimes consciously tell their alarmed parents about being abducted. The parents of one ten-year-old girl who had consciously described typical abduction events in detail took her to a gynecologist because she complained of pain. The physician found no evidence of sexual or physical abuse, nor did the child claim to have been abused. Although it is possible that parents would encourage their children to talk to a stranger about unusual events happening to them at night while in fact those parents were in the process of abusing them, it is highly improbable. To date, neither researchers nor therapists have found a single abduction case that is unequivocally generated from sexual or physical abuse.

Hysterical Contagion

Hysterical contagion, whereby people will believe that something has happened to them because they are aware that it has happened to others, is a real phenomenon that deserves discussion as a possible cause of abduction reports.[2] Although this phenomenon is rare, well-known incidences of it have appeared in the psychological literature.

For example, in 1954 residents of Seattle, Washington, reported that a mysterious force was pitting their automobile windshields. Investigators found no such force. People had become sensitized to the problem through publicity, and when they examined their windshields, they found the pits, which had remained unnoticed until the concerned citizen carefully looked for them.[3] In another example, in 1962 employees at a small clothing plant in Georgia reported being bitten by a mysterious "insect" that attacked their arms and faces, but no one could catch one of these bugs or even see them. Investigators found that no mysterious insects existed and that the employees were describing something that had no basis in objective reality.[4]

These classic examples of hysterical contagion contain several elements that must be considered in analyzing abduction cases and UFOs in general. In the Georgia incident, the workers were confined to one building where they could have daily mutual reinforcement about the reality of the "bugs." The workers, however, could neither describe nor catch any of the bugs. The only thing they perceived was the effect of the bugs. In a few days the hysteria had passed. It had been limited in time and space and relied heavily on the workers' mutual reinforcement within that space.

In the Seattle case, the "witnesses" actually saw nothing occur, but they had the pits as "evidence." Newspaper publicity suggested to them that the pits were caused by something extraordinary. When people found normal road-wear pits on their windshields, they assumed it was the mysterious force that had caused the damage and hence the phenomenon spread. In a few weeks the idea that the pits were being caused by a single force (e.g., radioactivity from recent H-bomb tests in the Pacific) was discredited, and the entire affair dissipated. Although much more widespread than the Georgia incident, the Seattle case was still limited geographically and involved media reinforcement of commonly held beliefs. Also the subjects had the pits as "proof." The phenomenon was short-lived with no recurrence.

Abduction claims do not fit the model of mass hysteria events. Although some claimants know each other, most do not. They are usually not in close proximity to one another; they do not engage in mutual reinforcement; prior to 1987 they were not subject to ongoing publicity about others with similar claims; and the phenomenon is not restricted in time or in geographic area. Furthermore, this is not collective behavior. Often the abductee claimant believes that he or she is the only person who has had an abduction experience. What we are dealing with is isolated individual behavior; only when taken together does it becomes collective.

Furthermore, the character of the abduction stories is quite different from that of hysterical contagion stories. The abduction claims sometimes involve more than one witness, and the narratives that are related are greatly detailed. They have a beginning, a middle, and an end. Recounting the episode often takes several hours. They do not involve only a single event, like the classic mass-hysteria cases. They contain a wealth of detailed information consistent with other abduction cases.

Unlike the people in hysterical contagion stories, abductees appear to have little in common. They usually do not know each other, and they often know little or nothing about abductions in general (although some may know about UFOs). While some abductees may have limited knowledge of the Barney and Betty Hill case, they also describe many common and critical parts of their experiences that are not in the Hill case. And some unpublicized parts of the Hill case routinely show up in the abduction accounts.

Finally, when first investigating their memories, the majority of abductees may suspect that something has happened to them, but most of the time they do not know what it is. This eliminates any overt conscious "hysteria" that they may be subject to. They are not reacting to events that they read about in the newspapers.

Prewaking and Presleeping States

Another psychological explanation involves hypnogogic and hypnopompic states—the periods between wakefulness and sleep, and between sleep and wakefulness during which the subject may feel paralyzed for a very short time. She might have vivid "dreams" in those moments that take on the shape of reality. Some people have great difficulty in telling the difference. Since many abductions take place when the victim is sleeping or about to sleep, hypnogogic and hypnopompic states are reasoned to be responsible.

But this explanation fails to account for those abductions that take place when the victim is awake, not tired, not in bed, and not even inside a room. A large percentage of abductions take place in broad daylight when the victim is pursuing normal activity or driving a car. Furthermore, hypnogogic and hypnopompic states have idiosyncratic, dreamlike content that does not match that of the abduction accounts.

The Will to Believe

Some critics say that the abduction phenomenon is a prime example of "the will to believe." In other words, people want to be abductees and therefore they allow themselves to believe that they are. This claim lumps abductees together with New Agers and occult practitioners who actively demonstrate the will to believe. But abductees differ in that they are unable to summon forth an experience at will. Furthermore, for the most part, their recollected stories are not dreamlike or surrealistic; they proceed in a consistent, step-wise fashion, and they are extremely disturbing to the abductee. Abductees universally wish the abduction had never happened, and they are often desperately frightened that it might happen again. For most, the trauma is so great that they refuse to confront it, fearful of bringing it into memory because of the terrifying feelings it might unleash. Some have even contemplated suicide as an escape from the buried horror's pressure. It seems absurd to suggest that the abductees would will themselves to believe in something so terrifying or destructive.

Channeling

Critics like to point to the popularity of channeling—wherein a subject goes into a trancelike state and contacts benevolent space alien spirits—and suggest that the abduction accounts are simply channeled variants that have the same point of origin: the mind. But channeled information is very different from abduction accounts. It is devoid of any physical aftereffects or other evidence. It is almost always personally directed toward the channeler, and the space spirits relay messages with much the same content as those given to the contactees. In short, these tales have virtually no points of congruence with the abduction information. For channelers, the spirits are benevolent, informative, advice-giving folks who have the best interests of the channelers and the human race at heart. They tell the channelers where they are from, how they got here, and what they are doing. Except in some broad areas, most of the channeled information is inconsistent with itself. Furthermore, channelers do not claim abduction events as the normal course of obtaining information.

Hallucinations

Some critics have suggested that people who claim to have been abducted are simply hallucinating, and that all humans have hallucinations at one time or another. Hallucinations are, according to Professor Ronald Siegel of the University of California at Los Angeles, "previously stored memories or fantasy images woven together or projected onto the mind's eye" that are "usually accompanied by simple geometric patterns."[5]

But the abduction phenomenon has no strong element of personal fantasy. There is nothing in our society or in people's backgrounds that would call forth such concepts as imaging, Mindscan, staging, and hybrid touching. Most abductees' lives contain nothing that would have such a strong effect upon them that they would hallucinate a full-scale, copiously detailed abduction event that they desperately do not want to have.

Abductions are profoundly alien. They contain few reference points upon which to hang personal content. Abductees do not know what is happening to them; they find nothing in the accounts that would allow them to lead better lives; and they find very little about the effect that relates to their lives.

Fantasy-Prone Personalities

Another theory is that people who generate abduction accounts have fantasy-prone personalities—in other words, that they spend an inordinate amount of time fantasizing about themselves as willing participants in erotic or dramatic adventures.

In order for the fantasy-prone individual to spin abduction yarns, she would have to be so inordinately affected by her daydreams that she would be unable to distinguish them from reality. Like hallucinations, the fantasies of fantasy-prone individuals are almost never completely divorced from idiosyncratic personal content, and simply dreaming up a complex abduction event is just as unlikely for them as it is for non-fantasy-prone individuals. Furthermore, the abduction accounts are not pleasant experiences designed to bolster or shield the ego of the abductee.

Of course, some people do spin fantasy-abduction tales. But their idiosyncratic stories do not match the accounts given by other abductees. They have not usually undergone competent hypnosis. They act more like a combination of channelers and contactees seeking publicity and perhaps money and yet still not fabricating a conscious hoax.

The Influence of Hypnosis

A popular theory suggests that it is the use of hypnosis itself in the hands of an incompetent practitioner that calls forth abduction stories. People can be suggestible while undergoing hypnotic regressions, and it is possible that the abductees might be responding to leading questions asked by the hypnotist. If so, their accounts might represent material that was confabulated, or invented from the unconscious mind, either to please the investigator or to "fill in" when the answer is not truly known.[6]

Yet experience has shown that most abductees refuse to be led. When asked intentionally leading questions by the hypnotist, they will nearly always reject the suggestion and reply in the negative ("No, it wasn't like that"). For example, while investigating the Barney and Betty Hill case, Dr. Benjamin Simon was intent on getting the Hills to admit that their incident had no objective reality. For months he deliberately tried to instill the idea while they were under hypnosis that events did not happen the way they described. He looked for contradictions and tried to get them to agree that it was just a dream. Still he was unable to get them to admit that any part of their stories did not occur as they had described.

Throughout the history of the abduction phenomenon, it has been the abductees who have taught the researchers. The abductees have outlined the major events of the experience and set its parameters. The investigators, hypnotists, and researchers have learned about abductions not by imposing some sort of purposeful structure on abductee accounts but by patiently listening to what the abductees say. Furthermore, a significant percentage of abduction accounts are related by the abductee without the aid of hypnosis. Their stories are essentially the same as those related while under hypnosis.

A comprehensive study of abduction accounts written by Dr. Thomas E. Bullard demonstrated that the "same key traits" (examination, table, etc.) showed up in accounts regardless of how the information was retrieved. He found no significant differences between material collected by experienced hypnotists, inexperienced hypnotists, and by hypnotists who believed in abductions and hypnotists who did not. His findings indicated that "hypnosis makes far less difference than critics have claimed."[7]

In 1978, Alvin Lawson, a professor of English at California State University at Long Beach, conducted an interesting study using eight volunteers to see if the abduction phenomenon was psychologically built into the unconscious minds of individuals. He screened each subject to filter out those who knew something about the UFO phenomenon (although he did not screen for abductions, a serious error because one of his subjects may have been an abductee) and had a physician hypnotize them; then he told them that they were to relate a UFO abduction event. They then proceeded to describe their "abduction." The stories they told were all different from each other. The details within the stories were also different from each other. The aliens all looked different from each other. One looked like a lizard, one was cone-shaped with no head, one had an asymmetrical head with no eyes, one looked like a wise man with a beard. The subjects reported no egg or sperm sampling. They had no secondary or ancillary experiences. Except for one, the subjects felt no emotional content in their stories. They described no natural progression of events during the course of the "abduction." For example, they were told that they would be taken aboard a UFO and were encouraged to describe how they got on board. They then described the interior and the aliens. Lawson specifically had to tell them that they were going to have a physical examination. Although a few details resembled those found in real accounts (e.g., they lay on a table, a machine was used to X-ray one, and a few said they could not move), the majority of them were not related to abductions and did not match what is known. Lawson showed that imaginary abductees were just that—imaginary.[8]

Hypnosis has been used to explore claims of "past lives." Under hypnosis, subjects deliver accounts of living lives in the past, complete with details about geography, society, and significant areas of personal life. Thus the case can be made that abductions are akin to past-life regressions in which subjects remember long, sometimes complicated scenarios about their former status. But past-life accounts are all different, more akin to "channeling." They lack the great mass of confirmatory detail that abductees report. They are personally idiosyncratic. Critics who claim that past-life stories and abduction accounts are related fail to take into consideration multiple abductions, the physicality of the event, psychological trauma, and the remarkable similarity of detail.

In truth, there are sincere people who are not channelers who make extravagant claims about being abducted that fit only loosely into the scenario that researchers have developed. These people might indeed be abductees but have not had the opportunity to undergo competent hypnosis. Therefore they carry mental images of atomic destruction, pollution problems, and kindly Space Brothers more typical of contactee accounts. Only competent hypnosis can reveal the origin of these images and feelings. When the hypnotist does not have an adequate knowledge of the subject, the true nature of the abduction may never be revealed.

Stigmata

Finally, it has been posited that the physical effects associated with abductions—scars, internal injuries, blood loss, and gynecological and urological sequelae—are a form of "stigmata" very much like the stigmata that can result in rare cases when a person is so extraordinarily obsessed with the crucifixion of Christ that he develops the wounds from it.

If abduction sequelae are stigmata, however, then stigmata or other psychosomatic physical symptoms can achieve a life of their own apart from the conscious thoughts and activities of the victims. For example, the abductee may have only a passing and vague concern with abductions, but she may develop marks on her body associated with them even though she is not in any way obsessed with the subject or aware that she might be an abductee. Far from being obsessed with it to the point of incorporating some functions of the abductions into the physical structure of her body, the aware abductee usually desperately wants the abductions to end. Moreover, scars are often found by accident: a friend will notice it behind the abductee's knee, or the abductee will feel something "funny" on her body and then notice the mark. Thus the physical aftereffects of an abduction do not conform to our knowledge about stigmata.

PSYCHIATRIC EXPLANATIONS

Psychiatric explanations of abduction accounts suggest that they originate either from organic brain problems or from serious mental disorders.

Psychosis

It is possible that abductee claimants are mentally disturbed people whose fallacious stories are an integral part of their illness. Psychiatrists believe that mental illness affects, in one degree or another, a significant percentage of the population of the United States and probably the world. To some debunkers the mere fact of claiming an abduction is prima facie evidence of mental illness. Even the eminent physicist Philip Morrison has said, "Go into a state hospital and every tenth person will tell you the same [abduction] story.[9]

It is true that mentally ill people will sometimes claim contact with Beings from other planets. But their claims are usually part of their psychoses and are consistent with a whole range of bizarre and confused thought patterns and behavior that characterize their lives. Their stories are inconsistent and incoherent. The details in their stories do not match the details in any other people's stories. Sometimes broad patterns of psychotic thought disturbances are similar ("The FBI is plotting against me," "Voices are speaking to me"), but even within this context the details are confused and jumbled.

Legitimate abductee claimants do not mistake fantasy for reality in the normal course of their daily existence. Most are productive members of society and are not mentally ill.[10] They claim events have happened to them that are inconsistent with anything else in their lives. For most of them, the abductions are unprecedented events that do not fit a pattern of other bizarre or unaccountable experiences.

And even though some of the abductees might seek psychological help, no evidence exists to show that they are schizophrenics, manic-depressives, or have delusionary personalities (although people with these traits may also be abductees). "Blind" psychological testing of nine abductees, including the administration of the Minnesota Multiphasic Personality Inventory, has shown that they exhibited characteristics of people who had been "violated," e.g., raped, and were more "wary" than usual. All the abductees were well within the psychologically "normal" range and exhibited no pathology.[11]

Multiple Personality Disorder

In spite of the lack of evidence for mental disease, some critics have said that the serious illness of disassociated personalities, or "multiple personalities," may have a bearing on the abduction phenomenon. The people who suffer from this unusual disorder may have one or more personalities separate from their dominant one, and they may or may not know about the others. The alternate personalities may engage in antisocial, immoral, or just different behavior from the other personalities.

In no case has an abduction researcher uncovered an individual who exhibited traits of multiple personality disorder. No abductee has spontaneously shifted into another personality during a hypnosis session, as if the abduction were happening to someone else. Nor has an abductee displayed other personalities independent of the regression session. When an abductee remembers the abduction, it is fully integrated into the structure of her life without resistance; it would not be if it were another person's problem.

Generally, people with multiple personality disorder come from backgrounds filled with severe and prolonged sexual abuse. Their disassociated personalities can be understood as a psychological attempt to escape from the traumas of their "real" existence. Although some abductees have been sexually abused, we have no evidence to suggest that the frequency of abuse is any higher among abductees than among the general population. Moreover, the abductees' accounts of abductions do not occur in response to the abuse and are exactly the same as those made by people with no known history of sexual abuse. Thus multiple personality disorder does not seem to be a likely candidate as the causative factor in the reports of abductions.

Psychogenic Fugue State

Psychogenic fugue state is a condition that has parallels with multiple personality disorder and with the missing time episode. In a fugue state, the individual will inexplicably travel to another geographic location, assume a new identity, and conduct her affairs with no recollections of what has happened in the past. A fugue state takes place when the individual is under a severe amount of pressure and stress. Usually a major conflict has just ensued with another person and the fugue victim lapses into this state. The act of going into a fugue state is an attempt to replace intolerable affairs with ones that are more psychologically manageable. Each experience is unique to that individual. The details of one person's life in a fugue state differ from the details of another person's life in a fugue state.

As with a fugue state, an abduction often takes place without the victim remembering the events. But the similarity ends there. People do not change their identities during an abduction, nor do they travel to another geographic location where other people see them. They consider themselves helpless victims of the abduction rather than new personalities forging new experiences. Their accounts contain no personal elements and are remarkably consistent with the accounts of other abductees. Finally, their memories are often filled with fear and terror. They wish to escape from the memories of the abduction rather than from any precipitating causative event.

Temporal Lobe Dysfunction

Dr. Michael Persinger, a professor of neurobiology at Laurentian University in Canada, has theorized that abduction accounts might stem from dysfunctions in the brain's temporal lobe. He says that the temporal lobe could be stimulated by electrically charged particles in the atmosphere unleashed as a result of the earth's geologic tectonic plate stress (sections of the earth's crust rubbing against each other). These electrical discharges might stimulate temporal lobe instability that could lead people to hallucinate. Or, says Persinger, abduction accounts might also be triggered by temporal lobe epilepsy. When the temporal lobe is electrically stimulated in a laboratory, he says, the subject will have a series of perceptual experiences that closely parallel abductions. For instance, they might have a sense of a "presence" around them; they might feel that they are having a mystical experience; they might interpret unusual events "as being meaningful or as special, personal messages," and they might have feelings such as a sense of unreality, internal vibrations, rising sensations, erotic thoughts, and anxiety. Persinger has even claimed that, with medication to control temporal lobe dysfunction, he has been able to "cure" an "abductee" of her "abduction" experiences.

Persinger's theory is based on precarious ground. The electrical effects of tectonic plate stress are extremely controversial and not yet accepted by the geologic community. The effect that the electrically charged particles might have on people's brains is highly conjectural and not accepted by the psychiatric community. Persinger presents no direct evidence to the contrary. Furthermore, the tiny population sample that Persinger worked with to obtain his abduction material was, by and large, not composed of abductees. Rather, it consisted of channelers, followers of mystically oriented Eastern religions and philosophies, and people with a few highly dubious "visitor" accounts that have never been fully investigated. And finally, their narratives, which he says contain "substantial fantasy," do not match the narratives of the abductees.[12]

CULTURAL EXPLANATIONS

Cultural explanations maintain that abduction accounts originate from the influence that prevailing culture and society have upon the individual.

Desire for a Baby

Some critics have stated that the abduction phenomenon is related to the societal awareness of new fertilization methods, such as in vitro fertilization, artificial insemination, and surrogate motherhood. Women, and presumably men, who desperately want children might unconsciously internalize these ideas and bring them forth in obsessive fantasies based on their desire to have children.

But the abduction phenomenon was known long before the new fertilization techniques were developed. And if abductions represent the unconscious longings of women for a child, then their reports of not wanting to hold or touch babies during the abduction would not make much sense. Also, teenage boys and men are shown babies and have sperm taken with no evidence that these men so want to have children that they are inventing fantasies around the event. Furthermore, the new fertilization techniques almost exclusively focus on women. Of the fifteen women in this study who were shown babies, ten already had children and had no plans for more, one was planning on having a child in the near future, and four had no desire to have a child at that time. Finally, young children are often shown babies and their concern with the new fertilization techniques must be assumed to be negligible.

The Influence of Science Fiction

Other critics claim that people pick up their ideas about abductions from science fiction motion pictures. While it is true that science fiction movies are popular, none has been released with themes or events similar to abduction accounts. No science fiction movies have been made that portray invading aliens as being uncommunicative and refusing to give information about their origin, mission, or methods. Nor have any shown aliens collecting eggs and sperm from their human victims with the intent of producing hybrid off-spring.

Science fiction movies have recognizable and even formulaic plots: Aliens come here to wreak destruction; aliens come here to take over the planet; aliens come here to help mankind, etc. The three most widely seen science fiction movies of all time, *Close Encounters of the Third Kind, E. T.,* and *Star Wars,* were not at all similar to the abduction accounts (although *Close Encounters* did have an off-camera abduction suggestion). Even *Star Trek,* which has been seen probably by more Americans than any other science fiction television show, had no plots that resembled the abduction scenario. Moreover, many abductees are not science fiction fans. They do not see science fiction movies or television shows. They do not read science fiction literature. They are not involved with the world of science fiction at any level. Thus to dismiss their abduction accounts as coming from science fiction is unwarranted.

Folklore

Some researchers have suggested that so-called abduction stories have occurred all through recorded history and that they are found in myth, legend, and folklore. However, these skeptics generally lump together all folklore accounts of "little people," gnomes, trolls, dwarfs, and so forth, no matter what the context, into the abduction phenomenon simply because these characters are small or because they are said to have supernatural powers. The adherents of this theory disconnect such folktales from their original social and cultural context and then present them as fact in a completely different milieu as if they have a life of their own. The only difference, they claim, is that abduction stories are now more technologically advanced. But they present only vague and general similarities to show that the abduction phenomenon is related to myth, legend, and folklore such as superficial stories about "changelings," little people, or gods who live in the heavens. For adherents of the folklore hypothesis, facile resemblances become complex modern duplicates.

The folktales also become evidence that the UFO abduction phenomenon has been going on for centuries. Of course, hundreds of folktales have been collected about little people, giants, gods, flying machines, people being kidnapped by trolls, and other material that the uninformed might decide were like the UFO and abduction phenomena, but the actual content of myths, legends, and folktales has almost nothing in common with abduction accounts. Typically, folktales, myths, and legends have been orally transmitted. They have been changed and altered over the years depending on the "spin" that the teller puts on the tale. That alteration is determined by the personality of the storyteller and the culture in which he lives. Folklore is a dynamic process that is constantly changing. Getting at the kernel of truth that may lie behind the tale is often quite impossible.[13] The victims of abductions are not telling stories that they had previously heard from other people. They are relating accounts of sometimes ongoing events that they believe happened to them.

EXOTIC THEORIES

Let us suppose that abductee claimants have no discernible psychological or psychiatric dysfunction and that they are not internalizing cultural events but are still relating episodes that have no basis in objective reality. Given this presumption, how can we explain these claims? Critics have often dipped into the exotic and bizarre to explain these accounts, as they try to replace one strange set of circumstances with another.

The Collective Unconscious

Some researchers have suggested that the abduction accounts embody certain archetypal memories that are inherent in all human minds, and that, when taken together, form part of what psychoanalysts call the "collective unconscious." The concept of the collective unconscious is a staple of Jungian and psychoanalytic dream interpretation. Freud and Jung found certain images in dreams that they thought had universal applications. When a person dreams certain images, they are symbolic of other more deep-seated desires and fears. The collective unconscious suggests that people can share the same thoughts across cultural and technological barriers.

Jung addressed the problem of UFO sightings from this point of view in his 1958 book *Flying Saucers*. His position was that if witnesses were not actually seeing objectively "real" objects, they might be seeing archetypal images, similar to those found in dreams. Like dreams, abduction accounts could be grand metaphorical stories masking or symbolizing more profound mental events.[14]

The collective unconscious challenges the theory that humans are

born with a "clean slate," suggesting instead that we have prepro-
grammed, richly detailed, and complex memories that can easily
generate abduction stories. To date, however, the psychological
community has made no discoveries to indicate that common, detailed thought patterns exist, lodged deep in the psychic lives of all
people. Of course, the healthy survival instinct makes all people
think about food, reproduction, and the prevention of death. But,
beyond such considerations, generalizations about what goes on in
people's unconscious minds are open to question.

If abduction events are part of the collective unconscious, then
the theory would have to be expanded to take into account any of
the abduction's unique characteristics: multiple abductions, physical
effects, disappearances, and so forth. Furthermore, it would have to
consider the puzzling fact that the abduction syndrome is a recent
phenomenon confined to the twentieth century. It would have to
prove that the collective unconscious is dynamic and can come into
being and change around the world at any given time regardless of
the culture.

If the collective-unconscious theory turns out to be valid, it is
revolutionary in the extreme. It fundamentally changes the way in
which human beings think and react to their environment. It re-
moves much of the control that people have over their own thoughts
and lives and places it within the genetic makeup of the species. The
implications for humanity are enormous. If the theory is true, a new
psychology of human experience based, to a large extent, on hypnosis would have to be devised because it is through the use of this
tool that the collective unconscious would be brought forth.

We must also bear in mind that Jung himself, writing in 1958 when
only minimal knowledge of the nature of the UFO phenomenon was
available, understood the dangers of trying to place UFOs within the
collective unconscious. He pointed out that although UFO sightings
might have a psychic component, "we are dealing with an ostensibly
physical phenomenon distinguished on the one hand by its frequent
appearance and on the other by its strange, unknown, and indeed
contradictory nature." [15]

Birth Trauma

Professor Alvin Lawson, who mounted the study of imaginary abductees, has also championed the birth trauma theory to explain
abduction accounts. He states that the profound mental effects of

being born are remarkably similar to abductee stories of going through a dark passage and then seeing little fetuslike people with large heads in bright rooms while lying on a table. The traumatic memories of being born are lodged deep within people's psyches, and abduction reports are transmuted manifestations of these memories.[16] However, advocates of the birth trauma theory fail to explain how a baby would see other fetuses. They fail to explain why people born in a cesarean procedure have related accounts similar to those of people born vaginally. They fail to demonstrate how the rest of the abduction material would fit into the birth trauma scenario.

If true, however, birth trauma, like the collective unconscious, would suggest that current theories about the development of fetal brains are wildly erroneous, and that all newborn minds are extraordinarily more sophisticated than the evidence indicates. The minds of newborn abductees would have to contain countless bits of specific identical information relating to their birth environment, regardless of whether their eyes were closed, whether they were born in a dark area, whether other people were present, and so forth. Presumably, all babies would retain the endless details of many other "traumatic" events as well.

Alternative Realities

Finally, some theorists—agonizing over the inability to explain abduction evidence—have resorted to suggesting that the human mind can in some way create a physical reality through mental processes. In other words, abductees "think up" a real, alternative universe that has aliens in it who can cause scars, disappearances, and the other physical phenomena of abductions. If abductees can do this, it would neatly answer all the problems created by their accounts.

This theory substitutes one bizarre series of events for another. If it was possible, then human beings would be creating many alternative realities and would have been doing so for all time. But the creation of an alternative reality that would terrorize its creator, cause her to experience physical damage, and then make her live in fear that it will happen again seems unreasonable when people might instead create physical realities wherein their deepest pleasurable fantasies could be played out. No evidence whatsoever has been presented to suggest that this theory has any viability.[17]

. . .

All of these explanations—psychological, psychiatric, cultural, and exotic—fail to account for critically important aspects of the abduction event. They ignore the richness and abundance of similar, frequently exact detail and the extraordinary convergence of the abductee narratives across all cultural boundaries. For example, Mindscan, visualization, and many other abduction procedures have never been publicized or written about even in the most esoteric UFO literature, yet virtually all abductees describe them. Abductees tell essentially the same story regardless of their age, race, religion, upbringing, occupation, economic status, educational level, intelligence, life-style, or ethnic or cultural background. This would not be so if the accounts were internally generated.

None of these theories explain the lack of strong personal content in the abduction accounts. For instance, the narratives contain little about the abductee's past life, personal life, or fantasy life. Abduction accounts contain almost no material related to a person's social, cultural, familial, or occupational activities. Events happen *to* them. They are unwilling participants.

None of the explanations account for the fact that when victims claim to have been abducted, they are physically missing from the place where they are supposed to be. Never has an abductee claimed to be abducted and later been physically accounted for during that exact time.

None of the explanations explain the unusual physical effects apparently derived from the abduction event, such as scars, bruises, cuts, hemorrhages, and bloody noses, to name a few. None account for the phenomenon of one person seeing another being abducted while the witness herself is not abducted. None explain the "switching off" phenomenon. And even if a theory can be made to account for one of two abductions, it still fails to deal with the great number of them.

To take the argument that abductions are internally generated one step further, we would logically expect certain things to take place. For example:

· We would expect reports of a great variety of sizes and shapes of aliens, as in the Lawson study. In fact, the opposite is true. Although abductees do see a limited variety, the vast majority of the accounts describe small beings with large heads, distinctive eyes, and so forth.

· We would expect that people would describe a vast array of procedures and events that happened to them during an abduction. As with the contactees, they might take trips to the moon, they might engage in leisure activities, they might eat lunch and dinner. In fact, the events that happen to abductees are narrowly focused, and virtually all abductee accounts fall within these narrow parameters.

· We would expect a significant number of abductees to say that the communication that takes place between them and the aliens is aural. In reality, virtually all abductees describe communication as telepathic.

· We would expect abductees to claim that communication that takes place with aliens is widespread and deeply searching. As with the contactee reports or channeled information, we would know about where the aliens came from, what their planets were like, why they were here, how many wives or husbands they have, what their children are like, whether they have death, taxes, divorce, and so forth. In fact, abduction accounts contain no such information. We know nothing about the aliens' home environment. We do not even know if they have a home environment. We have no knowledge about the aliens' lives outside the UFO.

· We would expect at least some of the abductees to conjure up aliens who show some interest in human affairs. But, in fact, according to the abduction accounts, the aliens virtually never express any overt interest in what people are doing, in human society, culture, politics, and economics.

· We would expect abductees to describe a wide range of intentions that the aliens would have. The aliens would want to take over the world, force world peace, benevolently cure disease, use humans for food, etc. In fact, we find a singular lack of information about the aliens' ultimate intentions except the tantalizing bits and pieces of information about what is going to happen to the babies.

· We would expect abductees to report that the aliens opened and closed the window to transport them out of the room. But virtually all the abductees who say they floated through a window or screen describe it as being closed.

· We would expect that the abduction events would have a strong personal content reflecting fears and other aspects of the abductee's life. In fact, we get the same accounts over and over again, regardless of the background and upbringing of the person who is relating them. The accounts do not draw on personal lives for their contents.

· We would expect that the baby and child presentations during abductions would be not only loving and happy but directly related to the person's inner desires for children. In fact, many of the instances of baby and child holding are described in horrific tones. Babies appear to be so oddly formed that the women often recoil when being told to touch them. Some women have to be physically forced to hold the babies. This unpleasant experience suggests the opposite of a deeply desired wish fulfillment.

· We would expect that the totality of the events would remain permanently random, without the congruence and richness of detail that characterize abduction accounts. In fact, we find many accounts to be so precisely similar that, in order to match other random, internally generated accounts, the abductees would have to be not only extremely well versed in published abduction literature, they would also have to know the minutiae of events that have never been published in the literature and, indeed, that even most abduction researchers are unaware of.

We are left with a puzzle. No viable alternative theory has emerged that takes into account the totality of the data in the abduction experience. Some theories address specific parts of abductions, but none even comes close to explaining the mechanism of the internal generation of these stories. No significant body of thought exists that presents strong evidence that anything else is happening other than what the abductees have stated.

If the abductees are relating events that do, in fact, have an objective reality, then we are presented with what might be one of the most important events ever to befall mankind. If, on the other hand, the events do not have an objective reality and the abductees are imagining abductions, then we have discovered something of immense importance. We have found a fascinating and inexplicable new psychological and sociocultural phenomenon unlike anything ever discovered in the human psyche before. It is obviously worthy of intense scientific attention. No matter what the origin of the abductions, whether subjective or objective, this phenomenon cannot be ignored.

Chapter 12

Questions

Suppose that everything the abductees report is essentially true. Suppose that we are dealing with extraterrestrial Beings and activities. From this admittedly precarious perspective, let us try to generalize about the meaning of these events.

When UFO research dealt merely with sightings, we could not answer any questions about the activities inside the objects or their purpose for being here. Speculation was rife and culture-bound: They are reconnoitering our atomic sites in preparation for takeover. They are surveying our geography for a scientific mapping expedition. They are here to prevent Earthlings from destroying themselves in a nuclear war. They are here because humans need help (for whatever reason) from benevolent, superior races. They are here to raise our consciousness about the multiplicity of life elsewhere. All of this speculation was based on little or no knowledge.

Today, if the abduction reports can be believed, we have gained knowledge. For the first time we can pose the correct questions and even supply some tentative answers based on new evidence.

Why are UFOs here? One of the purposes for which UFOs travel to Earth is to abduct humans to help aliens produce other Beings. It is not a program of reproduction, but one of *production.* They are not here to help us. They have their own agenda, and we are not allowed to know its full parameters.

Why are UFOs sighted at all? If people can be rendered invisible and float through solid matter to similarly invisible objects, and if secrecy is a priority of the abduction phenomenon, then the reason for UFO sightings is unclear. There have been, of course, many sightings by people who were not abducted. But it is possible that many, if not most, low-level sightings may be related to abductions. This may be true of a significant number of high-level sightings as well. Abductees might have only a few conscious sightings during their lives. If this is the case, then abductions might greatly outnumber sightings.

What is the magnitude of the abduction phenomenon? At first it appeared to be an isolated phenomenon that had occurred to just a few people around the country. That was wrong. We have evidence of thousands of abductions, and that is perhaps only a small fraction of the total number.

An unpublished survey that I conducted of more than 1,200 students at Temple University who answered a written questionnaire suggests that as many as 5.5 percent of them have potentially had abduction experiences. Similarly, a study done of 275 respondents to a magazine's survey searching for potential abductees came up with 6 percent. Projecting that number to the population as a whole yields as many as 15 million people in the United States who might have had abduction experiences. Let us assume that this number is ridiculously high, and that abductions are only happening to one half of one percent of the population. If that is true, we are dealing with over a million possible abductions in the United States.

Furthermore, abductions are not confined to the United States. British UFO researcher Jenny Randles has catalogued many abductions in the United Kingdom, and we have evidence that the geographic scope of the phenomenon might extend around the world. As researchers learn how to investigate these types of cases, the data are mounting not only that abductions are apparently taking place everywhere, but that the same material is beginning to come out of the accounts—namely, that the focus of the abduction is the production of children.[1]

If abductions have occurred for more than half a century, why have we not learned about them before? Abductees have been coming forth with accounts for many years, but in the past UFO researchers have not been well versed enough in the phenomenon to recognize them. For example, in 1977 I listened to an account about a UFO hovering above a group of stores in a shopping center in Ardmore, Pennsylvania. It was about 9:00 P.M. and an employee was going home from work. One of the last people out, she walked into an almost deserted parking lot. She was about to open her car door when she saw a UFO, which was quite close to her. She could see details of the craft, including the "windows." When I asked her if she could see inside the windows, she said that she could see white walls, the ceiling, and other details, although from where she was standing it would have been almost impossible to see these things. It did not occur to me then that she might well have been describing the interior of the object from *inside.*

In another case I investigated in 1972, an elderly couple was traveling at night near Madison, Wisconsin. They saw a UFO in front of the car and stopped to get a better look at it. They then felt the overpowering urge to go to sleep, which they did. When they woke up the UFO was gone and they resumed their journey. I listened to their story, but I was unable to recognize that something else might have happened to them.

Many other abductions have been couched in personal and cultural terms—visits from deceased relatives, encounters with angels, devils, and other religious figures, mystical meetings with animals, out-of-body experiences, and so on. We are now learning how to sift through these stories to see which ones indicate abduction activity. For the first time UFO researchers are recognizing potential abduction accounts, and they are actively seeking out possible abductees. The climate of opinion has made it "safer" for them to come forward.

Who is selected to be an abductee? The selection criteria are largely unknown. But the generational aspect of abductions is extremely important. There is a good chance that one or both of the abductees' parents may have had these experiences, and our research indicates that if a man or woman is abducted, the chances that his or her children will also be abducted may increase. The spouse, however, may not be an abductee and might be "switched off" during each abduction sequence. Evidence suggests that people who have been abducted only once are targeted as a matter of expediency and are in close proximity to an abductee during an abduction.

When do abductions begin? The evidence indicates that, with the exception of opportunistic abductions, all abductees have their first
experience in childhood. The youngest case I have found was that
of an abductee who reported her eight-month-old child being taken,
although most abductees remember their first episode occurring
when they were between the ages of four and seven. The aliens then
in some way "tag" the person and mentally and physically "mine"
him or her for a good part of their lives. I have no record of a series
of abductions that begin when the abductee is an adult.

Abductions sometimes take place in "clusters." They may increase
as the child approaches and goes through puberty, continue through
the teens, and then abruptly stop. Long periods of time may pass
without an abduction and then they begin again—intensely. Sometimes the abductee can have as many as one experience every few
nights for a week or two. For some women, frequency is linked to
their menstrual cycle. Abductions increase during ovulation and de-
crease during menstruation. The frequency of abductions for men
has not yet been adequately researched, but it appears to be less
predictable than for women.

Does location matter for an abduction? We used to think that UFOs were
sighted more often in secluded areas than in densely populated lo-
cations. This may still be true for the sightings, but it makes no
difference for abductions. With certain exceptions, abductions can
occur anywhere and location is no determinate.

An abductee cannot hide from the abductions. They occur in the
middle of Manhattan or in a farmhouse in Kansas. They occur within
an apartment complex or in a single dwelling in the suburbs. If an
abductee travels to other states or countries, he or she is often
abducted there. However, the specific locale might make a difference. For example, being in a room full of sleeping people at night
makes no difference, but being in a crowd of people at a sporting
event, in a market, or in a workplace seems to give some protection
against an abduction at that time. Methods have been found that, in
some cases, might postpone abductions, but no one has been able to
find a way to stop them permanently.

What do the aliens want? The reports indicate that they want to use
the ability humans have to recreate themselves. They want human

sperm and eggs. They want human physical involvement with the offspring. They want complete knowledge of the reproductive areas of human life. They also want knowledge of our mental and nonreproductive physiological processes. With Mindscan and other mental procedures they might also want knowledge of how humans function within society.

What do the aliens *not* want? They appear not to want human advice or consultation. They do not want to disclose information about their origins and purposes. Neither do they impart much information about the technicalities of what they are doing during the various procedures they conduct on humans. They do not want to be discovered. They do not want to be stopped.

How long have the aliens been doing this? It is possible that aliens have been abducting humans for hundreds of years, but we have found no evidence for it. It is very difficult to say exactly when the phenomenon began, but there are indications that it might have begun in the late nineteenth or early twentieth century. We have collected some reports suggestive of abductions in the 1900s, and we have investigated abductions that occurred in the early 1930s. The main bulk of the abductions seems to have begun in the mid-twentieth century, perhaps coinciding with the first UFO sighting waves in the 1940s. Our knowledge is limited by the age of the people who explore their experiences; most abductees who have come forth in the last five years are under sixty years old.

If we are dealing with a generationally based abduction program, then it could have started on a relatively small scale one hundred years ago; it may have grown exponentially as the children of the original abductees were themselves abducted, then their children in turn became abductees, and so on. The amount of time and effort that the aliens put into the breeding program would have grown as the abductee population increased. Such a scenario would account for the widespread abduction phenomenon of today.

How long will aliens continue abductions? The abduction program appears to be vast. Abductees routinely report rooms with as many as two hundred tables holding humans in various stages of examination. The aliens hustle them out as soon as possible after the procedures are completed, presumably so that more humans can be brought in. The evidence suggests that this goes on twenty-four hours a day, month after month, year after year. The amount of time and energy invested in the breeding program is enormous. This might indicate that the aliens will be here for a long period of time—possibly forever. It is also possible that the aliens could cease their operations tomorrow and never bother us again.

Are aliens malevolent or benevolent? The aliens appear to be neither malevolent nor benevolent. They do not seem to be here to help us or to harm us. They are here for themselves. They are doing what they want to do, without consideration for our wishes. They appear to have no concern with the central issues and problems of human survival. They do not share technology, impart knowledge, give advice, warn us about our course for the future, or tell us how to cure disease.

Modern anthropologists employ a policy of ethnical noninterference when they encounter a newly found tribal society so that it can survive without the disruptive shock of modern cultural and technological intervention. It is possible that the aliens are acting in the same way, although little evidence exists for this. However, it is also possible that they have instituted the practice of nonintervention so that they can continue to execute their program without threat of human attempts to prevent it.

Does the breeding program involve genetic interbreeding? Dr. Michael Swords, a professor of natural sciences at Western Michigan University, has argued that it would be biologically impossible for aliens to join their DNA with ours—assuming that they have DNA—just as it is impossible for humans to interbreed across animal species. Moreover, the lack of genitals on the aliens (some sexual reports notwithstanding) makes it clear that they are not interbreeding with us in the most usual sense.

It seems more likely that genetic alteration is taking place instead of interbreeding. The evidence seems to indicate the following sequence: (1) eggs and sperm are taken; (2) they are fertilized in vitro; (3) the fertilized egg is genetically altered; (4) the fertilized egg is implanted in utero; (5) after a short period of from two to ten weeks of gestation, the fetus is removed; and (6) the fetus is incubated externally. However the effect is achieved, the babies look like crosses between humans and aliens.[2]

Why do aliens need humans to touch offspring? Budd Hopkins has posited that the point of holding the offspring is for nurturance—to give them human love, just as humans do with their own children. However, touch seems to be more important than love. Experiments with premature human babies have shown that without touching the babies develop at a slower rate than premature infants who have been regularly massaged. Touching can stimulate hormones essential for physical and psychological well-being. For all human babies, the absence of touching can cause physiological deficiencies that lead to the serious condition of psychosocial dwarfism. If this is the reason the alien offspring need touching, then why the aliens cannot supply it is a mystery, as is why the offspring would need human touch so infrequently.

Are the offspring sick? Although abductees commonly report that the offspring look sickly or even close to death, we cannot substantiate the fact that they are ill. In fact, most abductees only see "sickly" babies and few, if any, see "healthy" babies. Thus, we must assume that either all the babies the abductees see are sick, or, more probably, that the babies' appearance of "wasting" is normal for them.

Why do aliens repeatedly abduct the same people? We do not know the answer to this. The abductee obviously fits some sort of criteria for use. It has been speculated that if the abductees' offspring cannot themselves reproduce in sufficient numbers to maintain the population, then repeated mining of abductees for reproductive material might account for the recurring nature of the abductions.

Do abductees take trips in the UFOs? Over the years researchers have reported cases of abductees traveling in UFOs. I have not uncovered an abduction-related trip to another planet in my research. I have had abductees say that they had the definite feeling of movement in the object as if it were traveling. Others have said that they could see the planet Earth outside a window. Some have seen stars against a black background outside a window. The travel that I have investigated has seemed incidental to the abduction, and I have found no procedures related to it. Further investigation may reveal deliberate travel experiences, but, based on what we know, it seems likely that some reports of travel might be due to envisioning or staging procedures.

Are aliens ultimately going to take over the planet? Based on everything we know, the aliens could have taken over many years ago if they had wanted to. The program they have instituted does not seem to be one of conquest, at least not in the common meaning of the word. The apparent lack of systematic interest in our culture and society probably precludes any type of program to "colonize." However, the aliens' meticulous attention to human thought processes and physiology suggests a far more serious interest in humans than just the mechanical production of babies. The clandestine character of the abduction event suggests that they do not want us to know what they are doing. This might mean that in the future they could make a sudden, widespread public appearance when they are ready. Of course, it could also mean that eventually they will complete their program and disappear.

What happens to the babies? This is the central question of abduction research. If the abduction phenomenon has been going on for at least fifty years, then the first of the offspring must be around fifty years old by now. But where are they? There is no evidence that the offspring are on Earth. We can surmise that the offspring are being taken somewhere else.

Some abductees have suggested that the babies are being taken elsewhere to populate another planet. Others have suggested that the babies are being used as workers somewhere. In one regression, Karen Morgan recalled a child-presentation procedure in which a voice came over the "telepathic P.A. system" summoning her to "behold the children of the future." She was shown ten children standing together. The voice told her they were playing.

And I think, "They're not playing. This is all manipulated. [Something bizarre is] happening here." But they're saying, "The children are playing." Or, "Observe the children at play. These are our children, and they're your children. They're the children of the future. Together we have done...built something." I'm looking at the children, saying, "I don't like this." "Observe the children of the future." It's like a speech. Everything's like a speech, you know? And the children are under a soft, yellow light, like a spotlight on them.

Can you kind of [remember] anything else?

Yes, I do remember. It said, "We're on the verge of a new horizon" or "beginning," or something. "We're on the verge of new 'something.'" . . .

What else do they say?

Nothing that I'm aware of. They just walk out of the room.

These babies have something to do with the future, then?

They definitely do. They said they're the children of the future. Whose future? I don't know.

(Karen Morgan, 38, 1987)

In another episode, Karen was once again in the media room when she heard more information about the possible purposes of the aliens.

Do they say anything about babies?

Children. There's some bullshit, David, I hear like, "Children of the future" or something. Children of the future, children of the world, children of the . . . it's like, these are impressions now, but it's something like, "This will be brought into being or inherited by children of the future." And something like, "the future that you help create," or "the future that you are part of," or "the future that . . ." I'd like to think that this was just wishful thinking on their part, but I'm not sure it is.

Now, are you sure that they're talking about Earth, or are they talking about another planet?

It looks a lot like Earth to me.... I have the feeling that it's not another planet, but it's a highly idealized version and a too-pretty picture of this planet.

(Karen Morgan, 38, 1987)

In one of Lynn Miller's abduction experiences, a Taller Being told her that the babies were being produced to be workers. She received the impression that he wanted her to have babies.

Why do you think he might want that?

He needs babies. . . .

When he says that he wants you to have babies, can you get a sense of why he needs babies?

No.

Can you get a sense of what he's going to do with the babies?

They need them for work.

For work?

Yes.

You mean they're growing babies to be workers?

Yes.

How can you get a sense of that?

I just get a sense of it.

Do you get a sense of what kind of work they'll be doing?

No.

Do you get a sense of where they'll be doing the work?

Not on Earth. . . .

So you suggest, then, that the babies will be in another place.

Yes.

By another place, does he mean another planet?

Another solar system.

So not in our own solar system?

No.

(Lynn Miller, 32, 1988)

A depressed Lynn said she felt as if she was being used as a baby-making machine for their purposes.

If the aliens' focus is on producing babies, then what do all the physical and mental procedures mean? Unfortunately, we do not have enough information about the purposes of these procedures to understand exactly how they fit into the larger context of abductions. The mental procedures suggest that the aliens are far more interested in human mental and emotional lives than the production of babies would warrant. It is possible that some Mindscan procedures might utilize human memories to learn about human culture and society. The aliens' meticulous physical examination of men and women also suggests greater curiosity than what might be assumed is necessary for physiological reproduction. The nonreproductive mental and physical procedures represent one of the more important, and perhaps ominous, mysteries in the abduction phenomenon.

Is it risky to investigate abductions? No investigator has ever been abducted as a result of his research. Yet, since we do not know the consequences of investigating abductions, it is necessary to proceed cautiously. For instance, the clandestine nature of abductions has been in effect since the beginning. But if abductions become commonly known through the work of investigators and are therefore no longer clandestine, we do not know what response the aliens might have to that situation.

What does the abduction phenomenon mean? We have been invaded. It is not an occupation, but it is an invasion. At present we can do little or nothing to stop it. The aliens have powers and technology greatly in advance of ours, and that puts us at a tremendous disadvantage in our ability to affect the phenomenon or gain some control over it. We do not know what is going to happen in the future, just as we do not know what the aliens' ultimate purposes are. We do know that the effect on abductees' lives can be devastating. The net effect of the abduction phenomenon on our society and culture at large could very well be the same over a long period of time.

Contact between the races is not taking place in a scenario that has been commonly envisioned by scientists and science fiction writers: two independent worlds making careful overtures for equal and mutual benefit. Rather, it is completely one-sided. Instead of equal benefit, we see a disturbing program of apparent exploitation of one species by another. How it began is unknown. How it will end is unknown. But we must face the abduction phenomenon squarely and begin to think rationally about what to do about it.

Afterword

Final Thoughts

When I first became involved with abduction research, it was easy to keep it at arm's length and treat it as an intellectual puzzle. But the more I learned about the abduction phenomenon, the more frightening it became, both personally and in the larger context of its potential effects on society.

This book is, in one sense, a warning. We must realize that the abduction phenomenon is too important to dismiss as the ravings of prevaricators or psychologically disturbed people. I hope the extraordinary lack of scientific concern to date does not in the long run prove to be a mistake with undreamed-of consequences.

We are just at the beginning of a systematic study of abductions. Amateur investigators and professional therapists are also beginning to do abduction research. *Extreme caution is necessary.* The researcher must protect the abductee from further harm. Abductees can be emotionally fragile, and incompetent memory recovery techniques can cause them psychological damage. The risk of the further victimizing of the abductees by well-meaning but unqualified individuals is high. Special training is required.

Investigating the abduction phenomenon has demonstrated to me how brave and resilient people can be. I am continually astonished to see people who come back from these terrifying experiences and retain their sense of humor and their optimism. I admire their fierce determination to gain control over their lives and the abduction

experiences. It is the triumph of the human spirit that is most remarkable in dealing with the abduction experience. And in the end,
I believe, the human spirit will prevail.

I am often asked how I would react if the entire abduction phenomenon should prove to be the internally generated product of
people's imaginations—if there are in reality no abductions and no
aliens, and never have been. If that were true, I would weep with
joy. I want to be wrong.

If you think you may have been involved with the
abduction phenomenon, I would like to learn about
your experience. Please write to:

Dr. David M. Jacobs
Department of History
Temple University
Philadelphia, PA 19122

All communications will be confidential.

A Few Words about Methodology

Anecdotal Data

For the most part, the material in this book is based on anecdotal evidence—stories that people relate. The quality of evidence of this nature has been a point of contention ever since the public began to make UFO sightings. But we must do the best with what we have. Wishing for better evidence does not advance knowledge; dealing with the evidence at hand does. No single book, no matter how much or what quality of evidence it marshals, is going to convince the majority of people that alien abductions are happening as described. Most probably, it will be the accumulation of evidence over a long period of time that ultimately will persuade people of the importance of the abduction phenomenon.

Recruiting Subjects

People who have had abduction experiences have come to me in a variety of ways. Some were referred by Budd Hopkins and other UFO researchers, others heard me discussing the subject on radio or television or saw newspaper articles about my work, and still others heard of my abduction work through word of mouth. I have also had abductees referred to me by mental health professionals who had them as clients.

When a person first contacts me and tells me that she thinks something might have happened to her, I first ask a set of twenty-five questions that enable me to discern whether her memories might be related to the abduction phenomenon. I try to get a "feel" for the person and gauge whether she is motivated by a sincere desire to find out what has happened or is simply inquiring on a lark. If the person demonstrates genuine concern, if she does not have serious mental problems, and if she has had unusual experiences that might be related to the abduction phenomenon, I give her a strong verbal warning about the psychological consequences of finding out that something might have happened to her, and I then send her an abduction information pamphlet that outlines the pros and cons of memory collection. The pamphlet emphasizes the problems that can be engendered from memory recovery and stresses that for some people it might not be the right time to explore these events. If the person still wants to go forward, I give her a second verbal warning detailing more of the problems that she might face. If she still wants to participate, then the memory recovery process begins.

Recall

Abductees have a wide range of conscious recall about any given abduction event. If I am investigating a series of abductions that have taken place over the course of the abductee's life, the subject may be able consciously to remember bits and pieces of some abductions, virtually nothing of other abductions, and virtually everything about still other abductions. The process seems dependent on the degree of consciousness alteration that occurs during the abduction. When abductees remember entire episodes consciously, hypnosis on that same abduction event often reveals that some of the details might be different and that entire parts are sometimes left out of the conscious recall. The consciously recalled elements of the abduction are often accurate, sometimes even to minute details. Just as often, however, they are untrustworthy because of the problems of screen memories, confabulation, dream material, and the visualization procedures.

The Use of Hypnosis

When I first begin the memory recovery process with a subject, I obtain a case history of the abductee, outlining many of the "suspicious" occurrences in that person's life that might be indicative of an abduction. I do not discuss anything about the specific content of abductions with the subject. Then, with the abductee's accord, I select a memory to be probed. The abductee then consciously re-lates all that she remembers about the incident, sometimes in sur-prising detail. We discuss this and then we begin a hypnosis session to ascertain the origin of the occurrences.

Hypnosis is an indispensable tool in unlocking the memories of an abduction. Ever since 1963, when Dr. Benjamin Simon first used it on Betty and Barney Hill, UFO researchers have employed it to learn about abductions. It is the best method available to gain detailed access to people's hidden abduction memories. Hypnosis, however, is not foolproof. Some abductees simply do not remember; when they do remember, especially details, it may be an incorrect memory that they are "filling in." This can be particularly true when the subject is asked to supply details of an event from childhood.

It is easy for a hypnotist to ask (consciously or inadvertently) leading questions that steer the abductee into an answer that may not reflect reality. This can be a problem for suggestible subjects. Confabulation, or the unconscious invention and filling in of memo-ries, can become an easy way of providing information to the eager hypnotist-investigator. In hypnosis, even asking questions about a specific event can put pressure on the subject to invent details of that event to provide the answers to those questions. This problem is compounded by the fact that in abduction research, questions about details are routinely asked in order to gather as much infor-mation as possible.

Even the milieu of the investigation might present problems. Cer-tain expectations are inherent in this situation. The hypnotized per-son might unconsciously invent information about an abduction because that is what is expected. Even the investigator's beliefs might subtly influence the subject to tell him "abduction" material. Intentional fabrication can be another problem. Even in deep hyp-nosis, the subject can consciously fabricate stories.

Yet, despite these potential problems, hypnosis is a valuable in-strument of data collection. The abduction accounts are recalled in a surprising manner. For many abductees, once the event is tapped into, the memories seem to pour out without much questioning. When the memories are finally out and discussed, they then are contained in "normal" memory and the abductees tend to forget them as they would any other more or less traumatic memory (thus, often these abductees find it difficult to recall details of the events later on without hypnosis). Other abductees, however, have a very difficult time remembering details of the abduction during the regression. Much of this depends on the specific abduction that they are trying to recall.

The hypnosis I employ consists of light relaxation induction. Basically, I tell the subject to relax in several different ways, use a small amount of visual imagery to "deepen" the trance, and then begin to ask questions. My inductions are usually about fifteen minutes long. The hypnotized subjects have complete control and are free to challenge questions, refuse answers, or get up and go to the bathroom.

I use a calm, informal style of inquiry, especially with those abductees who have had many sessions with me and with whom I have spent enough time to know their reactions to the questioning. When a person comes for her first session, my questioning technique is necessarily cautious and not pressing. With a new subject, I intentionally ask leading questions to ascertain whether she is "leadable" to any degree. The vast majority of the time she is not, demonstrating this by answering a definite "no" to my leading questions.

During a regression session, I try to be as rigorously systematic as I can. I go through the abduction one step at a time, from just before the incident began until the very end. This requires expending a great amount of time on each abduction account. I have developed a technique through which I can move the abductee backward and forward through the event, slowly expanding memories. Sometimes I will go through the event twice, asking questions in a slightly different manner based on what has already been said. If a person cannot remember something, I do not press for recall. Each session lasts between three and five hours, with the hypnosis itself lasting between one and three hours.

I use as nonconfrontational and supportive a manner as I can, often purposely not finishing questions so that abductees can "ease" into the line of questioning that I am developing or interpret the question for themselves. For the most part, I speak in low, conversational tones so that I do not in any way set up an environment that is hostile or suspicious. If I find what appear to be contradictions, I point these out and question them about it (e.g., "If you are lying on your back, how could you feel someone touching your back?"). If they say something that I have never heard before, I again question them very closely to make sure that it is not imaginary. It might appear in some of the transcript excerpts used in this study that a question is leading. In each case I have found that the abductee was not leadable; often the questions asked are from material that had already been discussed previously in the session.

During a regression, all abductees are quite aware of what is happening on two fundamental levels: (1) the information that they are remembering, and (2) the questions and answers that they are required to deal with while they remember. If possible, the abductees learn to observe and analyze the events from a dispassionate and systematic point of view. When they have had a number of sessions, they become adept in questioning themselves and their remembrances, and they can distance themselves to a greater degree from the event. They become "participant-observers" rather than just helpless victims. This has proved to be invaluable for my own research and for the way that the abductees learn to cope with the problems engendered by the abductions. After I have had a number of sessions with them and am sure that they cannot be led while undergoing hypnosis, I can be more blunt in my questions and they can evaluate their memories for themselves. After I bring them out of the hypnotic state, we engage in a thirty-minute to one-hour "talk down" period when other details may be recalled.

Occasionally I use a method I call "assisted recall," in which close and careful questioning techniques enable the abductee to remember most of the abduction without the use of hypnosis.

Questioning Techniques

Disentangling "legitimate" information from unreliable memories involves techniques calculated to produce an understanding of the structure of the abduction and a recognition of anomalies within it. But this is not easy. The most systematic method is patient and thorough questioning, minutely examining every detail and going over every minor contradiction and gap in the account, no matter how irrelevant it might seem, in a second-by-second chronological order. But the problem of confused memory is complicated by the fact that not only is the abductee usually in a hypnotic trance while recalling her memories, but she was also in an altered state of consciousness during the abduction itself. Furthermore, complex mental procedures might have been executed on her that further clouded her perceptions and placed pseudo-images and "memories" in her mind.

Experience in investigating these problems makes it possible to unweave an abduction account and have a reasonable assurance that false recall has been eliminated. Through patient and extremely cautious questioning, the researcher and the abductee can recognize that the events abductees sometimes describe might either not have happened at all or have happened in a different way than they first thought. For instance, one man talked about a beautiful young woman who was coming over to him for what he thought would be a sexual liaison. He described her as having "black hair." Through meticulous questioning about the minute details of her actions and her appearance ("If her head is on your upper chest, can you see the top of her head?"), the false memories fell away and the abductee independently realized that it was her black eyes that he had been describing and not her hair. In fact, she had no hair at all. He also realized that the sexual encounter that he thought he was having was not, in fact, taking place, and that he had been involved with sexual imagery before a sperm sample was taken.

Uncovering abduction memories and helping people come to terms with them is not an easy task. My investigative techniques have evolved and become more sophisticated during the five years that I have been involved in this endeavor. As I learned more about the content of abductions and their effects on the victims, my questioning changed to incorporate my new knowledge. Thus, I conducted my first investigations somewhat differently from later ones. This is bound to happen in a dynamic field where the influx of information is rapid and overwhelming, and where there is no large body of precedent to guide the investigator.

Multiple Sessions

The process of systematic and careful delving into abduction accounts can yield much previously unknown information. When abductees decide to do a series of hypnotic regressions on many different experiences in their lives, each session can generate both material previously known and new material never before encountered. Thus, abductees can have myriad experiences that might not be discovered with only one or two sessions. The investigation of abduction material over the course of a subject's lifetime can provide important information about whether the abductions have changed over time and demonstrates the full scope of activity that happens to each individual. Furthermore, multiple sessions allow for the establishment of the mutual trust that makes it easier for an abductee to reveal sensitive and sometimes embarrassing material, often sexual in nature, that might be difficult to discuss after only a few sessions.

Developing the Scenario

When I started this research, some events had been known for years and were easier to understand. For instance, since 1966 researchers have known about the physical examination. In the 1980s, Budd Hopkins's pioneering work uncovered reproductive procedures, such as egg removal, sperm collection, and baby holding.

Yet there were still many elements of abduction accounts that seemingly defied comprehension. Systematic questioning techniques and analysis have now revealed the origin of many of those incomprehensible events. Thus, some reports of extremely tall aliens might be the result of an abductee's lying down and looking up at them, which gives them the appearance of height. Images of atomic explosions are due to visualization procedures. Scenes of alien landscapes might also have their origin in mental procedures. Published accounts of alien "councils" during which aliens discuss abductees probably reflect the abductee's seeing aliens standing around the examining table. Even though the abductees may not understand the import of the information they are relating, I have found it to be amenable to rational explanation given enough data collected through correct questioning techniques.

The Transcripts

I have tape-recorded each abduction account I researched and then had it transcribed. These written documents, based on oral accounts, help in comparing and analyzing the reports. The transcripts are then analyzed, divided into constituent parts based on the type of event described, and stored in a computer for more detailed analysis.

Reading the transcripts can present a problem. My questioning might sound harsh or abrupt in places, which is unavoidable when the spoken word is written down verbatim. Inflection, nuance, timing, pauses, and the like are lost in a transcript. Therefore, much of the impact of what the abductees are saying is unavoidably omitted. Rather than extensively annotating each transcript, however, I allow the abductees to speak for themselves as much as possible without editorial comment that might interject too much of myself into the accounts.

Support Systems

Abductees are victims who, having gone through incredible and traumatic events without the ability to deal with them consciously, sometimes need help in overcoming the stress from the abduction events. I provide as much support as I can based on my experience, and I hold support-group sessions to allow abductees to discuss their ideas and meet others who have had the same experiences.

Some abductees find it very difficult to cope with their abductions. The tears and emotions that have emerged in many regression sessions from these often terrorized victims is a testament to the trauma they consciously confront for the first time. If a person is suffering emotionally from the effects of abductions and needs more help than I can give, it is important for them to have professional counseling from a sympathetic psychologist or psychiatrist. Dr. Stephen Greenstein in Merion, Pennsylvania, has proved to be invaluable in giving the support and therapy that some of the abductees require.

The proper methods of abduction research are still in the formative stage. Methodological and ethical protocols are being established. While this is happening, the possibility of abuse exists both from well-meaning but incompetent abduction investigators and from mental health professionals. It is extremely important for anyone seeking to examine potential abduction experiences to be certain that the person she or he consults for help in recalling the memories is well qualified for that task.

The Abductees

Below is a list of thirty-nine abductees with whom I investigated two or more abductions, and whose testimony appears in this book. In addition, twenty-two other individuals explored only one abduction experience with me.

Name, year born	Occupation	Number of hypnotic regression sessions
Barbara Archer, 1967	Newspaper reporter	6
James Austino, 1966	University student	5
Melissa Bucknell, 1960	Real estate management	30
Rick Caulfield, 1951	Bartender	4
Elaine Corrello, 1955	Dance instructor	2
Anita Davis, 1958	Transcriber	4
Janet Demerest, 1954 (Karen Morgan's sister)	Secretary	13
Alan Edwards, 1950	Commercial artist	4
John Franklin, 1966	University student	4
Andrew Garcia, 1955	Alcohol rehabilitation counselor	4
Cindy Goldman, 1957 (Lydia Goldman's daughter)	Registered nurse	4
Lydia Goldman, 1932	Secretary	8
Ruth Grossinger, 1943	Interior decorator, former nurse	4

Richard Heyward, 1956	Clerk typist	3
Jason Howard, 1959	Corporate insurance consultant	8
Marvin Josephson, 1966	Accountant	2
Gloria Kane, 1943	Cardiologist	14
George Kenniston, 1949	Attorney	2
Tracy Knapp, 1957	Musician	2
Patti Layne, 1962	High school teacher	24
Evelyn Livingstone, 1962	Graduate student in English	5
Michelle Mason, 1942	Apartment maintenance	2
Lynn Miller, 1955	Waitress	11
Laura Moore, 1948	Secretary	2
Karen Morgan, 1949 (Janet Demerest's sister)	Owner of public relations firm	26
Linda Nichols, 1957	University student	10
Will Parker, 1955	Radio announcer	9
Lucile Perino, 1940	Homemaker	5
Charles Petrie, 1951	Printer	13
Jill Pinzarro, 1948	Minister	7
Marva Roberts, 1954	Systems engineer	2
Ken Rogers, 1961	Professional bicyclist	16
Jason Sandburg, 1956	Graduate student in physics	10
Grant Sawyer, 1932	High school teacher, former army colonel	3
Belinda Schiffrin, 1951	Music teacher	2
Helene Thomas, 1950	Real estate sales	4
Steve Thompson, 1950	Apartment maintenance	8
Rodney Walker, 1959	Graduate student in urban planning	8
Victor Young, 1949	Computer programmer	2

Appendix C

Diagraming the Abduction

After studying abductions for several years I began to realize that the procedures I was uncovering fit together into a graphic form. This matrix represents the results of my investigations into diagraming the structure of the common abduction. All of the physical, mental, and reproductive experiences are linked together through the primary, secondary and ancillary experiences. By examining this matrix, we can get a visual sense of the continuity of these remarkable events. What is extraordinary is that there is a structure, and a fairly tight one at that. The existence of this complex structure suggests a greater sense of the purposefulness in the alien abduction program, and lends support to the theory that reports of abductions have a nonpsychological origin. Although most of the abductions that I investigate verify what is already in the matrix, I expect that as researchers learn more about the abduction phenomenon, the categories will be filled in and expanded upon.

I also expect that new categories will be added that shed further light upon alien activities. We are continually learning and continually being astonished.

COMMON ABDUCTION SCENARIO MATRIX

		Primary	Secondary	Ancillary
P R O C E D U R E S	**Physical**	*Examination* Tissue Samples Implants	*Machine* Enveloping Scanning Light Miscellaneous	*Miscellaneous Physical* Surgery Pool Cures Pain [Proto-People]
	Mental	*Staring* Mindscan Onset Calmative End-Pain Sexual Arousal	*Visualization* Imaging Envisioning Staging Testing	*Miscellaneous Mental* Media Display Knowledge Information Transfer
	Reproductive	*Urological-Gynecological* Egg-Sperm Collection Embryo Implanting Fetal Extraction	*Child Presentation* Incubatorium Nursery Baby Toddler, Youth Adolescent	*Sexual Activity* Involuntary-Compulsive Humans Hybrids

Notes

Chapter 2: Sightings and Abductions

1. Cf. Armando Simon, "The Zeitgeist of the UFO Phenomenon," in Richard Haines, ed., *UFO Phenomena and the Behavioral Scientist* (Metuchen, NJ: The Scarecrow Press, 1979), pp. 43–59.

2. For a more complete analysis, see David M. Jacobs, *The UFO Controversy in America* (Bloomington: Indiana University Press, 1975); Edward Ruppelt, *The Report on Unidentified Flying Objects* (Garden City: Doubleday, 1956); Paris Flammonde, *UFO Exist!* (New York: Putnam, 1976). For current government activity see also Lawrence Fawcett and Barry Greenwood, *Clear Intent* (Englewood Cliffs: Prentice-Hall, 1984). See also Timothy Good, *Above Top Secret* (London: Sidgwick & Jackson, 1987).

3. Edward U. Condon, in Daniel S. Gillmor, ed., *Scientific Study of Unidentified Flying Objects* (New York: Bantam, 1969), pp. 1, 5.

4. William Hartmann, in Daniel S. Gillmor, ed., *Scientific Study of Unidentified Flying Objects* (New York: Bantam Books, 1969), p. 407.

5. Coral and Jim Lorenzen, *Flying Saucer Occupants* (New York: Signet, 1967), p. 54.

6. John Fuller, *The Interrupted Journey* (New York: Dial Press, 1966).

7. Travis Walton, *The Walton Experience* (New York: Berkeley Books, 1978).

8. Leonard Stringfield, "The Stanford, Kentucky Abduction," *The MUFON UFO Journal,* January 1976, pp. 5–15.

9. Ray Fowler, *The Andreasson Affair* (Englewood Cliffs: Prentice-Hall, 1979); *The Andreasson Affair, Phase Two* (Englewood Cliffs: Prentice-Hall, 1982); *The Watchers* (New York: Bantam, 1990).

10. Berthold E. Schwarz, "Talks with Betty Hill: 1—Aftermath of Encounter," *Flying Saucer Review,* vol. 23, no. 2, 1977, p. 19n; Ann Druffel, *The Tujunga Canyon Contacts* (Englewood Cliffs: Prentice Hall, 1980).
11. Budd Hopkins, *Missing Time* (New York: Marek, 1981).
12. Thomas E. Bullard, *UFO Abductions: The Measure of a Mystery* (Mount Ranier, MD: Fund for UFO Research, 1987).
13. Budd Hopkins, *Intruders: The Incredible Visitations at Copley Woods* (New York: Random House, 1987).

Chapter 8: The Abductors

1. Richard Hall, Ted Bloecher, and Isabel Davis, *UFOs: A New Look* (Washington, DC: National Investigations on Aerial Phenomena, 1969), p. 5.
2. Once in a while an abductee will report that the aliens appear to be much clumsier than others report. They claim that the aliens have trouble unbuttoning and removing their clothes.

Chapter 9: Exploring the Evidence

1. Ron Westrum, "Post Abduction Syndrome," *MUFON UFO Journal,* December 1986, pp. 5–6.

Chapter 11: Answers

1. See David M. Jacobs, *The UFO Controversy in America* (Bloomington: Indiana University Press, 1975), chapter 5, for a discussion of the contactees and their effect on UFO research. Several of the contactees either confessed that their stories were untrue or were exposed by investigators.
2. For a discussion of hysterical contagion, see Neil J. Smelser, *Theory of Collective Behavior* (New York: The Free Press, 1962); Ralph L. Rosnow and Gary Alan Fine, *Rumor and Gossip: The Social Psychology of Hearsay* (New York: Elsevier, 1976).
3. Nahum Z. Medalia and Otto N. Larsen, "Diffusion and Belief in a Collective Delusion: The Seattle Windshield Pitting Epidemic," *American Sociological Review,* vol. 23, 1958, pp. 180–186.
4. Alan C. Kerckhoff and Kurt W. Back, *The June Bug: A Study in Hysterical Contagion* (New York: Appleton-Century-Crofts, 1968); Alan C. Kerckhoff and Kurt W. Back, "Sociometric Patterns in Hysteric Contagion," *Sociometry,* March 1965, pp. 2–15.
5. Ronald Seigel, "Long Day's Journey into Night," *Omni,* December 1988, p. 88.
6. Philip J. Klass, *UFO Abductions: A Dangerous Game* (Buffalo: Prometheus Press, 1989).
7. Thomas E. Bullard, "Hypnosis and UFO Abductions: A Troubled Relationship," *Journal of UFO Studies,* n.s. 1, 1989, pp. 3–40.
8. Alvin H. Lawson, "Hypnosis of Imaginary Abductees," in Curtis Fuller, ed., *Proceedings of the First International UFO Congress* (New York: War-

ner Books, 1980), pp. 195–238. One woman related some details about the examination and the aliens that were closer to abduction accounts. It is possible that she was an abductee and that neither she nor Lawson realized it.

9. Michael Capuzzo, "Exploring the Claims of UFO Abductions," *Philadelphia Inquirer,* March 8, 1987, p. 8-L.

10. One must be clear, however, that mentally disturbed people can also have abduction experiences. The ability of these people to describe and analyze what has happened to them is limited. Competent investigators usually refuse to work with them and refer such people to mental health professionals. One young woman with whom I worked in the course of writing this study fell prey to mental illness and was hospitalized. The factors leading to the breakdown were not related to the abduction phenomenon, and at no time did the abductions become involved with her thought disturbances.

11. Ted Bloecher, Aphrodite Clamar, and Budd Hopkins, "Summary Report on the Psychological Testing of Nine Individuals Reporting UFO Abduction Experiences" (Washington, DC: The Fund for UFO Research, 1984).

12. Michael Persinger, "Contribution of Temporal Lobe Factors to Visitor and Paranormal Experiences," paper, Society for Scientific Exploration, Cornell University, June 1988. Persinger has also suggested that geophysical events can precipitate temporal lobe instability.

I have worked with an abductee who had temporal lobe epilepsy. She took medication to stop her seizures. Once she was given medication that had been recalled by the manufacturer; instead of preventing seizures, it caused them. Within five days, she had 125 seizures before her epilepsy was brought under control. During that time, she did not have an abduction, imagine abductions, or think about abductions. Three months later, she forgot to take her medication and had a seizure while recounting an abduction event to me under hypnosis. She felt the onset of the seizure, asked to be brought out of the trance, and then had the seizure. At that time she did not confabulate, imagine other abduction events, or have vivid memories of the abduction event she had been describing. She experienced no sensory stimulation of any sort, nor did she think about the abduction event. In fact, the seizure prevented her from recalling the event and it added nothing whatsoever to her account. None of the other abductees with whom I have worked have had any type of epilepsy.

13. Jacques Vallee, *Passport to Magonia* (Chicago: Henry Regnery, 1969); Jacques Vallee, *Dimensions* (Chicago: Contemporary Books, 1988); Robert Bartholomew, *UFOlore* (Stone Mountain, GA: Arcturus Book Service, 1989); Thomas E. Bullard, "Why Abduction Reports Are Not Urban Legends," *International UFO Reporter,* July/August 1991, pp. 15–20, 24. See also Edoardo Russo and Paolo Grassino, "Ufology in Europe; or, What Is America Coming To?" *International UFO Reporter,* March/April 1989, pp.

4–7; Jerome Clark, "Two Cheers for American Ufology," *International UFO Reporter,* March/April 1989, pp. 8–12; Jerome Clark, "The Fall and Rise of the Extraterrestrial Hypothesis," *MUFON 1988 International UFO Symposium Proceedings* (Seguin, Texas: MUFON, 1988), pp. 58–71; Thomas E. Bullard, "The American Way: Truth, Justice, and Abduction," *Magonia,* October 1989, pp. 3–7.

14. Carl G. Jung, *Flying Saucers: A Modern Myth of Things Seen in the Sky* (New York: New American Library, 1959).

15. Ibid., p. 17.

16. Alvin H. Lawson, "A Touchstone for Fallacious Abductions: Birth Trauma Imagery in CE III Narratives," in Mimi Hynek, ed., *The Spectrum of UFO Research* (Chicago: The J. Allen Hynek Center for UFO Studies, 1988), pp. 71–98.

17. Ann Druffel and D. Scott Rogo, *The Tujunga Canyon Contacts* (New York: New American Library, 1988) (updated version). Rogo later felt that the mass of abduction evidence had weakened this theory.

Chapter 12: Questions

1. Jenny Randles, *Abduction: Over 200 Documented UFO Kidnappings* (London: Robert Hale, 1988).

2. Michael Swords, "Extraterrestrial Hybridization Unlikely," *MUFON UFO Journal,* November 1988, pp. 6–10; David M. Jacobs, "Hybrid Thoughts," *MUFON UFO Journal,* February 1989, pp. 10–11.

Acknowledgments

This book could not have been written without the help and encouragement of those who have been subjected to abductions. They were supportive and gave freely of their time and energy. Not only did I learn about the abduction phenomenon from them, but I also learned lessons about the human spirit in the face of adversity that have made me proud to have had our lives intertwine.

No study of this nature can be done in a vacuum. Dr. Thomas E. Bullard, folklorist and abduction researcher; Jerome Clark of the Center for UFO Studies; writer Michael Fare; Dr. Stephen Greenstein, psychologist; Dr. Charles W. Hieatt, Anglia College, Cambridge; Dr. Roger Keeran, Empire State College; art historian April Kingsley; Dr. Michael Swords, Western Michigan University; and Dr. Ronald Westrum, Eastern Michigan University, gave much of their time and offered invaluable comments on the manuscript.

Fred Hills and Daphne Bien of Simon & Schuster were extraordinarily helpful in shaping the final outcome of this book. They expended much time and energy editing the manuscript, and their work has enhanced the quality of this book immeasurably. I am in their debt.

Without Budd Hopkins this project would never have begun. His encouragement, advice, and critique of my work has helped me to clarify my thoughts and to work steadily toward my goal. Our countless hours of discussion provided me with an outlet for my thoughts, and he patiently suffered through the earliest days of this study when my ideas were just beginning to take shape.

My wife, Irene, has put up with the enormous disruption and turmoil that the research for and writing of this study have caused in our lives and the lives of our children. In spite of this, her sage comments, her clarity of vision, and her steadiness have kept me on the intellectual straight and narrow in the face of tremendous obstacles. Her thoughtful editing of the initial drafts of the manuscript strengthened it tremendously.